Kate Kirkpatrick is Lecturer in Philosophy at the University of Hertfordshire and Lecturer in Theology at St Peter's College, Oxford.

OXFORD THEOLOGY AND RELIGION MONOGRAPHS

OXFORD THEOLOGY AND RELIGION MONOGRAPHS

Sartre on Sin

Between Being and Nothingness

KATE KIRKPATRICK

OXFORD
UNIVERSITY PRESS

OXFORD

UNIVERSITY PRESS

Great Clarendon Street, Oxford, OX2 6DP,
United Kingdom

Oxford University Press is a department of the University of Oxford.
It furthers the University's objective of excellence in research, scholarship,
and education by publishing worldwide. Oxford is a registered trade mark of
Oxford University Press in the UK and in certain other countries

Published in the United States of America by Oxford University Press
198 Madison Avenue, New York, NY 10016, United States of America

British Library Cataloguing in Publication Data
Data available

Library of Congress Control Number: 2017942086

ISBN 978-0-19-881173-2

Printed and bound by
CPI Group (UK) Ltd, Croydon, CR0 4YY

Acknowledgements

This research would not have been possible were it not for the support of many individuals and institutions. I am grateful for the support of the AHRC's Block Grant Partnership for funding this project; to St Cross College, the Faculty of Theology and Religion, and the Udo Keller Stiftung Forum Humanum for travel grants that enabled me to present work in progress at several conferences during the period of research; and to the Beinecke Rare Book and Manuscript Library at Yale University and Grégory Cormann for their assistance in procuring the 'Sartre's Readings of Youth' manuscript and *mémoire*, respectively.

TORCH, the Maison Française d'Oxford, and the UK Sartre Society supported the 'Thinking with Sartre Today/Penser avec Sartre aujourd'hui' conference I co-organized at the Maison Française d'Oxford (30–31 January 2015), which was a source of both research leads and relationships—in particular with Ârash Aminian-Tabrizi and Marieke Mueller, whom I thank for their collaboration and camaraderie.

Several scholars have read and commented on aspects of this work at various stages of its development. I am especially grateful to Pamela Sue Anderson and George Pattison for the care and commitment they have shown this project; to OUP's anonymous reviewers; as well as to Graham Ward, Joel Rasmussen, James Hanvey SJ, Katherine Morris, Clare Carlisle, and Stephen Mulhall; and to Richard Parish, who generously met with me to discuss Pascal's works and twentieth-century reception.

Excerpts from Jean-Paul Sartre, *Being and Nothingness*, translated by Hazel Barnes © 1958 and the Philosophical Library (US & Canada) and Routledge (UK & rest of world), are reproduced by permission of the Philosophical Library Inc (philosophicallibrary.com) and by Taylor & Francis Books UK. All rights reserved.

Finally I would like to acknowledge, with gratitude, the support and love of my family. In particular, I would like to thank Matt—for his encouragement and partnership, in words and in deeds.

Contents

Chronology of Sartre's Works, 1924–46

Dates are dates of publication unless given in parentheses, in which case they are dates of writing for works that were published later or that remain unpublished. English titles are given in square brackets for works that have been translated into English. This chronology ends at 1946 because this book concerns Sartre's pre-humanist phase, i.e. Sartre's philosophy before *Existentialism is a Humanism*.

(1924–5)	*Carnet Midy*
(1927)	*L'Image dans la vie psychologique: rôle et nature* (unpublished *mémoire* for the Diplôme d'études supérieure)
1936	*L'Imagination* [*The Imagination*]
	La Transcendance de l'ego [*The Transcendence of the Ego*]
1938	*La Nausée* [*Nausea*]
(1939–40)	*Carnets de la drôle de guerre, Septembre 1939–Mars 1940* [*War Diaries*]
1939	*Esquisse d'une théorie des émotions* [*Sketch for a Theory of the Emotions*]
	Le Mur [*The Wall*]
1940	*L'Imaginaire* [*The Imaginary*]
(1940)	*Bariona* (staged) [*Bariona*]
1943	*L'Être et le néant* [*Being and Nothingness*]
	Les Mouches [*The Flies*]
1944	*Huis clos* [*No Exit*]
1945	*L'Âge de raison* [*The Age of Reason*]
	Le Sursis [*The Reprieve*]
1946	*La Poutain respecteuse* [*The Respectable Prostitute*]
	Existentialisme est un humanisme [*Existentialism is a Humanism*]
	La Liberté [*Cartesian Freedom*]

List of Abbreviations

B   *Bariona*, trans. Mary Mayer and Bernard Seal, *ADAM International Review*, Nos. 343–5 (1970), pp. 37–85.

BN   *Being and Nothingness*, trans. Hazel Barnes, London: Routledge, 2003.

CG   *Carnets de la drôle de guerre, Septembre 1939–Mars 1940*, ed. Arlette Elkaim Sartre, Paris: Gallimard, 1995.

CG Pléiade *Les Carnets de la drôle de la guerre*, in *Les Mots et autres écrits autobiographiques*, ed. Jean-François Louette, Paris: Bibliothèque de la Pléiade, 2010.

CM   *Carnet Midy*, in Jean-Paul Sartre, *Écrits de jeunesse*, ed. M. Contat and M. Rybalka, Paris: Gallimard, 1990.

E   *Sketch for a Theory of the Emotions*, trans. Philip Mairet, London: Routledge, 2002.

EH   *Existentialism is a Humanism*, trans. Carol Macomber, London: Yale University Press, 2007.

EJ   *Écrits de jeunesse*, Paris: Gallimard, 1990.

EN   *L'Être et le néant*, Paris: Gallimard, 1972.

F   *The Flies*, trans. Stuart Gilbert, New York: Vintage, 1989.

I   *The Imaginary*, trans. Jonathan Webber, London: Routledge, 2004.

IFI   'Intentionality: A Fundamental Idea of Husserl's Phenomenology', *Journal of the British Society for Phenomenology* I/2 (1970): 4–5.

IM   *L'Imagination*, Paris: PUF, 2010.

IN   'Intimité', in *Le Mur*, ed. Walter Redfern, Bristol: Bristol Classical Press, 1997.

IVP   *L'Image dans la vie psychologique: rôle et nature*, unpublished typsecript of the *mémoire* for the Diplôme d'études supérieure, équipe Sartre, ITEM, École Normale Supérieure, Paris.

LC   'La Liberté cartesienne' (introduction), in *Descartes* (Classiques de la liberté), ed. Jean-Paul Sartre, Paris: Trois collines, 1946. The 1946 edition is cited herein; the text is more widely available in Sartre's *Situations I* (1947).

LE   *Liberté–Egalité: manuscrit sur la genèse de l'idéologie bourgeoise*, in *Études sartriennes* 12 (2008): 165–256.

LL   *Lucifer and the Lord*, trans. Kitty Black, London: Penguin, 1965.

A Note on Translations

I have used the Hazel Barnes translation of *L'Être et le néant*, although there are some instances where I have found it necessary to cite the French, in particular where the same English word is used for different French words with different theological connotations. These instances are noted at relevant points in the argument. Where citations refer to other works in French (by Sartre or others) and cited matter is in English all translations are the author's own unless otherwise stated.

Part I

Sartre and Sin

1

Introduction

This book argues that Jean-Paul Sartre's early philosophy retained a recognizable inheritance from the Christian doctrine of original sin. In particular, his philosophical anthropology in *Being and Nothingness* presents the human condition as fallen. This contention may come as a surprise, given that in his time there was 'no more prominent atheist.'[1] But 'atheism' is by no means monolithic, and Sartre's atheism has recently begun to receive greater recognition—and greater scrutiny for being ambiguous.[2]

Where Sartre's prominence is concerned there is less ambiguity: in his own country he dominated the mid-twentieth century.[3] His output was astonishing on account of its diversity (it traversed several literary genres), quality (he was awarded, and famously refused, the Nobel Prize in Literature in 1964), and quantity ('once calculated at 20 published pages a day over his working life'[4]). In an age before global publishing and mass-market trends, his first novel, *Nausea* (1938), sold more than 1.6 million copies in his lifetime, and his play *Dirty Hands* (1948) nearly 2 million. Even *Being and Nothingness* (1943), his 700-page tome on phenomenological ontology, went through five editions in its first three years and has never been out of print.[5]

In light of such fame, one might be inclined to ask why this theme of sin—significant as I am about to argue it is—has not already surfaced in Sartre scholarship. It has surfaced: but it has not been pursued to the

---

[1] Hopkins 1994: 113.

[2] By 'ambiguous' I mean that there are many possible interpretations (see Gellman 2009; Kirkpatrick 2013; Gillespie 2013, 2014; Chabot 2016). I will elaborate on this in the next section of this chapter.

[3] Lévy (2003) dubbed him '*the* philosopher of the twentieth century'.

[4] *Economist* 2003.   [5] *Economist* 2003.

necessary depth. Several readers of Sartre have made passing comments on resemblances between *Being and Nothingness* and Christianity in general,[6] and in particular to the doctrine of original sin and to
its interpreters, St Augustine,[7] Kierkegaard,[8] or Kant.[9] In the English-
speaking philosophical literature Stephen Mulhall notes Sartre's
'Christian theological horizons';[10] Merold Westphal describes Sartre
as a 'secular theologian of original sin';[11] Robert Solomon and Jonathan
Webber note similarities between bad faith and original sin;[12] and
Hans van Stralen notes the close similarity between Sartre's later view
of history and original sin.[13]

That there is no sustained scholarly work exploring the reputed
relationship between Sartre and sin can be explained on historical,
textual, and theological bases. Historically, Sartre's existentialism is
just beginning to emerge from a period in scholarly *purgatoire*: it has
been seen by many as 'of its time'—a philosophy *of* the post-war
period *for* the post-war period—or even as the 'height of kitsch'.[14]
Textually, there is a neat proof text for Sartre's disbelief in sin: in the
War Diaries he wrote that 'what is certain is that from the start I had a
morality without God—without sin, but not without Evil'.[15] And
theologically, the most common objection I have encountered to
this project is that 'Sartre didn't have a theological formation!' How
could he *keep* theological concepts?

Cognizant that the latter two reasons for dismissal posed a greater
threat to my argument than the first, this research, therefore, initially
set out to test earlier scholars' claims of resemblance—to compare
Sartre's ontology of freedom to Augustine's ontology of sin—and to
see what case (if any) could be made for Sartre having a 'theological'
formation. On both historical and textual bases the research
found that Sartre's intellectual formation included a theological element which is often overlooked by Sartre scholars—especially in the

---

[6] See Kirkpatrick 2017 on the influence of theology on Sartre and Sartre on twentieth-
century theology.

[7] Westphal 2010: 172.

[8] Theunissen writes that 'In a certain sense, Sartre even incorporates Kierkegaard's
theological conception of sin' (2005: 31).

[9] Philonenko suggests radical evil, rather than 'original sin', as the problem Sartre
sought to address (1981: 154), although radical evil itself can be considered a 'secu-
larization' or, in Kant's case, a philosophical version, of original sin.

[10] Mulhall 2005: 13, 31. See also Harries 2004: 28.

[11] See Westphal 2010: 172.   [12] Webber 2009: 143; Solomon 2006: 13.

[13] Van Stralen 2005: 182.   [14] Lévy 2003: 3.   [15] WD 70.

English-speaking philosophical community, where his German phenomenological influences receive greater attention. Moreover, it found that this theology was indeed Augustinian, but it was the Augustinianism of *l'école française de spiritualité* and Jansenism, in both of which the concept of *le néant* (nothingness) plays a profound role.

Before presenting my own reading of *Being and Nothingness*, therefore, I must advance a preliminary contention: namely, that the reception of *Being and Nothingness* among English-speaking philosophers has placed such an emphasis on Sartre's position in (or deviation from) the German phenomenological tradition that it has missed significant formative influences on his thought. In particular, I argue, French theological and literary traditions are in evidence, but since these are less well known to Anglo-American philosophers—or not considered to be 'philosophy'[16]—the text is often not read for this register.[17]

Sartre himself is partly to blame for the ease with which it can be overlooked. In Sartre's self-contextualization in *Being and Nothingness* he frequently defines himself in agreement or opposition with 'les trois Hs'—Hegel, Husserl, and Heidegger—and with Descartes; theological figures are rarely named. But this, I argue, is because Sartre's own methodology involved what I will call a 'morganatic marriage'.

Sartre clearly drew on the German phenomenological tradition. But his philosophical education was well under way by the time he encountered phenomenology in the early 1930s. English-speaking commentators note his debts to Descartes and Bergson, but Sartre's intellectual formation did not just expose him to thinkers respected by the English-speaking canon of philosophy, but to theological writers—whether they went by the other names of *mystiques* or *moralistes*.

Where 'mystics' are concerned, Sartre's little-studied '*mémoire*' for the *Diplôme d'Études Supérieures* (written in 1926–7) was dedicated to the 'image' and included a section on Christian mystics. The work,

---

[16] Roger Scruton, for example, notes that the French have 'a completely different conception of what philosophy is' (2014: n.p.).

[17] See, e.g., Flynn's intellectual biography (2014), which starts in the 1930s with Sartre's discovery of phenomenology; or Catalano 1985, which moves from 'Descartes' to 'Husserl' in its treatment of Sartre's 'background'. Many English-language texts neglect his earlier intellectual development. Cormann 2015 (in French) examines one of Sartre's pre-phenomenological philosophical interlocutors (Alain), but there is very little work devoted to this early formation in English. The 'Sartre's readings in youth' MS is helpful in this respect, for showing the sources that Sartre took to be significant in his early development.

entitled *L'Image dans la vie psychologique: rôle et nature*, was written under the supervision of Henri Delacroix (professor of psychology at the Sorbonne and author of *Étude d'histoire et de psychologie du mysticism*, among other things—a work which included substantial treatments of St Theresa of Avila, Madame Guyon, and Fénelon). A heavily revised version of the *mémoire* was published in 1936, after Sartre's discovery of phenomenology, as *L'Imagination*.[18] And where *moralistes* are concerned, Sartre frequently cites them and relates his own works to theirs.[19]

What we find in *Being and Nothingness*, therefore, is a morganatic marriage of phenomenology and these 'lesser' methods: neither *les mystiques* nor *les moralistes* shared the high status of *les philosophes* in the intellectual climate of interwar France.[20] It is not surprising that Sartre did not acknowledge these influences: for in addition to feeling that they were methodologically lesser, sub-, or un-philosophical approaches, he could presume tacit familiarity on behalf of his French readership.[21]

I will outline the contours of my argument in greater detail in the concluding section of this Introduction. But before doing so it

---

[18] The relationship between Sartre and mysticism is complex. In part, this is because of the multiplicity of meanings assigned to the word 'mysticism'. In Sartre's historical context, in the throes of a renaissance of interest in mystical thought, it was a live question whether France herself had always had 'a mystical soul', or whether the crystalline light of *les philosophes'* reason shone brighter. It is clear from the endnotes for Sartre's *mémoire* that he read Baruzi (1924) and Delacroix (1908) as well as works by Tauler and Theresa of Avila.

[19] The French *moraliste* is not to be confused with the English 'moralist'; the former is often used to describe religious writers, 'bad' philosophers, or a particular group of seventeenth-century authors. Sartre refers to *les moralistes* as a group and by name in many of his works: In TE 17, for example, he refers to La Rochefoucauld and *les moralistes* because he is not content to have a 'purely psychological theory' that rids the presence of the *me* from consciousness. In the WD, Sartre describes himself as 'affected by moralism, and . . . moralism often has its source in religion' (WD 72). See also BN 574 and 583, which will be discussed in Chapter 7.

[20] See Kirkpatrick 2013 on Sartre and mysticism, and Connor 2000: 16, 19–20 on the intellectual climate in France in the interwar years. The notion that 'mysticism' was a departure from reason was particularly important in the 1930s, when the word 'mysticism' took on connotations of National Socialism. It was the antiphilosophy: where philosophy emphasizes doubt and critical reflection, mysticism was a kind of being carried away, often against reason (Connor 2000: 129).

[21] See Morris 2009: 10; the French educational system allowed Sartre to presume knowledge on behalf of his (French) readers. In BN we find allusions to theological controversies with which Sartre assumes his readers will be familiar: Manicheanism, Arianism, and the religious politics of Constantine's conversion (BN 467f.).

is necessary to make a few further introductory remarks about (1) Sartre's ambiguous atheism; (2) Sartre as secular theologian of original sin; (3) and the scope, structure, and methodology of this book.

SARTRE'S ATHEISM

As John Henry Newman wrote, 'The word "God" is a Theology in itself',[22] and where Sartre is concerned scholars have yet to reach precision about which God he spoke. Sartre's atheism is ambiguous, with its origins, nature, and duration subject to debate.[23] His philosophical rejection of belief in God in *Being and Nothingness* is simple: since no being can be both *en soi* and *pour soi*, God cannot exist.[24] But as I have written elsewhere, there is good reason to doubt that this argument persuaded its author: in conversation with Beauvoir, Sartre said that his real reasons for denying God's existence were 'much more direct and childish'.[25] Moreover, it is questionable whether any *argument* persuaded him. In *What Is Literature?* Sartre writes that 'thought conceals man': on their own, arguments are uninteresting. 'But an argument that masks a tear—that is what we're after.'[26]

Sartre provides several different accounts of the genesis of his atheism in *Words*, adding fuel to the fire of uncertainty. In addition to the genesis stories I have listed elsewhere,[27] he describes atheism as 'a cruel, long-term business' (W 157); himself as 'prevented' from being a Christian (W 82); and God as an 'old flame' (W 65). It is difficult, therefore, to define a precise philosophical position or provide a clear biographical account with respect to his atheism.

---

[22] Newman 1907: 26, 36–7.

[23] On origins see Gellman 2009 and Kirkpatrick 2013; on duration see Gillespie 2013 and 2014.

[24] T. Anderson 2010 also draws attention to Sartre's discussion of God as *ens causa sui*.

[25] Beauvoir 1984: 438.

[26] WL 22. Sartre continues, 'The argument removes the obscenity from the tears; the tears, by revealing their origin in the passions, remove the aggressiveness from the argument.'

[27] See Kirkpatrick 2013.

Despite its ambiguity, however, it is clear that Sartre's atheism is not of the same variety as the naturalist atheism that is popular (and perhaps, in some circles, the assumed meaning of the English word 'atheist') today. In this it is worth mentioning a passage in *Words* in which Sartre offers a description of 'the atheist'—and noting its Jansenist hues. The atheist, Sartre writes, was

> a man with a phobia about God who saw his absence everywhere and who could not open his mouth without saying his name: in short, a Gentleman with religious convictions. The believer had none: for two thousand years the Christian certainties had had time to prove themselves, they belonged to everyone, and they were required to shine in a priest's glance, in the half-light of a church, and to illumine souls, but no one needed to appropriate them to himself; they were the common patrimony. Polite society believed in God so that it need not talk of him.
>
> (W 62-3)

When Sartre uses the word 'atheism', therefore, it is wise not to assume his intended meaning was synonymous with that of the evidential atheism that is debated in the analytic philosophy of religion today. Bertrand Russell's famous account of what he would say to God should the two ever meet—'Not enough evidence, God! Not enough evidence!'—is unlikely to have been Sartre's mantra.[28]

Rather Sartre might better be viewed as belonging to the 'school of suspicion'.[29] As Merold Westphal describes it, the hermeneutics of suspicion involves 'the deliberate attempt to expose the self-deceptions involved in hiding our actual operative motives from ourselves, individually or collectively, in order not to notice how and how much our behaviour and our beliefs are shaped by values we profess to disown'. As such, suspicion must be distinguished from the scepticism that is characteristic of evidential atheism: 'Skepticism seeks to overcome the opacity of facts, while suspicion seeks to uncover the duplicity of persons.'[30]

---

[28] Quoted in Plantinga and Wolterstorff 1983: 17–18. Gellman 2009 argued that Sartre is a 'mystical atheist', but I have argued elsewhere (Kirkpatrick 2013) that, on the basis of the variety of Sartre's genesis stories, it is difficult to accept Gellman's categorization as conclusive. Gardner (2009: 205) similarly interprets Sartre's motivations as non-metaphysical, seeing them on 'the same *order* as Jacobi's assertion that the being of God is intuited directly, but with an exactly opposite *content*'.

[29] See Ricoeur 1970.

[30] Westphal 1998: 13.

SECULAR THEOLOGIAN OF ORIGINAL SIN

In *Being and Time*, Heidegger wrote that the 'ontology [of Dasein], as a philosophical inquiry, "knows" nothing about sin'.[31] On my reading of Sartre, we shall see, Heidegger's claim does not hold true for *Being and Nothingness*. If there is one aspect of Sartre's work that scholars do not dispute, it is that freedom played a central role in his thought. On the standard reading, Sartre's most fundamental and attractive idea—the idea that brought him his reputation as 'the best-known metaphysician in Europe'[32] or '*the* philosopher of his generation'[33]—is freedom.[34] It is, in Christina Howells's words, a 'critical cliché'.[35] But, as Sarah Richmond notes, Sartre's interest in phenomenology 'co-existed with and was an instrument for his wish to demonstrate the existence of human freedom, and his sense that the way to do this was by establishing an essential connection of consciousness with nothingness'.[36]

In Christian theology, since Augustine at least, *nothingness* is an alias of sin and evil. These concepts, on the Augustinian reckoning of them, are indistinguishable: both are privations (or absences) of the good, and both are possible on account of human freedom. The genealogy of the human condition Sartre presents—as a tensive state between being and nothingness—clearly has roots in sin.

This brings us back to the proof text cited above: for Sartre's claim there—that he believes in a world without God and without sin, but with evil—only throws us off the wrong scent. Although we will examine it in greater depth in Chapter 2, it is worth saying at this stage that, broadly construed, the Augustinian view of sin holds to a double meaning for sin as 'actual' and 'original', where actual sin consists of discrete actions deliberately done against the will of God and original sin is a state of corruption (which particularly affects the human will) that ensued from the actual sin of the first human couple.

The double meaning of sin is important because holding these two sides together has practical consequences: if actual sin, by definition, is against God, then sin is a theocentrically defined concept and humans can be held *accountable* for committing such sins. As actual, sin is something of which we are conscious and for which we are

---

[31] SZ 306, n. 1, cited in Harries 1995: 19.   [32] Murdoch 1999: 1.
[33] Bernasconi 2006: 9.   [34] Philonenko 1981: 145.
[35] Howells 1988: 1.   [36] Richmond 2013: 94.

responsible. However, if it is only defined as such then the concept of sin can seem moralistic and individualistic.

To call sin original checks both of these inferences, because our actual sins follow from a corrupted state. We cannot, of our own power, extricate ourselves from this state, however heroic our attempts. Sin is thus a shared problem: it is not only a matter of individuals in isolation, but also affects our relations with each other, producing injustices of both small and large scales. Such a state is tensive, simultaneously active and passive: active in that the individual can choose to perpetuate or resist actual sin, and passive in that the individual enters a fallen world that is not of her creation.

My training is in both philosophy and theology, and my intention is not to perpetuate the view that the boundaries of these disciplines are impermeable. Rather, in this work I aim to attend to the theological themes in *Being and Nothingness* in order to see what emerges from the text by so doing. The Sartre of *Being and Nothingness* clearly rejects the notion of actual sin—discrete violations of prohibitions would make no sense in a world without God to do the prohibiting. However, he retains a recognizable descendant of the Christian doctrine of original sin in *le néant*.

Redressing a deracinated reading of Sartre is not my only aim, however. I also argue that understanding Sartre's theological sources serves further conceptual ends. For philosophers, it clarifies Sartre's slippery conceptions of nothingness and bad faith; and for theologians, it opens up a new, theological interpretation of Sartre's account of human reality. Theologically, I argue that Sartre's phenomenology can be read as anti-theodicy and as a hermeneutics of despair. Moreover, this reading of Sartre may serve as a useful hamartiological resource: it provides a phenomenology of sin from a graceless position.

The idea of 'Sartrean theology' will strike some as counterintuitive or ill-advised. Turning to an atheist for theological insights may seem backwards, methodologically, particularly for those who think knowledge of God can only come from God and those who claim to know him. But my aim in this book (as Merold Westphal argued with respect to Marx, Nietzsche, and Freud) is to demonstrate that Sartre can be read as a 'secular theologian of original sin'. As such, his works should 'be taken seriously as a stimulus to self-examination rather than refuted as an error'.[37] In what follows, therefore, I read Sartre's

---

[37] Westphal 1998: xiv.

atheism 'for edification',[38] as a stimulus to be reflexive and learn more about one's own position.

SCOPE, STRUCTURE, AND METHOD

The primary exegetical focus of this book is *Being and Nothingness*. Its argument concerns the early, anti-humanist Sartre, which is to say, his existentialism *before* 'Existentialism is a Humanism' (1946).[39] In support of this argument I will appeal to other texts—philosophical and literary—written by Sartre in the early period up to 1946. In later life Sartre called *Being and Nothingness* an 'eidetic of bad faith'[40] and 'an ontology before conversion'.[41] But this book reads the text on its own terms—so the Sartre it concerns is the Sartre we find on the pages of *Being and Nothingness*, unless otherwise stated.

After this introduction, Part II (Chapters 2 and 3) outlines the Augustinian tradition by which, I argue, Sartre's account of the human as 'between being and nothingness' was informed. This part is both conceptual and historical: it lays the groundwork for the exegesis to follow in Part III.

Chapter 2 considers the philosophical and theological sources Sartre encountered in Augustine, Bérulle, Descartes, Jansen, Pascal, and Fénelon. It notes the importance of *le néant* and grace in seventeenth-century French accounts of the human person and demonstrates that Sartre was exposed to theological conceptualizations of *le néant*.

---

[38] Clark 1998: ix.

[39] As Stefanos Geroulanos notes, Sartre's early work was not humanist (2010: 218ff.); it was only after the war that he began to soften his opposition. The lecture 'Existentialism is a Humanism' was given at Club Maintenant in Paris, on 29 October 1945, and published in 1946. Sartre later repudiated it as over-simple. As Howells notes, 'it was given at the height of the vogue for existentialism, and in an attempt to refute accusations of immorality' (1988: 31). Simont (1999: 125) notes that at the stage of *La Nausée* (1938) Sartre considered 'humanism in all its forms detestable'. In the *War Diaries* Sartre wrote that one of the good things about war is that it deprives you of human dignity. The 'world of war' yields '*the complete loss of all human dignity*; and, in principle, this is not such a bad thing' (CG *Pléiade* 152; this *carnet* is not translated in WD). In WD Sartre explicitly treats his 'theoretical opposition to humanism' (WD 87). See Geroulanos 2010 (*passim*) and Simont 1999 on the shifting position of 'humanism' in Sartre's works.

[40] SIV 196; cited in Philonenko 1981: 160 and Busch 1989: 18.

[41] Cited in Busch 1989: 18.

In Chapter 3 we turn to French literature, to see examples of the 'literary fate' of Jansenism in the works of Racine, Voltaire, and Hugo. After having sketched this literary trajectory, we turn to the renaissance of sin in the Catholic novelists of the 1920s: Mauriac, Bernanos, and Claudel. It was in this literary context that—before Sartre's discovery of phenomenology—he studied Christian mystics when preparing his thesis on the imagination under the guidance of Henri Delacroix. And it was in this literary context that the hamartiological figure Søren Kierkegaard was first published in France.[42] This part concludes with a summary of relevant themes from Kierkegaard's *The Concept of Anxiety* and *The Sickness unto Death*.

Part III (Chapters 4 to 7) is dedicated to a part-by-part examination of Being and Nothingness. *Sartre, like Schleiermacher, would object to any claim to understand the whole of a work on the basis of considering a single part. The reader is asked to bear in mind, therefore, that individual chapters of this part cannot be separated from the whole.*[43]

Chapter 4 (on BN Part I) introduces Sartrean consciousness as 'the being by which nothingness comes into the world', bringing Sartre's account of human freedom into dialogue with the theorists of nothingness and negation introduced in Chapters 2 and 3. It argues that Sartre's *néant* in *Being and Nothingness*, like that of many of his Augustinian predecessors—is intimately connected with problems of epistemology—especially, self-knowledge.

Chapter 5 (on BN Part II) examines Sartre's for-itself in greater depth. It explores the character of consciousness as 'existing for a witness' and then turns to Sartre's discussions of internal relations and possibility, contingency, facticity, and lack. On Sartre's view, philosophical prejudices for the existent and the external have prevented an accurate understanding of them—for they are not only abstract concepts but *lived experiences*. Each demonstrates the futility of consciousness in search of lost being. We saw in Chapter 4 that Sartre's nothingness renders self-knowledge problematic; in Chapter 5 we see further the psychological effects of nothingness.

Chapter 6 (on BN Part III) follows Sartre in turning from the isolated consciousness to being-with-others. In particular, this chapter

---

[42] 'The Seducer's Diary' (extracted from *Either/Or*) was published in France in 1929.
[43] Cf. Catalano 1985: xi.

focuses on the revealing power of shame; the objectifying gaze of the other; and the ambiguity of embodiment, to argue that the problem of my being in relation to the other is that I am not the only being 'through whom nothingness comes into the world'. In theological idiom, I am subject not only to my own fallenness but the fallenness of others: the consequences of nothingness are ethical. Sartre's account of being-with-others as *conflict* can therefore be read not merely as affirming the Hegelian master–slave dialectic, but as affirming the Jansenist view of man under concupiscence: subject to the *libido dominandi*.

Chapter 7 (on BN Part IV) turns to consider Sartre's technical and philosophical concept of freedom. Reading his engagement with Leibniz here alongside his discussion of Descartes in *La Liberté cartesienne* (1946), I argue that Sartre's phenomenology of freedom in *Being and Nothingness* can be read as anti-theodicy. Sartre rejects 'freedom' as a 'sufficient reason' for the world's ills: it is the source of too many of them. Moreover, the resulting Sartrean pessimism is more extreme than that of his Jansenist predecessors. For Sartre's for-itself is free *to the extent that it refuses* any possibility of grace.

Part IV (Chapters 8 and 9) constructively argues that Sartre is a useful resource for contemporary hamartiology.

Chapter 8 argues (i) that Sartre's account of love provides further evidence of the Jansenist inflection of his pessimism. On this basis, it makes the case that (ii) *Being and Nothingness* presents a 'hermeneutics of despair' (to adapt Ricoeur's phrase). It then asks (iii) whether—and if so, *how*—this reading of Sartre might usefully inform contemporary hamartiology, arguing that some theological categories (such as sin and love) cannot be known merely conceptually, but must be acknowledged personally. Finally (iv) it presents the 'original optimism' of the Christian doctrine of sin, which is lacking in the situation Sartre describes. In both the Augustinian and Kierkegaardian accounts of Christianity, an important component of this original optimism is *love*.

Chapter 9 offers two provocations: one on wretchedness without God, the other on wretchedness with God. The first brings Sartre into dialogue with Marilyn McCord Adams's work 'God because of Evil', arguing that Sartre's account lends credence to her view that optimism is not warranted if one takes a robust realist approach to evil without God. Read as a phenomenologist of fallenness, Sartre may serve, to use the phrase of Stephen Mulhall, to 'hold open the possibility of taking religious points of view seriously'.[44] The second provocation—on the question of wretchedness *with* God—suggests that Sartre can be read 'for edification' in order to help us see our failures in love.

A final, methodological point should be made before concluding this introduction. Several of the chapters to follow include references to Sartre's literary works in cases where they illustrate the ideas expressed in *Being and Nothingness*. As Christina Howells writes, continental thinking

> has been keen to contest the traditional distinction between philosophy and literature, and to refuse the truth/fiction opposition which underlies it. Philosophy is no longer envisaged as giving a privileged access to 'objective' truth, but as presenting a partial perspective which creates rather than describes its object. And literature in consequence becomes no more fictive, false or imaginary than any other discourse about the world. In this perspective, Plato's poets are no longer seen as 'lying' or even fabricating, they are presenting a 'truth' as valid as that of the philosopher who would seek to banish them.[45]

The early Sartre does not go quite so far as this—he does not wish to break down the distinction between philosophy and literature entirely—but he does state that novels necessarily express the novelist's metaphysics: 'une technique Romanesque renvoie toujours à la métaphysique du romancier' (SI 66), where by 'metaphysics' Sartre means an exploration of the situation of the novelist in the world.[46]

As Simone de Beauvoir wrote, Sartre 'deployed his ideas through the medium of the story.... He had to replace proposition by demonstration.'[47] He sought to marry the conceptual and the imaginative in the narrative mode. In the words of one of Sartre's early characters, Frédéric, the novel should be 'as difficult as a philosophical work [... it should] occupy our intellectual life as much as our affective life [... and] show a man at work, reasoning' (EJ 229).

Plays, on the other hand, are taken by Sartre to 'pose problems' without resolving them.[48] Unlike novels, plays present characters and situations directly to their audiences, without the mediation of a

---

[44] Mulhall 2005: Conclusion.   [45] Howells 1988: 46.

[46] See SII: 251, where we read 'la métaphysique n'est pas une discussion sterile sur des notions abstraites qui échappent à l'éxperience, c'est un effort vivant pour embrasser du dedans la condition humaine dans sa totalité'.

[47] Beauvoir 1962: 50.   [48] See TS 247.

narrator's[49] omniscience. Plays are polyphonic, and the plurality of voices, it might be argued, renders it difficult—if, indeed, it is possible at all—to isolate *the* voice of the author. Even so, I have decided to include references to Sartre's plays because sin is a leitmotif that recurs in most of them. My argument concerning *Being and Nothingness* does not depend on my interpretation of Sartre's theatre, but I have included reference to the plays because they provide concrete and particular illustrations of possible readings of Sartre, including my own.

While Sartre was a prisoner of war in 1940, the first of his eleven plays, *Bariona*, was written and staged. It was never professionally produced or commercially published (on Sartre's instructions),[50] but Sartre described the experience of performing it as a profound discovery: 'As I addressed my comrades across the footlights, speaking to them of their state as prisoners, when I suddenly saw them so remarkably silent and attentive, I realized what theatre ought to be: a great, collective, religious phenomenon ... a theatre of myths.'[51]

After this amateur début, Sartre went on to write ten plays which were all published and professionally produced (see table 1.1). His theatrical characters are overshadowed by a preoccupation with their acts. Whether they are acts that were committed (or *not* committed) in the past, or contemplated acts in the future, acts are the determining feature of human existence. In keeping with Sartre's dictum that 'existence precedes essence', acts are inventions rather than products. But they are not always discrete, past events; rather, even once committed they require an effort of clarification—the human person must clarify the relationship between herself and her action. Guicharnaud suggests that Sartre's plays, therefore, are 'investigations of the different relations of man to his acts'. Sartre's characters' frequent use of the phrase 'my act' emphatically expresses the idea of an act being 'both an outer object and a reciprocal bond between man and what he does',[52] whether that bond is one of denial[53] or resolute ownership.[54]

---

[49] Unless the devices of prologue or chorus are employed by the playwright.
[50] See section on *Bariona* in Chapter 7.
[51] See TS 63–4.
[52] Guicharnaud 1967: 138.
[53] e.g. Estelle's bad faith in *Huis clos*; the madness of Franz in *Altona* or Electra in *Les Mouches*; Heinrich's devil in *Le Diable et le bon dieu*.
[54] e.g. Orestes in *Les Mouches*.

Table 1.1. Sartre's plays

Date of Theatrical Production	Title of Play	In Context of Publication of Philosophical Works
1940 (Christmas)	*Bariona*	*L'Imaginaire*
1943 (June)	*Les Mouches*	*L'Être et le néant*
1944 (May)	*Huis clos*	
1946	*Morts sans sépulture*	
1946	*La Poutain respectueuse*	*L'Existentialisme est un humanisme*
1948	*Les Mains sales*	
1951	*Le Diable et le bon dieu*	
1954	*Kean*	
1955	*Nekrassov*	
1959	*Les Séquestrés d'Altona*	(1960) *Critique de la raison dialectique*
1965	*Les Troyennes*	

The existentialist tenet that whatever I do, *I* am the one who does it—that there is no appeal to a predisposition or nature to mitigate my responsibility for my conduct—means there are no legitimate excuses for any action. The dramatic intensity of Sartre's plays, therefore, rests on the seriousness of the acts committed. Whereas Sartre's novels demonstrate his philosophy in everyday contexts and mundane actions (e.g. the famous tree scene in *La Nausée*), in his plays 'dramatic economy demands that the weight of dilution be replaced by the shock of concentration'.[55]

The majority of Sartre's plays contain explicitly religious language. Whether it is explicitly Christian (*Bariona, La Poutain respectueuse, Le Diable et le bon dieu, Huis clos, Altona*) or an anachronistically Christian portrayal of the religion of ancient Greece (*Les Mouches, Les Troyennes*), the language of sin is plentiful in Sartre's theatrical works—as it is in his philosophy.[56] The use of language is not necessarily to be equated with the use of concepts; and in some cases of Sartre's use of the word 'sin' an ironic or rhetorical reading seems most obvious. However, Sartre also uses the word in ways that betray familiarity with the concept and related theological metaphors.

Consider *Lucifer and the Lord* [*Le Diable et le bon dieu*], for example. We will not return to it in subsequent parts of the book because of its late date (1951), but the words 'sin' and 'iniquity' occur

---

[55] Guicharnaud 1967: 139. For this reason, some conclude that 'Sartre the philosopher makes a better dramatist than novelist' (Blair 1970: 103), and others that theatre, for Sartre, was 'a snare and a delusion' (Weightman 1970: 31).

[56] On Sartre's religious language see King 1974; Howells 1981; Hopkins 1994; Gellman 2009; Wang 2009; Meszaros (2012: 181, n. 312) writes that religious references in BN 'are numerous, and none of them could be described as nihilistic'.

frequently in this—reputedly Sartre's favourite—play.[57] The word is presented in almost a dozen ways:

1. as debt (LL 60);

2. in term of particular sins, plural; specific actions such as allowing oneself to die (LL 63) or lust, 'the most degrading of vices' (LL 174);

3. as deserving (or even requiring) punishment (unless indulgences bought) (LL 126);[58]

4. as something to expiate (LL 131);

5. as something which is impossible to expiate (LL 131);

6. as 'nothing' (LL 131)—such that 'nothing can expiate nothing';

7. as 'the world itself' ('The world itself is iniquity; if you accept the world, you are equally iniquitous', LL 110);

8. as despair (LL 110);

9. as 'inequality, servitude and misery'—these are the 'original sin' Goetz sees himself as chosen by God to efface (LL 118);

10. as something which must be suffered for, on behalf of mankind (LL 146–7);

11. as woman's body (see LL 178, in dialogue with Hilda about desire).

These suggest a level of theological sophistication that is underexplored in Sartre scholarship. The first presentation of sin, for example, as debt, uses one of the two dominant metaphors for sin in the Hebrew Bible.[59] And, as we shall see in Chapters 2 and 3, sin as nothing has a long provenance with which Sartre was demonstrably familiar, as does sin as despair.

In her well-known article 'Sartre and Negative Theology', Howells writes that while Sartre clearly rejects mystical knowledge, 'the parallels

---

[57] The title of the play, as well as its setting in the Reformation, makes clear that religion is one of its key themes. But it is difficult to parse any systematic understanding of the religion at stake, and Sartre's considered position in relation to it. One possible reading is that, in the aftermath of the death of God, human beings must realize that there will be no divine trial to condemn our actions: the only trial we undergo concerns how we are seen by other human beings. But the polyphonic nature of the play leaves open other possibilities.

[58] In one of the many allusions to the Gospels in the plays, after selling an indulgence the priest Tetzel says, 'Go home and sin no more' (LL 126).

[59] See G. Anderson 2010.

between the mystical conception of God and the transcendent *néant* of Sartrean consciousness are striking. Moreover,' she continues, 'Sartre's attitude towards the mystical tradition itself is ambiguous and repays closer scrutiny.'[60] Recent research by John Gillespie, Jerome Gellman, and myself supports the latter claim. But this book disputes the former: it agrees that Sartre's *néant* owes a conceptual debt to theology. But it is not the mystical conception of God that influenced Sartre's *néant*: it is the concept of sin.

In 'Je ne suis plus réaliste', an interview from 1972 which is still unpublished in English,[61] Sartre was asked outright whether his early philosophy retained 'a kind of original sin'.[62] Sartre's response was: 'You are right. I did not speak in terms of "sin" but I remember something Aron said about *Being and Nothingness*: "Everyone chooses, but they all choose badly!".'[63] In the same interview Verstraeten asked Sartre whether he needed something akin to 'grace' to overcome it. But Sartre explicitly rejects such a notion: 'I do not see why I need to be visited by a "grace". But even so it is an interesting problem, because in a certain sense it is the problem of freedom.' The reason grace must be rejected, on his view, is that: 'If it is really a superior possibility which enables some to see clearly and come to the revolutionary side, then "grace" cannot come from anywhere but God! How could we tolerate it if the future of man came from elsewhere and not from himself?'[64] The problem with grace—and, we read in *Liberté-Égalité*, another recently republished MS dating from *c*.1952,[65] with Lutheranism, Jansenism, and eighteenth-century materialism—is *determinism* (LE 51). Grace renders the human person *passive*,[66] and has been used to justify inequality.[67]

Having made these introductory remarks, it is to the 'Doctor of Grace' and his followers that I now turn.

---

[60] Howells 1981: 550. In addition to Howells 1981, Salvan 1967, Gellman 2009, and Kirkpatrick 2013 also address Sartre's relationship to mysticism.

[61] This interview was originally published in *Gulliver* in November 1972 (no. 1, pp. 39–46), and was recently republished in *Études sartriennes* (Sartre and Verstraeten 2010).

[62] Sartre and Verstraeten 2010: 13.

[63] In Sartre's words: 'Vous avez raison' (Sartre and Verstraeten 2010: 13).

[64] Sartre and Verstraeten 2010: 11–12.   [65] See de Coorebyter 2008: 156.

[66] See LE 214, where Sartre describes 'quietism, Cartesian intuition, and Jansenist passivity'.

[67] In LE Sartre takes 'grace' to be the root of bourgeois ideology. For more on Sartre's non-Marxist account see de Coorebyter 2008, 2010.

Part II

A Genealogy of Nothingness

Part II

A Genealogy of Worldliness

2

French Sins, I

'Les mystiques du néant' and 'les disciples de Saint Augustin'

> Il n'y a point de doctrine plus propre à l'homme que celle-là qui l'instruit de sa double capacité de recevoir et de perdre la grâce à cause du double péril où il est toujours exposé de désespoir ou d'orgueil.[1]

This chapter demonstrates that theology played a significant part in Sartre's formation as a phenomenologist. In the proto-existentialist writings of Augustine and Pascal, for example, we find descriptions of the lived experience that underlay their conceptions of original sin.[2] We saw in Chapter 1 that some scholars have noted a resemblance between Sartre's phenomenological description of human reality and the Christian doctrine of original sin, and that there has not been any sustained study of this resemblance.[3]

In this and the next chapter, I introduce the conceptions of sin from which Sartre drew. Taken together, the two chapters in this part are intended to offer material to support the claims that are defended in parts III and IV. This part will demonstrate (1) that Sartre's formation—before his discovery of phenomenology in the early 1930s—included a theological element (which is neglected in the English-language scholarship on Sartre); and (2) that the content of this theology was

---

[1] Pascal, *Pensées*, L354/B524.
[2] See, e.g., the experience described in *The Confessions* or the *Pensées*, both of which Jean Wahl took to be proto-existentialist.
[3] Although see Kirkpatrick 2015.

indeed Augustinian—but more specifically, it was the Augustinianism of *l'école française de spiritualité* and of Jansenism: the 'mystiques du néant' and 'disciples de Saint Augustin'. For readers unfamiliar with these French conceptions of sin it is easy to overlook their influence on Sartre. But they are present, and as we shall see in Part III, recognizing this genealogy illuminates some of the 'slippages' philosophers have difficulty explaining in Sartre's use of *le néant*.[4]

In this chapter, therefore, I will explore Augustine's ontology of sin, its origins and effects, before turning to the seventeenth-century French revival of Augustinianism. Seventeenth-century France—*le grand siècle*—is also known in French scholarship as *le siècle d'Augustin*.[5] Augustine's influence on the French theology, philosophy, and literature of this period has been documented in many scholarly works over the past century and a half, and the story of *la querelle des augustinismes* is a complex one that cannot be treated in full here.[6] For the purposes of this book, therefore, I will consider the *néantisme* of Pierre de Bérulle, the legacy of Descartes, the Jansenism of Pascal, and the mysticism of Fénelon. My aims in so doing are (1) to lay the necessary historical and conceptual groundwork for the exegetical and constructive accounts to follow in parts III and IV; and (2) to open up this vein of enquiry for readers who are not familiar with this tradition and its influence.[7]

AUGUSTINE

Any study of original sin must acknowledge the importance of Augustine's expression of it, and Sartre's case is no exception.[8] But the source and interpretation of Augustine's doctrine of original sin is

---

[4] See Chapter 4.

[5] This expression, now widely used, was pronounced first by Jean Dagens at the Congrès international des études françaises de 1951 (published in Dagens 1953).

[6] See the introduction to Sellier 1970 for an excellent summary of these 'three Augustines'; and also Magnard 1996 and Dagens 1953 on the seventeenth century as the 'century of Saint Augustine'.

[7] Although the present work concerns only the early Sartre, given that Sartre's criticism of bourgeois ideology may have had a non-Marxist, *theological* origin, it is clear that this aspect of his formation is as significant as it is underexplored. See Coorebyter 2010.

[8] See Kirkpatrick 2015 on Sartre's 'Augustinian' atheism. Cohen-Solal indicates that Augustine was among those Sartre read in the mid-1920s, citing the Archives of the École Normale Supérieure. See Cohen-Solal 1987: 67.

contested. For Augustine, the origin of 'original sin' is Adam's literal historical sinful act in Eden, as recounted in Genesis 3. This is transmitted to subsequent generations by concupiscence,[9] which is to say that following Adam's fall, sexual reproduction with Eve altered human nature such that their descendants—namely, all of humankind—live in a state of sin from the moment of conception. After the fall, humans are separated from God, others, and their true selves. In the terminology of the Apostle Paul,[10] sin is *hamartia*—'falling short' or 'missing the mark'. As outcasts of Eden, human beings are deficient. We exist in a state of lack and long to be restored to our right relation to God, others and ourselves.

The problem of evil plagued Augustine's thoughts both before and after his conversion to Christianity.[11] In answer to the perennial question 'How could a good God let bad things happen?' Augustine's answer was that humanity—through the exercise of free will—chose nothingness over Being. The problem of evil, therefore, is a problem of freedom. Human willing is the source of sin—and evil—in the world.

Augustine's original sin, therefore, is explicitly ontological. On Augustine's account, the ontology of the fallen human subject—between being and nothingness—has phenomenological and psychological repercussions. For Augustine, the self is central to any understanding of being because ontology is integrally linked to personal questions of desiring, willing, and seeking to know.[12] Moreover, on his view, to be human is to be restless, constantly beset by questions. In the *Confessions* he writes that 'I had become to myself a vast problem';[13] he was 'not himself', not 'at home' but rather constantly uncertain and uneasy. In the *Soliloquies* we read that:

> For long I had been turning over in my mind many various thoughts. For many days I had been earnestly seeking to know myself and my chief good and what evil was to be shunned . . .

---

[9] Augustine 1957: V.iv.18; I.ix.42.   [10] See 1 Corinthians 6:18, for example.
[11] Augustine 1961: VII.3.
[12] See Smith 2001: 275. Indeed, Augustine is widely acknowledged to have anticipated 'existentialist' themes; in Jean Wahl's introduction to Sartre's *The Philosophy of Existentialism*, for example, Wahl traces the philosophy of existence back to Kierkegaard, but also to Pascal and Saint Augustine, 'who replaced pure speculation with a kind of thinking closer to the person, the individual' (Wahl 2012: 205).
[13] Augustine 1961: IV.4.

REASON: What then do you wish to know?
AUGUSTINE: All that I have mentioned in my prayer.
REASON: Briefly summarize it.
AUGUSTINE: I desire to know God and the soul.
REASON: Nothing more?
AUGUSTINE: Nothing less.[14]

In investigating himself Augustine considered the subject of his study to be both closest to and farthest from his understanding.[15] The self is 'a house divided against itself',[16] containing 'feelings so much at variance, in such conflict with each other'.[17] This is not our natural state, however; such division is symptomatic of sin.

For Augustine, evil did not enter creation through any evil act, but through the evil wills of Adam and Eve: an evil will 'is the cause of all evils'.[18] If the evil will is the origin of evil, one might be tempted to ask, what then is the origin of the evil will? In Babcock's gloss, for example, Augustine's reading of Genesis 3 merely shows us 'how human beings, already evil, enacted their first misdeed'.[19] But Augustine is agnostic on this question, relegating it to the realm of mystery.[20] By making pride purely voluntary (for only in their prelapsarian state did Adam and Eve have truly free wills), divine providence is absolved of the charge of direct authorship of sin.

On Augustine's view there is no cause of the evil will. Moreover, to enquire into the origins of the evil will is misguided. It erroneously presupposes that evil is a substantial reality:

> The truth is that one should not try to find an efficient cause for a wrong choice. It is not a matter of efficiency, but of deficiency; the evil will itself is not effective but defective... To try to discover the causes of such defection—deficient, not efficient causes—is like trying to see darkness or to hear silence.[21]

Rather, for Augustine evil is (famously) conceived as the privation of good (*privatio boni*). Forged against Manichean philosophy, his account of evil attempts to reject metaphysical dualism by denying evil any substantial reality. Since God created all things, anything

---

[14] Augustine 1948: I.i.1; I.ii.7.   [15] Augustine 1961: X.16.
[16] Augustine 1961: VIII.8.   [17] Augustine 1961: IV.14.
[18] Augustine 2010: II.xv.48; III.49.   [19] Babcock 1988: 42.
[20] Augustine 2003: XII.xii.477.   [21] Augustine 2003: XII.vii.479–80.

which *is* is good.[22] Like silence, deficiency does not need to be accounted for because it is not a thing in itself.

Evil is unnatural—not according to nature (that is, measure, form, and order) as God created it—and therefore it has no being per se. For Augustine, God is the Good, Being, the source of all being; there is nothing contrary to him in nature. For this reason, evil cannot be a substance or essence in itself.

The Movement from Nothingness

Nothingness therefore plays a crucial role in Augustine's theology, for God's grace can only truly be understood 'in terms of the evils it is to cure'.[23] For Augustine sin is 'a movement that comes from nothingness', turning the soul 'away from true Being, the originator of the created Being'.[24] Sin has a corroding effect on the soul's being; it is a 'fall movement, which brings about in the soul a failing of essence'.[25] This, then, is what constitutes evil: 'falling away from essence and tending not to be.'[26] As we will see later in this chapter, many of the quarrels that took place among seventeenth-century French interpreters of Augustine concerned how far human beings had fallen: did they fall away to the extent of losing all being? Is the human, separated from God, *un néant pur*?

Augustine repeatedly emphasizes that human beings, as God's creations, are good.[27] But when we choose 'the will's own line and not God's', we frustrate our own perfection and are plagued by dissatisfaction—we slip towards non-being and cannot of our own power satiate our desire to be, our 'ontological hunger' (to borrow Zum Brunn's phrase).[28] When we live according to nature, by

---

[22] Augustine 1961: XIII.ii.2; XIII.4.5.
[23] Gilson 1961: 143.   [24] Augustine 2010: II.xx.54.
[25] Augustine, *De Mus.* VI.xi.33, cited in Zum Brunn 1988: 51.
[26] Augustine, *De Mor.* II.ii.2, cited in Zum Brunn 1988: 51.
[27] It is worth noting, as Mann does, that there is no textual evidence that Augustine thinks God must create the 'best possible world': 'Creation is indeed very good (*De Genesi ad litteram imperfectus liber* 1.3, echoing Genesis 1.31; created out of the "fullness of [God's] goodness" (*Conf.* 13.2.2; 13.4.5) [. . . and] God will not create a thing unless he *knows* that it is good (*De civ. Dei* 11.21)' (Mann 2001: 43). See also Augustine 1982: VIII.14, in which he describes two purposes of God's love of creation: that it should exist and that it should abide.
[28] Zum Brunn 1988: 53.

contrast, 'we are and are on our way to becoming fully ourselves'.[29] Sin thus illuminates a spectrum of ontological possibility; we may either enact evil and decrease in being or participate in God, in the plenitude of Being. Augustine's use of language in characterizing the ontological depletion of the soul led astray from Being leaves little question as to the scalar nature of his view: '*minus minusque esse*, to be less and less; *ad nihilum uergere, tendere, inclinari*, to come close to nothingness; *inanescere*, to nihilate oneself'.[30]

The self, Augustine writes, is disposed to seek its own happiness.[31] But by abandoning the rule of God who *is* the truth, we come to live in falsehood, 'not living in the way for which [we are] created'.[32] This involves us in a great irony. We want to be happy, yet we pursue happiness by the most futile means, by fleeing its source.[33] We desire flourishing; we enact destruction. This is a moral failure on our part, but it is also an ontological deformity:

> Man did not fall away to the extent of losing all being; but when he had turned towards himself [*inclinatus ad se*] his being was less real than when he adhered to him who exists in a supreme degree. And so, to abandon God and to exist in oneself, that is to please oneself, is not immediately to lose all being; but it is to come nearer to nothingness [*nihilo*].[34]

Evil is nothing. Its only power is the power of perversion, the capacity to corrupt creation.[35]

Disordered Love

But this capacity to corrupt is frequently exercised by human beings. And when we turn to ourselves (*inclinatus ad se*) instead of adhering to God, there is a shift in the relatedness of the self. Augustine vividly portrays this dynamic in his description of sin as disordered love. 'Sin in a human being is disorder or perversity, that is, an aversion to the more preferable creator, and a conversion to the inferior creatures.'[36]

---

[29] Jenson 2007: 21.   [30] Zum Brunn 1988: 53.
[31] The *beata vita* (Augustine 1961: X.xx.29).   [32] Augustine 2003: XIV.iv.552.
[33] Augustine 1961: X.xxiii.34.   [34] Augustine 2003: XIV.xiii.572–3.
[35] In this respect Augustine's account of evil is heavily indebted to Neo-Platonism: Plotinus writes in the *Enneads* that 'Evil cannot have place among Beings or in the Beyond-Being; these are good. There remains only, if Evil exist at all, that it be situate in the realm of Non-being, that it be some mode, as it were, of the Non-being' (*Enn.* I.8.3; cited in Pattison 1996: 9). For Porphyry's influence cf. Zum Brunn 1988: 35f.
[36] Augustine 1953: I.ii.18.

In the *Confessions* Augustine describes his own turning from Creator to created, writing 'my sin was this, that I looked for pleasure, beauty, and truth not in him but in myself and his other creatures, and the search led me instead to pain, confusion and error'.[37] The temptation to succumb to the power of others—which Augustine describes as 'the desire to be loved or feared'—is a perpetual temptation 'though in such pleasure there is no true joy'.[38] We are easily ensnared by custom[39] and social hierarchy, for the 'enemy of our true happiness . . . knows that when men hold certain offices in human society, it is necessary that they should be loved and feared by other men. He sets his traps about me, baiting them with tributes of applause, in the hope that in my eagerness to listen I may be caught off my guard. He wants me to divorce my joy from the truth and place it in man's duplicity.'[40] Only God, on Augustine's view, can see 'the hidden merits of our souls'.[41] And it is only by turning to God— away from nothingness—that our restless selves can return to their eternal home.[42]

Unde bonum? Grace

But we cannot 'turn to God' by ourselves. It is only the grace of Christ— the love of God poured out in our hearts by the Holy Spirit[43]—that enables us to love God and delight in the good. Left to our own, we delight in our concupiscence. Augustine's doctrine of grace was developed in opposition to Pelagianism and semi-Pelagianism,[44] so it is worthwhile to turn to pertinent features of that debate. The central issue was the doctrine of original sin, and particularly the extent to which the will of the fallen human can be called free. Indeed, as Adolph

---

[37] Augustine 1961: I. 20.   [38] Augustine 1961: X.36.
[39] Augustine 1961: 1.16.   [40] Augustine 1961: X.36.
[41] Augustine 1961: VII.6.
[42] Book IV of the *Confessions* concludes: 'For in you our good abides and it has no blemish, since it is yourself. Nor do we fear that there is no home to which we can return. We fell from it; but our home is your eternity and it does not fall because we are away' (Augustine 1961: IV.16).
[43] Augustine 1961: XIII.7.
[44] The Semi-Pelagian view held that salvation is accomplished through the cooperation of the human will and divine grace, and that predestination should be understood as God's foreknowledge of free human decisions. Since Pelagianism is more pertinent to the argument of this book, it will be the main focus of the following section.

von Harnack wrote, there has 'never, perhaps, been another crisis of equal importance in church history'.[45]

The debate between Augustine and Pelagius is complicated both historically and theologically.[46] For the present purposes, however, it is important to note a few major points of disagreement: concerning freedom of the will, sin, and grace. For Pelagius, unlike Augustine, human beings possess total freedom of the will and are totally responsible for their sins. On Pelagius' view, any imperfection in humanity reflects negatively on the goodness of God, and for God to intervene directly in such a way as to influence human decisions would undermine human freedom and integrity. Humans, therefore, are equipped with perfect scales on which to weigh the merit of their actions, free from bias, and any evil decisions are theirs alone. There is no need for divine grace on this view; humans are perfectible by their own lights. God would not lay on human beings commands which they were unable to bear; consequently, Pelagius thought, we can live out the commands we are given. In his own words: 'since perfection is possible for humanity, it is obligatory'.[47]

Since, on Pelagius' view, human beings are perfectible by their own effort, any human sin is an act wilfully committed against God. In the language of actual and original sin, Pelagius accepts the possibility of actual sin, but denies any original element. This is seen most clearly in his doctrine of grace. Whereas Augustine frequently refers to John 5:5, 'apart from me you can do nothing', seeing the human as totally dependent on God for salvation, and grace as a 'gift' of divine assistance that renews and restores us, Pelagius did not think such a gift was necessary to live sinlessly. On his view, human reason was not corrupted or compromised. Consequently, faith was a meritorious human decision to which God responds by providing the grace of further human understanding.

For Augustine, by contrast, in creating Adam God gave him a 'sufficient grace', which gave him the ability to choose the good, but not the will to do so. Adam was *free* to choose whether to cooperate with it. But Adam chose to sin, leading to the guilty conception and condemnation of each subsequent human. All humanity fell in Adam's

---

[45] Harnack 2005, 169 (section V/IV/3).

[46] Historically, for example, it is important to note that Pelagianism is best regarded as a mix of ideas put forward by several writers in Rome at the end of the fourth century AD, by Pelagius and others, including Rufinus of Syria and Caelestius.

[47] Cited in Kleist 2008: chapter 1, n. 7 (n.p.).

fall; all tend to nothingness; and all are thus inexcusable before God. There is no reason God should offer grace to anyone: all deserve damnation. But God chose to elect some to salvation, not because of their foreseen merits but because he gives them the ability to cooperate with his grace. This grace 'grants that the delight of sin may be conquered by the delight of what is right'.[48]

On Augustine's view, the evil of the world—and the 'divided houses' we call ourselves—are part of a *felix culpa*, a 'fortunate fall'. As Mann writes, Augustine emphatically affirms that 'some things, even when corrupted, are still better than other things that remain uncorrupted. According to human estimation, at least, corrupted gold is better than uncorrupted silver, and corrupted silver is still better than uncorrupted lead.'[49] The fall is fortunate because God 'judged it better to bring good out of evil, than to allow no evil to exist'.[50]

Rowan Williams writes of Augustine's account of nothingness that it is not 'tidy or exhaustive'.[51] But describing sin in Augustine's onto-logical terms—that is, as a process of relational loss or corruption through which our being is diminished—enables the human person to approach God in search of 'temporal processes of clarification, reconciliation, self-discovery in love, the processes that lead us beyond rivalry and self-protection'.[52] Augustine's relational ontology—his inclusion of the threat of nothingness as well as the plenitude of Being—reveals a self which exists in relation to others and which, in finding rest and ordering its loves in God, discovers that to be most fully is to be for others—not merely for oneself.

This relational ontology survived in a tradition of French mysti-cism which assigned a leading role to the Augustinian anthropology of nothingness. And to understand this thread in the tapestry of seventeenth-century French Augustinianisms, we must look to a little-known figure, the Cardinal Pierre de Bérulle (1575–1629).

BÉRULLE: *LE MYSTICISME DU NÉANT*

Pierre de Bérulle's influence far exceeds his reputation. His obscurity outside France—with very little of his work available in English even today—derives, in part, from his obscurity in his own country. In an

[48] Augustine 1999: 2:217. [49] *De nat. boni c. Man.* 5, cited in Mann 2001: 44.
[50] Augustine 1947: xxvii. [51] Williams 2000: 120.
[52] Williams 2000: 121.

anthology of French mysticism published in Paris in 1941, Bérulle is introduced as someone who has been 'neglected' by 'official literary history'.[53] Despite his historical significance in both philosophical and theological circles—as Descartes's spiritual director,[54] for example, and an influence on Malebranche,[55] and indeed as the founder of the Oratory of France—his political fall from grace (in a dispute with one of the better-known cardinals of his epoch, Cardinal Richelieu) led to a prolonged period in *purgatoire*.[56]

But after Henri Brémond published the third volume of his *Histoire littéraire du sentiment réligieux en France*[57] in 1921 Bérulle and the school of spirituality he founded—referred to by Brémond as 'l'école française de spiritualité'[58]—began to receive recognition as one of the 'masters of the masters' of French mysticism.[59] Bérulle's exposition of Augustine, as we shall see, was to have a profound influence on seventeenth-century French philosophy, theology, and literature—not least through his mentee Saint-Cyran, and Saint-Cyran's own Mère Angélique of Port-Royal.[60] And although he was not treated at great length in them, Bérulle's importance was noted in books Sartre read and cited in his *mémoire* for the Diplôme d'Études Supérieures.[61]

In what follows it must be emphasized that there is only space to paint a partial portrait of Bérullian spirituality; the cardinal is renowned for his theocentrism, and for rejecting the 'abstract mysticism' of his predecessors on account of its 'Christological gaps'—that is to say, for ignoring the humanity of Jesus. For Bérulle, theology and spirituality are inseparable. In his own words: 'Some distinguish

---

[53] Daniel-Rops 1941: 133.   [54] Bachmann 1964: 44.

[55] See Cochois 1963: 158.

[56] In a study of Bérulle published in 1933, Claude Taveau—himself a priest of the Oratory—notes that Bérulle's *Oeuvres complètes* were published in two editions, one in 1644 and one in 1856, but that still there was no work suited to the needs of novices reading Bérulle for the first time (Taveau 1933: 11). The editions were Bourgoing (1644) and Migne (1856).

[57] Published in eleven volumes between 1916 and 1936.

[58] Although this term gained currency following Brémond's use, it had been employed earlier; Thompson attributes its coinage to the Sulpician G. Letourneau around 1913 (1989: p. 89, n. 1).

[59] See Taveau 1933: 12; Daniel Rops 1941: 37 quotes Brémond referring to de Sales and Bérulle as *les maîtres des maîtres*; on Bérulle's formative role see also Cognet 1949: 53.

[60] See Doyle 2000: 17ff. for Bérulle's influence on Saint-Cyran.

[61] See Chapter 1, n. 18.

between a mystical and a practical theology, but this is a distinction which I do not wish to employ,' says Bérulle. 'All God's graces distributed upon earth are to enable us to act better.'[62] But rather than focusing on God, Christ, and grace—central though they are to a complete understanding of Bérulle—what concerns us is Bérulle's anthropology and the place of nothingness (*le néant*) in it.[63]

Throughout Bérulle's works nothingness plays a profound role; it is one of the most frequent of his themes.[64] Indeed, Thompson describes *l'école française* as 'rigorous in its phenomenology of human depravity', noting that 'it moves beyond the surface to the *fond*, from a symptomatology of evil and sin to its roots.'[65] It is a question of debate whether this emphasis on nothingness resulted from 'an excessively pessimistic interpretation of St Paul and St Augustine' or 'as a reaction to the unwarranted exaltation of human nature and freedom at the hands of the humanists', but Bérulle looked on man as 'the most vile and useless creature of all; indeed, as dust, mud, and a mass of corruption'.[66]

For Bérulle, the first quality of being human is to be in a relation of inferiority or superiority with the world, in a relationship of dependence.[67]

> There is nothing better known in the world, by the senses or by reason, than the difference between and condition of being master and servant. It is the most general and applicable quality in the world. It applies to all men: it enters into their sentiments and affections; it enters into or even invades every state and condition . . . and if they are masters of some, they are servants in the eyes of others.[68]

---

[62] Quoted in Thompson 1989: 32.

[63] It is worth noting, nonetheless, that Bérulle's notion of God is thought to be 'pseudo-Dionysian and Platonic, as transmitted by St Augustine and the Rhineland mystics'. Like Augustine, he considered unity the principal attribute of God (Aumann 1985: 223).

[64] See e.g. Bellemare 1959: 19; Cognet 1949: 66. Problematically, some render the French *néant* 'nought' in English, which loses the ontological and cosmological connotations of the original (see e.g. Dupré and Saliers 1989: 51).

[65] Thompson 1989: 86. Thompson also notes here that this accent in Bérulle became even more pronounced in the thought of his successor Olier.

[66] Aumann 1985: 221; latterly citing Bérulle's *Oeuvres complètes*, ed. J. P. Migne, Paris, 1856, p. 880.

[67] Bachmann 1964: 1. See also Cognet 1949: 58 on this theme, which Cognet attributes to Bérulle's Augustinianism.

[68] Bérulle 1944: 1145.

This condition of dependence and servitude is inseparable from being human, on Bérulle's view: we are creatures, and our creaturely origin is such that, though made *by* God, we were made *from* nothing.[69]

Bérulle clearly distinguishes between the order of nature and that of grace. One of the differences separating humanity from other creatures 'is that they were created perfect in their state and without the expectation of a further new degree which they lack; but man's nature was not created to remain in the limitations of nature; it was made for grace, and destined for a state raised above its power'.[70] In a frequently cited passage Bérulle describes human beings as 'a nothingness that tends to nothingness':

> Nous sommes un néant qui tend au néant, qui cherche le néant, qui s'occupe du néant, qui se contente du néant, qui se remplit du néant, et qui enfin se ruine et se détruit soi-même pour un néant. A lieu que nous devons être un néant à la vérité—car cela nous convient par nature—mais un néant en la main de Dieu, un néant destiné à Dieu, un néant consacré à Dieu; un néant rempli de Dieu, et enfin un néant possédé de Dieu et possédant Dieu, et cela nous convient par grâce.[71]

As Taveau notes, on Bérulle's account there are three types of nothingness: the nothingness of nature, the nothingness of sin, and the nothingness of grace.[72] With respect to the first, the created nature of humanity contains the traces of the nothingness whence it came: humanity is 'pulled out of nothingness',[73] and in fact every creature is 'but a nothingness'.[74] In a frequently cited passage Bérulle writes that 'our being is full of nothingness; our understanding is full of ignorance, our power is full of weakness and impotence; because there is more nothingness than being in our being'.[75]

Where the nothingness of sin is concerned, Bérulle was the first to use *amour-propre* to translate Augustine's *amor sui*—it is the *figmentum malum* of the self.[76] For Bérulle, like Augustine, sin is the absence of good; it explicitly presented in ontological terms as the privation

---

[69] Bérulle 1859: 219.
[70] Bérulle 1944: 132, 3, and 27, 3, cited in de Lubac 1969: 270.
[71] Bérulle 1944: 1129.   [72] Taveau 1933: 248–51.
[73] In French, 'tirée du néant'; G 219, cited in Bachmann 1964: 2.
[74] In French, 'toute créature n'est qu'un néant'; L II 5, cited in Bachmann 1964: 3.
[75] '... notre être est rempli de néant; notre lumière est remplie d'ignorance, notre puissance est remplie de faiblesse et impuissance; car il y a plus du nu néant que de l'être dans notre être...' (Bérulle 1944: 1014).
[76] Thweatt 1980: 79.

of being; a spiritual death. This nothingness reveals the creature's weakness: the creature cannot, of its own strength, stand out from nothingness. It is worse than the nothingness of nature in the sense that it rejects grace; in sin nothingness opposes the being of God. What is needful, on Bérulle's view, is that we recognize that 'on all sides we are nothing but impotence, indigence, nothingness... and this nothingness must be surrounded by grace on all sides'.[77] If humanity seeks its origins outside of God, we will find nothing but the nothingness from which we issue.[78]

The third form of nothingness, the nothingness of grace, appears in this context. After original sin, our nature includes inclinations to evil—and indulging in actual sins does nothing but exacerbate this inclination. Salvation is ours in Christ, but on the condition that we fight our flaws, whether hereditary or personal. In doing so grace becomes more active, and we find ourselves *anéanti*. But the nothingness reclaimed by grace is, like the grace of nature, a relative nothingness. By making ourselves nothing—through *anéantisation*—we are released from the spell of self-love and can glimpse the perfection of Christ. But in this state of grace we realize that 'our being is a *relation* [*rapport*] to God';[79] of ourselves, we are nothing. But in the right relation to our creator, we *are*; we share in God's being.

Human life, therefore, rests on two principles: nothingness and divine power (*puissance*). Both are present in creation and perdure in the creature who, in consequence, constantly tends toward nothingness and is always kept from it by divine intervention. Human existence is precarious: there is nothing between us and nothingness but the creative hand of God.[80] In each moment of his life, man is on the point of falling back into nothingness, but at the same moment the [divine] force of continuous creation keeps him from it: God perpetually wills being into being.[81] For Bérulle, therefore,

---

[77] Bérulle 1944: 1140.

[78] '[...] je vous [dis] que le fonds de votre esprit est à Dieu... Si vous contemplez votre origine sans regarder Dieu, vous ne trouverez que le néant, duquel nous sommes tous issus, et qui est notre unique et premier état hors la main de Dieu, et ainsi le néant nous appartient par le fond de la nature; le néant, dis-je, absolu, néant d'être...' (Bérulle 1944: 1237).

[79] Bérulle 1944: 1150.   [80] Bérulle 1944: 1165.

[81] Bérulle writes that humanity needs to receive the continual influence of God, because human dependence is more absolute even than the dependence of light rays on the sun; if one is separated from God for a single moment, one loses one's being at

true self-knowledge can be found—but only 'par le regard pur de Dieu',[82] by the pure gaze of God.

Those who know Sartre's works well may note how much of the mystical language which has perplexed philosophical commentators on *The Transcendence of the Ego* resembles key themes in Bérulle's works. In particular, in order to explain the appearance of perdurance in affects like anger (given the discontinuity of the self), he invokes the concept of 'emanation' (TE 26), which plays a significant role in Bérulle's thought.[83] Richmond writes that 'If this were the only item of religious vocabulary in TE, one might think its appearance accidental. In fact Sartre draws, without inhibition or comment, on a wide range of theological notions: the Ego creates itself *ex nihilo* (p. 32), relates to its states by a kind of *procession* (p. 33), and maintains its qualities by "a veritable continuous creation" (p. 32).'[84]

In addition to the explicit use of mystical language and concepts in Sartre's early work,[85] there is biographical evidence that Sartre thought 'mysticism' worthy of serious study. In particular, we read in Beauvoir's *The Prime of Life* that Sartre 'took an interest in the psychology of mysticism' in the early 1930s, which prompted Beauvoir herself to read the likes of Catherine Emmerich and Angela of Foligno.[86] And later, in *What Is Literature?*, he wrote the intriguing statement that 'God, if he existed, would be as the mystics have seen him, in a *situation* in relationship [rapport] to man' (WL 14; italics original).[87]

I have found no evidence that Sartre read Bérulle directly. However, there is direct evidence that Sartre read Bérullian thinkers: Bérulle's anthropology of *le néant* left a lasting legacy[88] in French thought with which Sartre was demonstrably familiar. The remainder

the same instant. Everything that is created is always dependent on the uncreated being (Bérulle 1859: 251).

[82] Bérulle 1987: 32.   [83] See Howells 2009.

[84] Richmond 2004: xxv.

[85] The use of mystical language has been noted. See Barnes 1958; Howells 1981; Salvan 1967; and Richmond 2004.

[86] Beauvoir 1962: 51. It is perhaps worth noting that Beauvoir's mentor, Jean Baruzi, published his *Saint Jean de la Croix et le problème de l'expérience mystique* in 1931—even if Sartre did dismiss Baruzi's language as 'hazy and obtuse' (WD 85).

[87] For more on Sartre and mysticism, see Kirkpatrick 2017: chapters 1–3; Kirkpatrick 2013.

[88] Howells 2009: 227 notes that Henri Brémond's view of Bérulle—as leading the seventeenth-century French mystical tradition—remains current.

of this chapter will sketch three trajectories of that legacy which are pertinent to the claims of this book: philosophical (in Descartes), theological (in Jansenism and Pascal), and mystical (in Fénelon).

RENÉ DESCARTES

Descartes, clearly, is well known—and well known to have influenced Sartre.[89] But he is included here because there is a danger, as Hegel wrote, that 'the familiar, just because it is familiar, is not really understood'.[90] Descartes is familiar in the English-speaking analytic philosophical tradition for his radical scepticism, mind–body dualism, and rationalist foundationalism. I will take it for granted that my reader is familiar with this Descartes of the cogito and the ontological argument. But considered in his historical context, another side of Descartes emerges, which, though less familiar, is no less important in the development Sartre's theological thinking.

As has already been noted, Descartes's spiritual director was Pierre de Bérulle. Bérulle was said to have encouraged Descartes in his pursuit of truth, and many scholars—particularly those writing in French—consider the cardinal's influence to have been profound. Etienne Gilson writes that 'L'influence du cardinal de Bérulle sur Descartes aurait été telle... qu'il faudrait le considérer comme l'un des facteurs le plus importants parmi ceux qui agirent sur son activité philosophique.'[91] Another commentator, Baillet, describes Bérulle as 'celui qui après Dieu a exercé la plus grande influence sur l'esprit de Descartes';[92] some even take 'complete dominance' to be a more apt description than 'influence'.[93]

Descartes's Augustinianism has also received substantial scholarly treatment: Michael Friedman has noted that Descartes follows an Augustinian 'method of ascent', wherein we seek knowledge of God by seeking knowledge of ourselves; and Stephen Menn has shown that Descartes used the authority of Augustinian metaphysics to legitimate

---

[89] We will explore this influence at greater length in Part III.
[90] Hegel 1977: 18.   [91] Gilson 1913: 161.
[92] Baillet, *Vie de Descartes*, p. 163, cited in Lavelle 1948: 4.
[93] See Alfred Espinas, cited in Read 2012: 60.

his own radically anti-Aristotelian approach to physics.[94] But more significant, for the present argument, is Descartes's use of Augustinian theodicy in his epistemology. In the Fourth Meditation, Descartes uses theodicy to derive a method—which is to say, a discipline of judgement which will help the thinker not to err. Indeed, Menn writes that it is 'possible to suggest that Descartes is not simply *applying* Augustine's doctrine of original sin, but *transforming* it, secularizing it, replacing it in his account of error by its structural equivalent, the childish condition'.[95] Descartes follows Augustine so closely, on Menn's reading, that 'the only difference we can observe in their accounts of this condition is that Augustine adds the historical account of its origin in the sin of Adam, on which Descartes is silent'.[96]

Whether or not Descartes was (wittingly or unwittingly) doing theology is open to dispute. But in the fourth meditation we read

> I am, as it were, an intermediary between God and nothingness, or between supreme being and non-being:[97] my nature is such that insofar as I was created by the supreme being, there is nothing in me to enable me to go wrong or lead me astray; but insofar as I participate in nothingness or non-being, that is, in so far as I am not myself the supreme being and am lacking in countless respects, it is no wonder that I make mistakes. I understand, then, that error as such is not something real which depends on God, but merely a defect.[98]

The Augustinian pedigree of this defect is clear, even if Descartes gives it a particular epistemological inflection: on Descartes's view, error is not 'a pure privation, but rather a lack of some knowledge which should somehow be in me'.[99] However much his successors would protest that Cartesian philosophy was atheistic,[100] Descartes's sceptical project can be read a study of the noetic effects of sin— a theodicy for evils not in the world, but of the mind. And it is this passage from which Sartre is thought to have taken his title, *L'Être et le néant*.[101]

---

[94] See Friedman 2010; Menn 2002.   [95] Menn 2002: 318, n. 14.

[96] Menn 2002: 318, n. 14.

[97] In French, 'entre le Dieu et le néant, c'est-à-dire placé de telle sorte entre le souverain être et le non-être' (Descartes 1981: 70; méditation quatrième).

[98] Descartes 1988: 99–100 (fourth meditation, 'On Truth and Falsity'). The *Meditations* were first published, in Latin, in 1641.

[99] Descartes 1988: 100.

[100] For the 'atheism' of Cartesianism, see Goldmann 1964: 11, 35–9.

[101] See Morris 2008: 9.

Bachmann persuasively argues that the 'spiritual climate' inaugurated by Bérulle paved the way for the *Meditations* of Descartes: 'After having discovered existence in the moment,' he writes,

> Descartes drew the consequences with full rigour. The *cogito* detaches a unique moment of existence, a moment which does not rely in any way on what precedes it nor on anything that follows in the course of its existence. . . . The Cartesian man also must be conserved; to be recreated at each instant. In the nakedness of the Cartesian moment one unerringly arrives at the notion of continual creation . . .[102]

As we shall see, this spiritual climate of Descartes had a legacy that affected the philosophical climate of Sartre. But before turning to Sartre, we must explore the legacy further.

JANSENISM: THE AUGUSTINE OF *AUGUSTINUS*

Bérulle's theological anthropology was to provide fertile soil for another cultural force, a 'specifically French'[103] movement that came to be known as Jansenism.[104] In 1640 a posthumous work was published which resurrected the ancient Pelagian controversy.[105] Although it is but one incarnation of the early modern revival of Augustinianism, according to Michael Moriarty 'the most influential restatement in the Catholic world of the Augustinian conception of original sin' was this work of Cornelius Jansen (1585–1638), Bishop of Ypres.[106] Jansen's 1300-page Latin treatise, *Augustinus* (published in France 'almost immediately' thereafter as *l'Augustin*[107]), was to leave an enormous political, theological, and literary legacy.

Politically, even though the epithet 'Jansenist' was denied by those to whom it was applied,[108] Cardinal Richelieu opposed it

---

[102] Bachmann 1964: 45.   [103] de Coorebyter 2008: 155.

[104] This is not to make the anachronistic claim that Bérulle was Jansenist (although some describe his circle as 'une première génération de jansénistes' (Foreaux 2010: 225)).

[105] See Doyle 2000, chapter 3, for a fuller consideration of the historical and political factors that contributed to the work's reception.

[106] Moriarty 2006: 110.

[107] See Sellier 2000, vol. 2: 139; it was published in both Paris and Rouen.

[108] Arnaud's *Phantôme du jansénisme* (published in 1686) reports that the label was not accepted by anyone to whom it was applied in the seventeenth century; they saw themselves rather as the 'disciples of Saint Augustine' (see Sellier 2000, vol. 2: 44).

vigorously.[109] But Bérulle's disciple Saint-Cyran, who led the Abbey at Port-Royal from 1633 to 1636, was among those who promoted a French edition of *Augustinus*—indeed, Saint-Cyran's emphasis on the depths of human depravity has led some scholars to comment that 'Cyranism' might have been a more apt name for the movement than 'Jansenism'.[110] When Jansenism's central 'five propositions' were condemned by Innocent X in 1653, condemnation did not put a stop to the controversy. Within French Catholicism, Jansenism became a reformist movement which opposed both the doctrinal compromise of the Jesuits and the claims of devout humanism. 'Port-Royal' defended the individual's freedom of thought against the absolutist authorities of church and state.[111]

Theologically, Jansen wrote to defend 'the doctor of grace' against the 'Pelagianism' of the Jesuits, arguing that salvation could not be achieved without God's grace and that grace, once imparted, was irresistible. Even in his prelapsarian state, on the Jansenist view, Adam needed a *sufficient* grace in order to desire the good. But for his postlapsarian successors, only *efficacious* grace could prevent them from sinning, and their own wills—no matter how intense their efforts—could not guarantee the giving of grace.[112] God, in his wisdom, had already chosen the haves and the have nots.

The *Augustinus* is 'undisguisedly polemical in intention'.[113] After the Council of Trent (1545–63) reaffirmed both the reality of the human free will and the necessity of divine grace, the Jesuits (as the

---

[109] For the debate about whether 'Jansenism' ever existed (or was rather 'une illusion créé par le langage qui lui a fait attribuer une unite substantielle'), see Sellier 2000, vol. 2: 53, which gives a good overview of the Laporte school, Goldmann, and Orcibal.

[110] Doyle 2000: 20. Sartre cites Saint-Cyran in LE 211.

[111] The people usually known as Jansenists often denied the existence of such an 'ism' (claiming to be true Christians, or true successors of Augustine), but despite their protest Jansenism was nevertheless, as one scholar puts it, 'the most persistent problem afflicting the Catholic Church for almost two centuries' (Doyle 2000: 1). Its origins concerned theological disputes between factions of the Church, but these theological disputes affected the wider world, in particular by raising questions about the relationship between the French crown and episcopacy, and indeed between France and Rome. By the eighteenth century, precisely what had happened in the seventeenth century was the subject of dispute and further disagreement. And although Jansenism as a movement did not survive the French Revolution, there were old antagonisms that survived it in historiography (and which have resurfaced in recent historiography: see Van Kley 2006; Doyle 2000).

[112] In LE (a MS from c.1952) Sartre explicitly discusses Jansenius's doctrine of efficacious grace.

[113] Abercrombie 1936: 125.

Jansenists saw it) erred in following the approach pioneered by Luis de Molina (1535–1600), on which God distributes a sufficient grace to all and each individual is left to choose whether or not to make use of it. According to Molina, grace is effective when the human recipient cooperates with God through free will.[114] But on the Jansenist view, grace is entirely unmerited and is only granted by God through predestination:

> depuis la chute d'Adam, l'homme a perdu son libre arbitre; que les bonnes œuvres sont un don purement gratuit de Dieu, et que la prédestination des élus est un effet, non de la prescience qu'il a des œuvres, mais de sa pure volonté.[115]

Merited or not, the Jansenists developed a reputation for pessimism, rigorism, and austerity.[116] They emphasized depravity, the refusal of the world (including, in some cases, its literary and theatrical representations), complete dependence on grace, and the fear that grace would be withdrawn.[117] Angélique Arnauld (1591–1661)[118] repeatedly emphasizes her tendencies toward sin, especially pride, in her letters:

> I am miserable from the continuation of my infidelities and resistance to [God's] grace. I cannot fully express to you what I am suffering...
> I believe that my whole life is only lies and hypocrisy. With this I have a fear of God which is servile and horrible and such an apprehension of death and of hell that it seems that I have no love [for God], nor true confidence in him. All my prayers and actions appear...to be only products of human spirit...not of grace.[119]

Because humans could contribute nothing to their salvation, they must beseech God to overcome their wills and their resistance to grace.

Jansenism became known as a doctrine of 'unrelieved pessimism',[120] and indeed—whether or not it is a fair characterization of the teachings of Cornelius Jansen—it is this unrelieved pessimism that merits the

---

[114] See Luis de Molina, *De liberi arbitrii cum gratiae donis, divina praescientia, praedestinatione et reprobatione concordia* (1588).

[115] Jansen, *l'Augustin*, cited in Louandre 1847: 714.

[116] Sartre's LE 209 confirms that this is the reputation Sartre received; there he describes Jansenist *austerité* as 'l'avarice sacrée'.

[117] See Rex 1977: 13.   [118] Another Jansenist figure Sartre cites in LE 254.

[119] Letters to Jeanne de Chantal (1572–1641), 9 November 1637 (cited in Gazier 1915: 153).

[120] Thweatt 1980: 77.

reader's attention. For though there may be fine distinctions between what Paul Bénichou calls 'les moralistes jansénistes ou jansénisants',[121] a pessimistic psychology is 'inseparable from Jansenist theology'.[122]

PASCAL

In addition to its political and theological legacies, in literature Jansenism was to be immortalized by one of France's great polemicists: Blaise Pascal. For readers familiar with the French literary tradition, Pascal's importance *va sans dire*. The *Pensées* drew responses, biographies, and commentaries from several of France's illustrious men of letters, including Voltaire and Condorcet in the eighteenth century; Chateaubriand in the nineteenth;[123] and Valéry in the twentieth.[124] The *Provinciales* were also enveloped into the French literary canon, and above all—as Leszek Kołakowski notes— 'a part of the libertine-liberal-anti-clerical-Voltairian canon. It functioned as a pamphlet that unmasked "Jesuit hypocrisy" and, by extension, the hypocrisy of the Catholic clergy and, by a further extension, the hypocrisy of the Christian religion.'[125] Pascal's influence was widespread: Nietzsche wrote that 'Pascal's blood flows in my veins';[126] and Stendhal once confided that 'when I read Pascal, I feel that I reread myself.'[127]

It is no great surprise, therefore, that the young Sartre should consider him worthy of attention. It is surprising, however, that the English-speaking literature on Sartre has not studied this attention in greater depth. Before returning to Jansenism and Pascal's place in it, therefore, it is worth noting a few textual and historical reasons in defence of taking Pascal's influence on Sartre seriously. In the historical sources we have concerning Sartre's formation, both

---

[121] Bénichou 1948: 100.   [122] Bénichou 1948: 88.
[123] Chateaubriand, *Le Genie du Christianisme* (1802).
[124] See Valéry 1960 for his essay on the *Pensées*.   [125] Kołakowski 1995: 63.
[126] Friedrich Nietzsche, *Gesammelte Werke* (Munich: Musarion Verlag, 1922–9), XXI:89, cited in Melzer 1986: 1.
[127] 'Quand je lis Pascal, il semble que je me relis. Je crois que c'est celui de tous les écrivains à qui je ressemble le plus par l'âme' (Stendhal, *Pensées*, cited in Victor Del Litto, *La Vie intellectuelle de Stendhal: genèse et évolution de ses idées (1802–1821)*, Geneva: Slatkine, 1997, p. 177).

the 'Sartre's readings in youth' manuscript[128] and the *Carnet Midy* attest to the significance of Pascal in Sartre's own estimation of his influences. In the former, Sartre places his reading of Pascal at the age of eighteen—the same year (1923) in which the tercentenary celebrations of Pascal's birth provoked widespread fanfare, including a special issue of the *Revue hebdomadaire* dedicated to Pascal—with contributions from major public intellectuals of the time including Paul Valéry, l'abbé Bremond, Maurice Barrès, Jacques Maritain, Robert Valléry-Radot, Jacques Chevalier, François Mauriac, Charles Du Bos, Paul Desjardins, and Lucien Fabre, among others.[129]

The *Carnet Midy*, a notebook thought to have been compiled by Sartre at some time between 1920 and 1924, includes eighteen aphorisms from the *Pensées* and the *Discours sur les passions de l'amour*.[130] In 1926 (that is to say, two years before Sartre's first, failed, attempt), Pascal appeared on the programme for the *agrégation de philosophie*, where the scope of the historical composition section was: 'The Theory of Method in Descartes, Pascal, Malebranche, and the Port-Royal *Logique*'.[131] Moreover, the edition of the *Pensées* current in Sartre's time was edited by the Sorbonne's Léon Brunschvicg, under whose supervision Beauvoir wrote her *diplôme* on Leibniz in 1928.[132] Indeed, Beauvoir's diaries from this period also include reflections on Pascal.[133]

---

[128] An annotated note in Sartre's own hand, listing books or authors he read and when. Pascal is included on p. 1, under the heading '18 ans'.

[129] *La Revue Hebdomadaire*, 32e année, tome VII, no. 28, 14 juillet 1923: *Troisième centenaire de Pascal*. For more on the tercentenary, see Philippe Olivera, 'Commémorer Pascal en 1923 (I)', *Les Cahiers du Centre de Recherches Historiques*, 28–9 (2002): 'Quelques "XVIIème siècle": fabrications, usages et réemplois'. A number of publications coincided with the anniversary, e.g. Filleau de la Chaise, *Discours sur les Pensées de M. Pascal*. Introduction and notes by Victor Giraud, Paris, 1922. And on Port-Royal more broadly: Jean Laporte, *La Doctrine de Port-Royal*, I, *Les Vérités de la grâce*, Paris: PUF, 1923.

[130] The *Carnet Midy* is a notebook Sartre filled in (largely with notes and quotes) in the early 1920s. The Pléiade edition places the date around 1922–3, but Michel Sicard, relying on Sartre's correspondence, suggests that it was completed in the early months of 1924 (see Sicard 1990: 439).

[131] Schrift 2008: 457.

[132] Moriarty 2006: 127ff. includes a useful examination of Pascal's editors' views of the role played by the fall in the *Pensées* (unfortunately Brunschvicg is not among those considered).

[133] See the entry dated 21 May 1927, in which Beauvoir writes that 'there is only one problem and one that has no solution . . . It is the one formulated by Pascal . . .

It is clear from a passage in Sartre's *Imaginary* that he considered Pascal's 'old and profound' 'theory of love-esteem'—and its successors in French literature and psychology—worthy of study (I 68). In subsequent works, too—as we shall see in Part III—Pascal is cited by name and by work.[134] It is curious, therefore, that despite being acknowledged as an important influence in some French-language texts on Sartre—even in introductory, illustrated, volumes[135]—he is so often neglected in the English-language writings on the subject.

Pascal was not a systematic philosopher, and *Pensées* is a fragmentary, unfinished work.[136] In what follows, therefore, the aim is not to provide an 'account' of the *Pensées* or *Provinçiales*, therefore, but rather a *précis* of Pascalian themes that are pertinent to Sartre's reception of what I will call the Jansenist–Augustinian tradition. Scholars dispute whether or not Pascal would have called himself Jansenist; but he nevertheless has a wide reputation for being 'more Jansenist than the Jansenists themselves'.[137] As Vivien Thweatt writes, '[a]mong the Augustinian writers, whether

I would want to believe in something—to meet with total exigency—to justify my life. In short, I would want God' (Beauvoir 2006: 262).

[134] See I 68; IM 88. Sartre's works from the 1940s include several references to Pascal: In *What Is Literature?* we find a line describing French literature as 'a perpetual colloquy between Pascal and Montaigne' (although the tone is mocking) (WL 23). Pascal is mentioned several times in Sartre's works, both by name alone (e.g. six times in WL and two in BN) and with reference to specific works—the *Pensées* are invoked numerous times in 'The New Mystic', and the *Provincial Letters* are mentioned by name in *What Is Literature?* (WL 16). In addition to discussing particular works, Sartre makes use of (and acknowledges) Pascal's accounts of the pernicious effects of custom (WL 139) and *divertissement* (see, e.g., NM 258; BN 583; WD 250-1).

[135] E.g. Guigot 2000: 7. In more scholarly articles he is also mentioned: Philonenko notes the resemblance between the Pascalian and Sartrean self (*Moi*) at a distance from itself (1981: 152; see also 164).

[136] Because the MS was left unfinished, different editions of the *Pensées* have proliferated, as have debates concerning the best way to interpret it. Louis Lafuma respects the provisional classification suggested by the order of MS copies, whereas Léon Brunschvicg rearranged the fragments thematically, rejecting the possibility of any 'true' ordering (see Van Den Abbeele 1994). In the following references to the *Pensées* I have provided the Lafuma/Brunschvicg fragment numbers; the former because Lafuma's edition is still widely respected, and the latter because it was the edition prevalent in Sartre's time (and, indeed, cited in the *Carnet Midy*). All translations are my own, but were made in consultation with the Levi and Krailsheimer editions (Pascal 1995a and 1995b).

[137] Geberon (quoted by Goldmann 1964: 54). See Maurice Blondel's 1923 'Le Jansénisme et l'anti-jansénisme de Pascal' in the *Revue Métaphysique et de Morale* for a contemporary treatment of the question.

clerical or lay, whether Jansenist or not, it is the Pascal of the *Pensées* who dominates his century.'[138] We shall see the importance of this reputation in the literature of subsequent centuries in Chapter 3, before turning to *Being and Nothingness* in Part III.

Know Thyself: Greatness and Wretchedness

Pascal's thought begins, like that of Montaigne and Socrates, Augustine and Calvin, with an injunction to 'know thyself': 'the order of thought is to begin with oneself' ('l'ordre de la pensée est de commencer par soi').[139] But this poses a problem, for the human condition is 'inconstancy, boredom, anxiety'[140] and any attempt at self-knowledge is foiled by the continual flux within ourselves. 'We are incapable both of total ignorance and certain knowledge,' Pascal writes, 'so obvious is it that we were once in a state of perfection from which we have unhappily fallen.'[141]

In the famous fragment 'Disproportion of man' (*Disproportion de l'homme*), we read that man in nature, 'is a nothingness with respect to the infinite, an everything with respect to nothingness, a place between everything and nothing'.[142] For Pascal, there are only two certainties, and together they prove the double nature of man: greatness and wretchedness. Pascal's juxtapositions are well known: 'grandeur/misère' (L114/B397; L116/B398; L117/B409), 'bassesse et grandeur' (L308/B793; L398/B525); 'excellence et corruption' (L449/B556). He writes that 'cette double capacité' (L386), 'cette duplicité de l'homme' has made some think that we have two souls' (L522).[143] This double capacity—for grace and for sin—is common to all human beings (L208/B435).

At root, therefore, the problem of self-knowledge is inseparable from the problem of sin. Pascal admits that original sin is 'foolishness to men'. But, he objects,

---

[138] Thweatt 1980: 88.   [139] L620/B146. See also L72/B66.
[140] L24/B127.   [141] L131/B434.
[142] L199/B72. Pascal asks: 'N'est-il pas clair comme le jour que la condition de l'homme est double? Certainement' (L131/B434). NB In addition to *néant* Pascal also juxtaposes *rien* et *tout*.
[143] There are two 'états de la nature de l'homme' (L273), or human nature can be considered in two manners, 'en deux manières' (L160).

You must not then reproach me for the want of reason in this doctrine, since I admit it to be without reason. But this foolishness is wiser than all the wisdom of men, *sapientius est hominibus*. For without this, what can we say that man is? His whole state depends on this imperceptible point. And how should it be perceived by his reason, since it is a thing against reason, and since reason, far from finding it out by her own ways, is averse to it when it is presented to her?[144]

On Pascal's Jansenist–Augustinian anthropology, human beings are *un néant*, alienated (*éloigner*) from understanding both the nothingness from which we issued or the infinite that engulfs it (L199/B72).[145] For Pascal original sin is 'folie' in human eyes, but 'though its transmission is the mystery furthest from our understanding' it is something 'without which we can have no understanding of ourselves' (L131/B434).

It is worth quoting this fragment—another of the *Pensées*' most famous—at length, for its exploration of 'the double condition of man':

> It is an astonishing thing that the mystery furthest from our understanding—the transmission of sin—should be something without which we can have no knowledge [*connaissance*] of ourselves. For it is beyond doubt that there is nothing which more shocks our reason than to say that the sin of the first man has rendered guilty those, who, being so removed from this source, seem incapable of participation in it. This transmission does not only seem to us impossible, it seems also very unjust. For what is more contrary to the rules of our miserable justice than to damn eternally an infant incapable of will, for a sin wherein he seems to have so little a share, which was committed six thousand years before he was in existence? Certainly nothing offends us more rudely than this doctrine; and yet, without this mystery, the most incomprehensible of all, we are incomprehensible to ourselves.[146]

---

[144] L695/B445.

[145] The *Pensées* include thirty-two uses of *néant* or *anéantir* in total, and we will see the psychological importance of nothingness for 'diversion' in what follows. See L199/B72: 'Toutes choses sont sorties du néant, et portées jusqu'à l'infini.'

[146] L131/B434. 'Chose étonnante cependant que le mystère le plus éloigné de notre connaissance qui est celui de la transmission du péché soit une chose sans laquelle nous ne pouvons avoir aucune connaissance de nous-mêmes. Car il est sans doute qu'il n'y a rien qui choque plus notre raison que de dire que le péché du premier homme ait rendu coupables ceux qui étant si éloignés de cette source semblent incapables d'y participer. Cet écoulement ne nous paraît pas seulement impossible. Il nous semble même très injuste car qu'y a(-t-)il de plus contraire aux règles de notre misérable justice que de damner éternellement un enfant incapable de volonté pour un péché où il paraît avoir si peu de part, qu'il est commis six mille ans avant qu'il fût

But even with this mystery our selves are difficult to comprehend. Where Descartes was optimistic that he could answer the question 'What then am I?',[147] Pascal shows greater suspicion. The self— *le moi*—is not simply the 'doubting, understanding, willing, thing' of the *Meditations*.[148] But what is it? In the important fragment 'Qu'est-ce que le moi?' we find a question that remains open:

> *What is the self?*
>
> A man goes to the window to see the people passing by; if I pass by, can I say he went there to see me? No, for he is not thinking of me in particular. But what about a person who loves someone for the sake of her beauty; does he love her? No, for smallpox, which will destroy beauty without destroying the person, will put an end to his love for her. And if someone loves me for my judgement or my memory, do they love me? me, myself?

Augustine wrote (albeit of a different beloved), 'what is not loved for itself, is not loved at all'.[149] And Pascal's response to his own question is in keeping with this sentiment:

> No, for I could lose these qualities without losing my self. Where then is this self, if it is neither in the body nor the soul? And how can one love the body or the soul except for the sake of such qualities, which are not what makes up the self, since they are perishable? Would we love the substance of a person's soul, in the abstract, whatever qualities might be in it? That is not possible, and it would be wrong.
>
> Therefore we never love anyone, but only qualities.
>
> Let us then stop scoffing at those who win honour through their appointments and offices, for we never love anyone except for borrowed qualities.[150]

And thus the Socratic injunction to 'know thyself' becomes a painful irony. Stripped of its borrowed qualities, we realize that the 'self' (*le moi*) of this world is 'le moi haïssable'. It is hateful because false—more concerned with appearing (*paraître*) than being (*être*).

---

en être. Certainement rien ne nous heurte plus rudement que cette doctrine. Et cependant sans ce mystère, le plus incompréhensible de tous, nous sommes incompréhensibles à nous-mêmes.'

[147] Descartes 1988: 83, Meditation II.

[148] See Wood 2013: 95ff. for a helpful discussion of the polyvalent French *moi*, which can mean 'me', 'myself', 'the I', or identity generally. See LE 215 for Sartre's notes on the historical development of the *moi* concept in French thought.

[149] Augustine 1948: I.2.13.   [150] L688/B323.

On Pascal's view the 'self' (*le moi*) is imaginary. It is 'the story I tell myself about myself, my subjective narrative identity'.[151] But this *moi* does not correspond to how I am; it is how I imagine that I am seen by others. 'My subjective narrative identity is therefore the story that I imagine that other people would tell about me: my fantasy about your fantasy about me.'[152] In his own words, Pascal writes that:

> We are not satisfied with the life we have in ourselves and our own being. We want to lead an imaginary life in the eyes of others, and so we try to make an impression. We strive constantly to embellish and preserve our imaginary being, and neglect the real one. And if we are calm, or generous, or loyal, we are anxious to have it known so that we can attach these virtues to our other existence; we prefer to detach them from our real self so as to unite them with the other. We would cheerfully be cowards if that would acquire for us a reputation of bravery. How clear a sign of the nothingness [*le néant*] of our own being that we are not satisfied with one without the other and often exchange the one for the other![153]

To be a true self, for Pascal, is to be an object of love. But the loves of fallen selves are idolatrous and disordered. Pascal writes that the 'most indelible quality of the human heart' is to 'enjoy the good opinion of his fellows'.[154] But rather than spurring us on to self-improvement, Wood writes, 'the desire for esteem creates the desire to seem'.[155]

> This is why *le moi* is hateful:

> In a word, the self has two characteristics: it is unjust in itself, in that it makes itself the centre of everything; it is a nuisance to others, in that it wants to assert itself over them, for each self is the enemy, and would like to be tyrant to all the others . . . Whoever does not hate the self-love within him, and this instinct which leads him to make himself into God, is truly blind.[156]

The self desires to make itself the all in all; but this disordered self-love, as Melzer writes, 'is the very essence of sin'.[157] In the *Pensées* we read that 'everything tends towards itself: this is contrary to all order . . . The bias toward self is the beginning of all disorder.'[158]

---

[151] Wood 2013: 94.   [152] Wood 2013: 94.   [153] L806/B147.
[154] Quoted in Wood 2013: 99.   [155] Wood 2013: 99.
[156] L597/B455.   [157] Melzer 1986: 27.   [158] L421/B477.

We attempt to disguise our own ugliness by doing good to others. But this is only a 'false image of true charity', pride's insidious way of whitewashing our tyrannical desires. The unpalatable truth, Pascal writes, is that

> All men naturally hate each other. We have used concupiscence as best we can to make it serve the common good, but this is only pretence and a false image of true charity, because at bottom it is only hate. We have created and drawn from concupiscence admirable rules of government, morality, and justice, but, at root, this evil root of man, this *figmentum malum*, is only covered up; not pulled up.[159]

The self, as Moriarty writes, 'tends towards the form of *libido dominandi*, the desire to subordinate all things and persons to itself, but in so doing it merely engraves all the deeper the message of its own contingency and dependence'.[160] To remove the blindfold and 'know yourself', then, is to realize that 'you are only a king of concupiscence'.[161] No wonder we would rather not see clearly.

Valéry would mock Pascal for this negative view; 'Que si le *moi* est haïssable, aimer son prochain *comme soi-même* devient un atroce ironie.'[162] Indeed, certain fragments support the view that there can be no legitimate Pascalian self-love: in one passage he writes that 'the true and unique virtue is therefore to hate oneself (*se haïr*), because one is hateable by one's (*par sa*) concupiscence'.[163]

But Moriarty highlights a passage in one of Pascal's letters which may provide an answer to this charge. He describes the 'superb exposition' of self-love in a letter Pascal wrote to his sister Gilberte on the death of their father. In this letter, Pascal describes pre- and post-lapsarian loves:

> Man was created with two loves, a love of God for his own sake, an absolute value limited by no other, and a love of self, limited by subordination to God; self-love was therefore a duty, part of obedience to the laws of his creation. The Fall extinguished the love of God, and self-love expanded to fill the resultant infinite void (an image we found in Jansenius). Henceforth man loved himself, and all other things, for his own sake, absolutely and thus infinitely (without limit), and his self-love, formerly natural and righteous, became wicked (*criminel*) and immoderate. The crucial point here is the origin of

[159] L210–11/B451. [160] Moriarty 2006: 186. [161] L796/B314.
[162] Valéry 1960: 489. [163] L564/B485.

self-love (as we experience it) in a loss, a lack, an overflow into an empty
space: it is the very opposite of a natural function.[164]

Unable to take root in God, the self restlessly and relentlessly attempts
to secure itself in human others, to fill its infinite emptiness with
finite ends.

If there is a God, Pascal writes, then we should love him only—for
passing creatures can not meet our eternal longing.[165] Attaching
ourselves to the created world prevents us from serving and knowing
(*connaître*) God. But we are full of concupiscence, and therefore of
evil, so 'we must hate ourselves, and all that encourages us to become
attached to anything other than God alone'.[166] This imperative,
however, is difficult to follow, for the fall has resulted in a disorder
of our loves and an aversion to truth.[167]

The Hidden God

In the aftermath of Eden, on Pascal's view, it seems as though we
must face life and its end alone: God has become *deus absconditus*. As
a consequence of sin he withdrew his presence from the world and his
communication with humanity. 'This religion consists in the belief
that man is fallen from a state of glory and communication with
God.'[168] On Goldmann's reading, Pascal is utterly unable to share the
epistemological optimism of Descartes, seeing no possibility of *knowing* (*savoir*) God's existence.[169] 'What is seen on earth indicates neither
a total exclusion nor a manifest presence of divinity, but the presence
of a God who hides himself. *Everything bears this character.*'[170]
But Pascal writes that it is 'useful' for God to be partly hidden and
partly revealed, because fallen humanity is tempted toward two poles
of sinfulness: pride and despair. It is 'equally dangerous for man to

---

[164] Moriarty 2006: 185.   [165] L618/B479.   [166] L618/B479.

[167] For an excellent extended consideration of the 'evaluative' aspect of Pascal's fall,
see Wood 2013.

[168] 'Cette religion ... consiste à croire que l'homme est déchu d'un état de gloire et
de communication avec Dieu' (L427/B194).

[169] Goldmann 1964: 69.

[170] 'Ce qui paraît ne marque ni une exclusion totale, ni une présence manifeste
de divinité, mais la présence d'un Dieu qui se cache. Tout porte ce caractère'
(L449/B556).

know God without knowing his own wretchedness as to know his wretchedness without knowing God.'[171]

Goldmann argues that Pascal's 'most urgent and essential task lay in proving against the Cartesians that human reason was limited and inadequate'.[172] There are limitations which mathematics and science 'cannot escape when they try to deal with man'.[173] And where misery and God are concerned, *savoir* is impossible: the intellectual faculties will always fail us because these things can only be seen truly with the eyes of faith. Descartes and others who succumb to the *libido sciendi* therefore miss the means by which we approach God and ourselves: It is not *reason* that 'senses' God, but the heart.[174] This is the essence of faith: 'one can recognize that there is a God without knowing that there is' ('on peut bien connaître qu'il y a un Dieu sans savoir ce qu'il est').[175]

The problem is that even when one treads carefully between pride and despair the absence is still palpable. God no longer seems to speak, Pascal writes, and 'the eternal silence of these infinite spaces terrifies me'.[176] Where we expect loving words of guidance, we find an unwelcome quiet: 'the universe [is] mute'.[177]

Hiding from Ourselves

According to Pascal, once the blindfold is removed and we recognize our misery for what it is, we observe that much of our time is spent pursuing illusory goods, attempts to escape reality through *divertissement*. If our condition was truly happy, he writes, 'we should not have to divert ourselves from thinking about it'.[178] But human beings are capable of 'feeling' (*sentir*) their nothingness without knowing it (*le connaître*).[179] In a fragment on boredom, Pascal writes that:

> Nothing is so intolerable for man as to be in a state of complete tranquility, without passions, without business, without diversion, without effort.

---

[171] L449/B556. See also L192/B527: 'La connaissance de Dieu sans celle de sa misère fait l'orgueil. La connaissance de sa misère sans celle de Dieu fait le désespoir.'
[172] See Goldmann 1964: 221.   [173] Goldmann 1964: 242.
[174] L424/B278.   [175] L418/B233.
[176] 'Le silence éternel de ces espaces infinis m'effraie' (L201/B206).
[177] L198/B693. Moriarty notes that in this Pascal differs from Augustine, who had spoken of 'les psaumes chantés par toute la terre' (the psalms chanted by the whole earth) (Augustine 1961: IV.iv.8; cited in L1/B596). In the post-Cartesian world, however, these can be heard only with the ears of faith.
[178] See L132/B170; L136/B139.   [179] L36/B164.

> Then he feels his nothingness, his abandonment, his inadequacy, his
> dependence, his helplessness, his emptiness. At once from the depths of
> his soul arises boredom, gloom, sadness, grief, vexation, despair.[180]

Our unhappiness 'springs from one thing alone, [our] incapacity to
stay quietly in one room'.[181] That is why we prefer the hunt to the
kill—for the distraction the hunt offers[182]—and that is why we covet
positions of power—because kings, judges, and magistrates are too
busy to be bored. With other people constantly vying for one's
attention, and important matters to resolve, there is little time to
think about oneself. But diversion is futile; it is vain to 'seek in
yourselves the medicine for your miseries'.[183]

Pascal's choice of word is significant: the French *divertissement* is
derived from the Latin *deuerto*, which means 'se détourner de son
chemin' or 's'échapper vers autre chose'. In verb form, the French
divertirer had two senses: 'to swerve away', or 'to entertain'. Pascal
uses this etymological flexibility to take the notion of *divertissement*
further than other Jansenists, such as Nicole.[184] For Pascal, *divertissement* is not simply a moral category—though, like Nicole, he does
insist that entertaining diversions such as the theatre and the luxuries
of the world are dangerous and to be avoided. But as Kołakowski
notes, for Pascal there is a second, metaphysical sense. Metaphysic-
ally, *divertissement* is a 'fundamental manner of living' through which
'we flee into the irreality of mundane amusements of all sorts ... in
order not to face death and the dilemma it compels us to think about.
The dangers of entertainment are a Jansenist topic, "divertissement"
as a mode of existence is not.'[185]

God of Grace?

Pascal describes human existence as wretched: 'humanity is Chaotic,
contradictory, prodigious, judging everything, mindless worm of the
earth, storehouse of truth, cesspool of uncertainty and error, glory

---

[180] L622/B131.   [181] L136/B139.   [182] L136/B139.
[183] L149/B430.
[184] He also draws heavily on Montaigne's essay 'On Diversion'. See the Sellier edition
of the *Pensées*, which 'illustrates the extent to which Pascal rewrote the *Essais* by
carefully citing in footnotes the passages borrowed from Montaigne' (Melzer 1986: 126).
[185] Kołakowski 1995: 134.

and reject of the universe'.[186] Indeed, his rhetoric has led some to comment that 'he uses every device of style to instil in his reader a feeling of desperate insecurity'.[187] But there is hope: for though we are not 'in the state of our creation', and though it is hopeless to seek a remedy in ourselves, God's grace is sufficient to overcome this plight.[188]

But only for those to whom God gives it. On Pascal's view as expressed in the *Écrits sur la grâce*, Augustine provided the orthodox statement in his writings against Pelagius (and his followers, of whatever century): because the fall radically corrupted human nature, humanity could no longer obey God's commands without grace—a gift of God which modifies the human will.[189] Moreover, since it is we who carry out acts of the will, we still contribute to our own salvation in the state of grace. Nevertheless, the prerequisite of grace implies that God bestows grace only to those whom he predestines for salvation:

> God has willed to redeem men, and to open salvation to those who seek it. But men render themselves so unworthy of it, that it is right that God should refuse to some, because of their obduracy, what He grants to others from a compassion which is not due to them.[190]

Pascal's theology of grace required delicate navigation between the libertinism of the Jesuits and the stark brutality (as he saw it) of Calvinism. At root, the issue is the character of God: for Pascal, God is just but his ways are inscrutable, whereas for Calvin (on Pascal's view) God is neither just nor inscrutable. He is straightforwardly cruel, the cause of evil as well as good. Thus Pascal writes,

> *Calvinists*: In creating humanity in Adam God had an absolute will, before regarding any merits and demerits, to save some and condemn others. To this end God made Adam sin, and made all of humanity sin in him, so that, all of humanity being criminal, He would be just in damning those that He had resolved to condemn at their creation, and sent Jesus Christ to save only those that He had resolved to save when He created them . . .
> The Calvinists' opinion is so horrible, and so strikes the mind so forcefully with its image of God's cruelty, that it becomes unbearable . . .
> Thus the Calvinists pose God's will as the only source of salvation and damnation.

---

[186] L131/B434.   [187] Krailsheimer 1980: 52.   [188] L149/B430.
[189] Jean Mesnard suggests that the *Écrits sur la grâce* is 'one of the clues to Pascal's entire oeuvre' (see Pascal OCM, vol. 3: 'Introduction' to the *Écrits*).
[190] L149/B430.

Thus the Church poses the only source of salvation, and the human will as the only source of damnation.[191]

This is problematic on two fronts: it makes God culpable for damnation and it makes it impossible to impute culpability to humanity. Such a God is arbitrary, and 'effectively abolishes free will out of existence (as opposed to Pascal's, who creates it in chains following the fall from Eden). Pascal, following Paul and Augustine, argues for an ethics of voluntary enslavement to God; on Pascal's view, Calvin's God creates a humanity whose enslavement to him is ready-made.'[192] Nothing is left to human will; whereas Pascal believes that even in the postlapsarian state humanity still has just enough agency to turn towards God, to receive his grace.

The Jesuits (the Molinists of the *Écrits sur la grâce*), by contrast, err in the opposite extreme, imputing both salvation and damnation to humanity,[193] instead of recognizing the role of God's grace in salvation. The sinner's soul should be grateful to God for the undeserved gift of grace: 'it must worship God as a creature, to praise him as one obliged, to satisfy Him as one guilty, to beg Him as one indigent'.[194] But the Jesuists were lax, the very definition of casuistry; like the papacy Calvin criticized with such vitriol, the Jesuits of the *Provincial Letters* are presented as having gravely misunderstood the doctrine of sin, and as overlooking the eternal consequences of so doing.[195]

Kołakowski writes that '[n]o unprejudiced reader can fail to be won over to the side of the author when he peruses the *Provincial Letters* or to be amused by quotations from various Jesuit writers who seem to have a ready-made excuse for all kinds of human depravities and crimes'. To give but a few of the many examples:

---

[191] Pascal OCM, vol. 3: 766–8.   [192] Elmarsafy 2003: 74–5.
[193] Pascal OCM, vol. 3: 768.   [194] Pascal OCM, vol. 4: 44.
[195] It is worth noting that Calvin dedicated considerable time to discussing the medieval doctrine of sin, which required payment for the sacrament of confession and absolution, in books 3 and 4 of the *Institutes*, and he pulls no punches. The forgiveness of sins is 'the most serious matter of all' (Calvin 1980: 3.4.2). But in its practice, the Church 'butchered souls', dividing 'sins into arms, branches, twigs and leaves', claiming that it could weigh the 'qualities, quantities, and circumstances' (Calvin 1980: 3.4.17). In light of Calvin's view of the noetic effects of sin, no priest could ever know with certainty that faith and repentance were truly present in the one confessing (Calvin 1980: 3.4.18). The result is that priests heard and absolved 'the worthy and unworthy indiscriminately', usurping 'power without knowledge'. Only the eyes of God see clearly enough to offer true absolution.

Did not Father La Moine argue that no action is sinful unless God inspires in the agent the knowledge of his weakness, the desire to be healed, to pray and beg for help—so that people who simply do not care a damn about God cannot commit a sin? Did not others argue that one becomes a murderer only if one takes money in order to kill someone in a treacherous way? Or that a monk may take off his habit without incurring excommunication if he does so for a shameful reason like going to a brothel? . . . That a woman of good society has more right to demand money for secret fornication than a whore because her body is more precious, in the opinion of Father Fillintius?[196]

It is clear that for Pascal, like Augustine, our loves—or 'pleasures'—shape us. Quoting Augustine's maxim for the will's behaviour—the more something pleases us, the more it will necessarily affect us—Pascal affirms that 'this is where all these discourses begin'. The Jesuits failed to recognize that humanity is either enslaved to its pleasures or freed by following the path of the Spirit; we can 'only be liberated from one of these two by the other'.[197] Man is double-natured. And our true liberty, for Pascal, comes from becoming nothing. He uses Bérullian language of *anéantisation*: 'The finite *anéantit* in the presence of the infinite becomes a pure nothing-ness', and in the same way 'is our spirit (*esprit*) before God', our justice before divine justice.[198] For once we make ourselves noth-ing, we see that 'it is right that God should refuse [grace] to some, because of their obduracy, what He grants to others from a com-passion which is not due to them':[199] because our justice is made nothing before his.

Views such as this led Pascal—and Jansenism—to become known for expressing 'extreme aspects of the Augustinian view of the self without communicating to any significant degree the serenity of faith and the redemptive love that undergird Augustinian thought'.[200] Whereas in Bérulle the human has being through her *rapport* with God, and finds self-knowledge in God's pure gaze, the Pascal of the *Pensées* can be read as denying the possibility of such respite, seeing in himself only an 'abyss of pride, curiosity, and concupiscence'.

---

[196] Kołakowski, 1995: 61–2.   [197] Pascal OCM, vol. 3: 704–5.
[198] L418/B233. Pascal's doctrine of *anéantisation* may depart from the Augustinian tradition, in which there is good in the human: Thweatt calls it 'a death *of* self rather than a death *to* self' (1980: 98).
[199] L149/B430.   [200] Thweatt 1980: 82.

Indeed, in the same fragment he writes that 'There is no *rapport* between me and God, nor even Jesus Christ.'[201]

Given the fragmentary form of the *Pensées* one can argue for many different Pascals. On Lewis's reading, for example, 'the apologist's aim is to prepare his interlocutor for salvation through a redemptive grace that restores a sacred relation between the human and the divine'— which is to say, a restorative *rapport*.[202] But on the Jansenist–Augustinian typology that was to influence subsequent centuries of French literature, it is difficult to distinguish Pascal's absent God from Calvin's arbitrary one. Jansenism became known as a 'Catholic Calvinism'[203]—though, on Bénichou's reading, Jansenism can be distinguished from Calvinism because Jansenism is purely negative with respect to real life.[204] The emphasis on the nothingness of the creature in the face of God—called *néantisme*—by Sellier[205] marked a departure from the Augustinianism of Augustine. For the Doctor of Grace, as we saw, did not affirm that sin affected the human person to the extent of losing all being. The human person, made in the image of God and whom God loves, is not a pure nothingness.

Threefold Concupiscence: *Volupté, autorité, curiosité*

What is needful, on Pascal's view, is that we recognize that our fallen nature is characterized by excessive, distorted desire. There is, in humanity, a natural desire for truth and the good, but we are incapable of attaining them because original sin diverts us away from seeking these things where they can be found: in God.[206] We know that our good exists, and that it must be sought beyond ourselves, but concupiscence misdirects our efforts to attain it. In several fragments in the *Pensées* Pascal refers to the threefold concupiscence of Jansenism: the *libido sentiendi, libido dominandi, libido sciendi*.[207]

---

[201] 'Je vois mon abîme d'orgueil, de curiosité, de concupiscence. Il n'y a nul rapport de moi à Dieu, ni à J.-C. juste' (L919/B553).

[202] Lewis 1994: 326. Some fragments support such a reading, e.g. L502/B571: 'Mais ceux qui n'avaient de bien qu'en Dieu, les rapportaient uniquement à Dieu.'

[203] This is demonstrably the case for Sartre, for whom Jansenism was a 'crypto-protestantism' (Donneau 2010: 68).

[204] Bénichou 1948: 127; see also p. 115 on Jansenism and the Reformation.

[205] Sellier 2000, vol. 2: 21.　　　[206] L148/B425.

[207] See L143/B464; L145/B461; L148/425.

In *l'Augustin* Jansen, following Augustine,[208] divided concupiscence into three forms: of the flesh, the eyes, and of pride ('concupiscence de la chair, des yeux, et de la superbe'). On his view, all human vice could be classified in this tripartite taxonomy of disordered desire.[209]

On Pascal's account we are 'thrown' outside ourselves; 'our instinct is that we must search for our happiness beyond ourselves', and 'our passions push us outside'.[210] He derides the wisdom of philosophers, which is nothing other than the counsel to follow 'one of the three concupiscences'.[211] God is the good, but instead of turning away from ourselves to God, some philosophers encourage us to seek good in authority, others in curiosity and the sciences, and others in carnal pleasure.[212]

In a postlapsarian state this is only natural, because concupiscence has 'become natural'; it is our 'second nature'. After the fall, there are two natures in us: one good, the other evil.[213] And the evil one inclines us to follow the philosophers' advice. In the *libido sentiendi* (naturalized in French Jansenism as *volupté*), we look to satisfy the desires of our bodies: bodily pleasures, laziness, and excess.[214] The *libido dominandi* (*autorité*) urges us to dominate others, expand the domain of our own will, and seek prestige and the feeling of superiority—whether social or intellectual. The *libido sciendi* (*curiosité*), literally 'the desire to know', is the origin of original sin, because it was of the tree of knowledge that Adam and Eve ate the apple. The desire to know is vain, on the Jansenist view; and Pascal derides too high a confidence in reason, which is clearly fallen and feeble—so feeble, in fact, that it is deterred from clear thinking by the buzzing of a fly.[215]

Whether it is the buzzing of a fly, the bleeding of a wound, or the unequal distribution of strength, health, and beauty, much human misery arises on account of being embodied. And indeed, passages in the *Pensées* have led scholars to conclude that Pascal harboured an

---

[208] Cf. the three temptations of Christ in Augustine 1959: XXXVIII.70.
[209] See Jansen 1640: II.2.323.   [210] L143/B464.
[211] L145/B461.
[212] 'Les uns le cherchent dans l'autorité, les autres dans les curiosités et dans les sciences, les autres dans les voluptés' (*Le Souverain bien*, L148/425).
[213] L616/B660.
[214] Or 'sloth' and 'gluttony'/'paresse' et 'gourmandise', as they are otherwise known.
[215] L48/B366.

odium corporis, a hatred of the body. He writes that we are 'thrown' into bodies, into having 'number, time, dimensions',[216] which are unnatural prisons for our souls: 'what is natural in animals we call misery in man'.[217] Such suspicion is supported by Pascal's sister Gilberte's biographical account: Pascal didn't approve of her hugging her children because he believed this carnal practice harmful.[218] Rather than indulging the pleasures of the flesh, Pascal thought we should love death in order to detach the soul from the 'body impure'. While scholars such as Kołakowski note that this *odium corporis* can be dismissed *ad hominem*—Pascal was tormented by his own body, which caused him pain every day of his adult life—it is important to emphasize that this semi-gnostic disgust was typical of Jansenism,[219] and indeed of Augustinian Christianity more broadly.[220]

Needless to say, the body can be the source of pleasure as well as pain. But to those who lose themselves in carnal pleasures—indulging the *libido sentiendi*—Pascal's message is simple: You will die! Kołakowski highlights this as Pascal's 'crucial and most pervasive message'. It is obvious: all men are mortal. But this universal fact is almost as universally avoided. 'It is easier to bear death without thinking of it than to think of death without danger.'[221] This is the question 'that really matters', which is 'stupid to avoid' because it is life's only certainty. But, as Tolstoy's Ivan Ilyich discovers, human beings are reticent about such recognition.[222]

The body is not the only source of our feebleness: we are also led astray by the mind—in particular, by imagination. Imagination can make a mountain out of 'un néant';[223] orienting the will towards things that turn it away from its infinite home. It creates substitutes for God—it can make idols even of the truth itself: 'because the truth without charity is not God'.[224]

---

[216] '*Infini—rien.*—Notre âme est jetée dans le corps, où elle trouve nombre, temps, dimensions. Elle raisonne là-dessus et appelle cela nature, nécessité, et ne peut croire autre chose' (L418/B233).

[217] L117/B409.　　　　[218] See Kołakowski 1995: 128.

[219] Kołakowski 1995: 129.

[220] See Kołakowski 1995: 87ff., for more on the 'gnostic temptation' in Christianity.

[221] L138/B166.　　　　[222] See Tolstoy 2010.　　　　[223] L531/B85.

[224] L926/B582. For more on imagination see Ferreyrolles 2000: 157. The imagination is linked to both the *libido sentiendi* (p. 168) and the *libido sciendi* (p. 170).

FÉNELON

The final figure to be considered here, like Bérulle, enjoyed religious and political influence during his lifetime. And like Bérulle, he fell from grace.[225] François de Salignac de la Mothe-Fénelon (1651–1715) was preceptor of *les enfants de France* under Louis XIV—a post occupied by Bossuet a generation before.[226] Under the guidance of an uncle (whose spiritual director was Jean-Jacques Olier, one of Bérulle's disciples),[227] Fénelon spent some time studying at Saint Sulpice in 1672, during which time he was introduced to the writings of the mystics.[228]

In Fénelon's *Treatise on the Existence of God* we find an enquiry framed in Cartesian doubt. Its second part opens with the assertion that 'the only way to avoid all error is to doubt—without exception—everything for which there is not plain evidence . . . I want to believe nothing,' Fénelon writes, 'if there is nothing that is perfectly certain' (1880: 102).[229]

But we also find a Bérullian refrain: that the *ego cogito* cannot, of its own power, pull itself out of nothingness. Only the Plenitude of Being can call something out of nothing.[230] *Le néant* is present in Fénelon's writings as that from which God created. Somehow human heritage involves 'a passage from nothingness to being'.[231] But here

---

[225] There is not space to discuss the question of Fénelon's *quietism* here; rather, our focus will be his use of *le néant* in his anthropology and spirituality.

[226] Helms 2006: 3.

[227] Leduc-Lafayette notes Fénelon's indebtedness to Bérulle and also to the Spanish mystics whose thought Bérulle introduced to France: Teresa and St John of the Cross. In particular, she highlights the conceptual scheme Fénelon inherited, including 'creaturely dependence', the 'first nothingness' which is creation, and also 'le néant où Adam nous met par le péché' (Leduc-Lafayette 1996b: 98 (citing Bérulle, *Opuscules de Piété*, Paris: Aubier, 1944, CXXXVI)). Sellier writes that Fénelon was 'imprégné de l'oeuvre augustinienne' (2000, vol. 2: 73).

[228] Paris at this period was '[s]till in the flush of Counter-Reformation piety' (Helms 2006: 9), having recently seen the ministries of—in addition to Pierre de Bérulle—Vincent de Paul, François de Sales, Madame Acarie, Benoît de Canfield, Charles de Condren, as well as the previously mentioned Olier (Helms 2006: 5). Sartre refers to him in WL 71.

[229] On p. 104 we read that 'doute philosophique . . . seul est raisonnable'; but on the next page this doubt is described as 'une espèce de tourment'.

[230] Fénelon 1880: 112. For the Plenitude of Being see also p. 174. Fénelon is self-avowedly Augustinian, as can be seen here and in his use of privation theory (1880: 120).

[231] Fénelon 1880: 120. The formulation 'passer du néant à l'être' is used several times; see also 1880: 122.

(as in Bérulle's account), though we have 'come out of' (*sorti du*)
nothingness, we are always on the verge of falling back into it (*prêt à y
retomber*).[232]

The nature of created beings is dependent, for 'that which has no
being except by another cannot keep it by itself'.[233] Human existence
is not essential; it is accidental, contingent,[234] and subject to the
ravages of time. The notion of time plays an important role. Fénelon
calls it 'the change of created being'; 'time is the negation of a very real
and supremely positive thing that is the permanence of being'. Unlike
God, we are changing, subject to 'la défaillance de l'être'.[235]

On Fénelon's view, 'everything which is not truly being is nothingness'.[236] Consequently, human being requires a 'don actuel' (1880: 76)
to be kept from nothingness.[237] There must be some link—a *rapport*—
between the Creator and the created.[238]

It is in the context of this thinking on time that the passage Jacques
Salvan uses as an epigraph for his chapter on Sartre and mysticism is
found (and it is worth quoting here at length):

> I am not, O my God, what is; alas, I am almost what is not. I see myself
> as an incomprehensible intermediate between nothingness and being.
> I am the one who has been; I am the one who will be; I am the one who
> is no longer what he has been; I am the one who is not yet what he will
> be; and, in this in-between that I am, something unknowable that
> cannot be held in itself, that has no consistency, that flows away like
> water; something unknowable that I cannot seize, that flees from my
> hands, that is no longer as soon as I wish to grasp or perceive it;
> something unknowable that finishes at the very instant in which it
> begins; so that I can never at any moment find myself stable and present
> to myself, so as to say simply that *I am*. Thus my duration is nothing but
> a perpetual failure/lack [*défaillance*] of being.[239]

---

[232] Fénelon 1880: 121.   [233] Fénelon 1880: 123.   [234] Fénelon 1880: 132.
[235] Fénelon 1880: 176.
[236] Fénelon 1880: 140. [Tout ce qui n'est point réellement l'être est le néant.]
[237] Fénelon, too, invokes an idea of continual creation [*un don perpétuel*] to solve
the problem of *durée*, invoking the imagery of manna from heaven to illustrate the way
in which future needs will be met: 'Le jour de demain aura soin de lui-même. Celui qui
nourrit aujourd'hui est le même qui nourrira demain. On reverra la manne tomber du
ciel dans le désert, plutôt que de laisser les enfants de Dieu sans nourriture' (Fénelon
1827, vol. 6: 329).
[238] Fénelon 1880: 183.
[239] 'Je ne suis pas, ô mon Dieu, ce qui est: hélas ! je suis presque ce qui n'est pas. Je
me vois comme un milieu incompréhensible entre le néant et l'être; je suis qui a été, je

For Fénelon, being escapes us on account of being composed of parts, mixtures of truth and lies, being and nothingness.[240] In this respect, Fénelon follows the trajectory of Bérulle, drawing out the painful consequences of human nothingness. He writes, 'I do not know how to assure myself that the me [*le moi*] of yesterday is the same as today's. They are not necessarily linked together. One could be without the other.'[241] For Fénelon, the lack of a link between moments results in a loss of consistency of the self. The self escapes its own self-knowledge at each instant, its fluidity eludes definition. According to Bachmann, 'in the course of the seventeenth century the part of non-being [*non-être*] in the existence of the creature would assert itself more and more. If Bérulle and Descartes could still say, in knowing themselves in the present moment, "I am", the driving force of being unmade [*entraînement de la défaillance*] was too great for Fénelon; he did not discover that he was, but rather that he was lacking [*défaillant*].'[242]

SARTRE AND THE MYSTICISM OF NOTHINGNESS

There are other thinkers from this epoch who might relevantly have been considered here were it not for constraints of space—notably Malebranche and La Rochefoucauld, whose *Maximes* have been called 'more truly Augustinian than Pascal'.[243] Augustine's name was frequently invoked in this century, with opposing parties citing different passages in defence of their views.[244] And the controversies

---

suis celui qui sera, je suis celui qui n'est plus ce qu'il a été, je suis celui qui n'est pas encore ce qu'il sera; et dans cet entre-deux que suis-je? ... un je ne sais quoi que je ne puis saisir ... ; un je ne sais quoi qui finit dans l'instant même où il commence, en sorte que je ne puis jamais un seul moment me trouver moi-même fixe et présent à moi-même pour dire simplement: Je suis. Ainsi ma durée n'est qu'une défaillance perpétuelle' (Fénelon 1880: 180; translation adapted from Salvan 1967: 188).

[240] Fénelon 1880: 180.

[241] Fénelon, *Oeuvres*, ed. Gaume 1851, vol. 1. p. 117, cited in Bachmann 1963: 45.

[242] Bachmann 1963: 46.

[243] Thweatt 1980: 99. Sellier (2000, vol. 2: 74) notes that La Rochefoucauld was 'nourished on *The City of God*' and took for his themes 'the corruption of fallen man and *amour de soi*, the principle of the earthly city'. Sartre writes about La Rochefoucauld's treatment of *amour-propre* in TE (17), and also refers to him in WL 71.

[244] See Magnard 1996.

that arose in this period—most notably in the debates surrounding Jansenism and Quietism—were not contained to what we might today call 'religious' spaces: if Madame de Sévigné is to be believed, theological matters were the pillow talk of illicit liaisons[245] and, as Vivien Thweatt puts it, original sin 'was served with the soup'.[246]

I will show in Part III that the themes that preoccupied these seventeenth-century thinkers recur in Sartre's work: being and nothingness, freedom and determinism (whether 'determinism' goes by the name of sin or grace), self-searching and self-loss. In *Being and Nothingness*, where Sartre discusses the elusive nature of the self, we hear a distinctly Fénelonian refrain:

> [A] nothingness has slipped into the heart of this relation; I *am* not the self which I will be. First I am not that self because time separates me from it. Secondly, I am not that self because what I am is not the foundation of what I will be. Finally I am not that self because no actual existent can determine strictly what I am going to be. Yet as I am already what I will be (otherwise I would not be interested in any one being more than another), *I am the self which I will be, in the mode of not being it.*   (BN 56)

I have argued elsewhere that Sartre clearly took issue with mysticism as a method, rejecting mysticism as bad faith.[247] When previous readers such as Howells and Salvan have written on Sartre and mysticism, they have correctly noted this rejection.[248] But he did not reject the mystic's problem: that nothingness—or in theological idiom, *sin*—haunts being.

On my reading (as given in Part III), *Being and Nothingness* can be read as a continuation of these French theological, philosophical, and mystical explorations of the human condition as fallen. For the Augustinianisms described here, *and for Sartre*, the human exists in a tensive state between being and nothingness. The difference, for Sartre, is that while there exists a nothingness of nature and (arguably) a nothingness of sin, there is no nothingness of grace. Bérulle writes that self-knowledge can be found—but only 'par le regard pur de Dieu',[249] and that 'our being is a *relation* [*rapport*] to God'.[250]

---

[245] See Marie de Rabutin-Chantal, marquise de Sevigné, *Lettres*, ed. Gérard-Gailly, 3 vols (Paris: Gallimard, Bibliothèque de la Pléiade, 1953), vol. 2, no. 444, p. 146, cited in Thweatt 1980: 44.
[246] Thweatt 1980: 44.   [247] Kirkpatrick 2013.
[248] See Howells 1981; Salvan 1967.   [249] Bérulle 1987: 32.
[250] Bérulle 1944: 1150.

This is significant because scholars such as Sellier have questioned whether there is any distinction to be made between Jansenism and Augustinian Christianity. Both, on Sellier's view, share features such as 'le sentiment de la faiblesse et de la corruption de l'homme, insistence sur le péché originel, méfiance à l'égard du corps, pédagogie du soupçon, tout cela faisait partie des réprésentations collectives'.[251] However, I defend the view that there is a distinction to be made: for despite these ills Augustine viewed the fall optimistically, as a *felix culpa* out of which greater good would be wrought by a God of love.

For Jansenist–Augustinians such as Pascal, by contrast, this optimistic reading of the fall is hard to make: the *juste pecheur* of Jansenism, the just sinner who does not know whether he will receive God's grace, is a tragic figure whose metaphysics warrants pessimism and distrust.[252] I will return to this point in Chapter 8, after showing in Part III that Sartre explicitly rejects Bérulle's optimism, denying the possibility of self-knowledge, and making every negation an estrangement from being. In *Being and Nothingness*, Sartre writes that '[Anxiety] as the manifestation of freedom in the face of self means that man is always separated by a nothingness from his essence' (BN 59).[253] Without grace, there is nothing that can 'ensure me against myself, cut off from the world and from my essence by this nothingness which *I am*' (BN 63).

Sartre accepts the mystics' diagnosis: to be human is, as Fénelon puts it, to be 'in-between', to be 'something unknowable that cannot be held in itself'.[254] But he rejects their cure. Before turning to *Being and Nothingness*, however, another source of Sartre's theological formation must be considered: literature.

[251] Sellier 2000, vol. 2: 47.
[252] See Goldmann 1964 for the definitive study of Jansenist tragedy.
[253] I have inserted '[anxiety]' here because the French *angoisse* was translated by Hazel Barnes as 'anguish', and I take 'anxiety' to be more closely collocated to the Kierkegaardian concept we will meet in Chapter 3 (and, indeed, to Sartre's account of *angoisse*, which will be considered in Chapter 4).
[254] Fénelon 1880: 180.

3

French Sins, II

Individuals and their Sins

The Bishop of Nantes, in his wisdom, taught me a saying of Saint Augustine's which has greatly comforted me: that he who is not satisfied with God alone as a witness to his actions is too ambitious.[1]

The last chapter showed that seventeenth-century France—*le grand siècle*—was preoccupied by questions of sin and salvation, nature and grace.[2] Doctrine was the stuff of salon conversation and political suicide. More importantly, for the purposes of this argument, it was to become the stuff of literature.[3]

Indeed, Moriarty writes, the Jansenist debate was dragged out of the theology faculty into the public sphere when Pascal attacked it in *Les Lettres provinciales*.[4] Any tacit convention that theological issues were only for professional theologians was no longer followed. And thus theology found its way into a broader culture. Indeed, Jean Mesnard, in his essay 'Jansenism et littérature', stresses that the magnitude of Jansenism's contribution to French literature was so great that 'one can even wonder if its destiny wasn't literary, above all'.[5] Similarly, Philippe Sellier writes that literature and theology have

---

[1] Mother Angélique de Sainte-Madeleine, letter to Arnauld d'Andilly, 9 January 1623, cited in Goldmann 1964: xii.
[2] Leduc-Lafayette 1996a: 5.
[3] See Sellier 2000, vol. 2 on 'l'augustinisme littéraire'.
[4] See Rex 1977: 9 and *passim*.
[5] Mesnard 1992: 'On peut se même demander si sa destinée n'a pas été surtout littéraire.'

'never known a similar osmosis'.[6] Even after the seventeenth century much of French literature was bathed in what Sellier calls a 'diffuse Augustinianism'.[7]

Given that Jansenism was such a cultural force, it is safe to say that an educated French person (of whatever religious or non-religious persuasion) would know about it. And Sartre is no exception. Recent Sartre scholarship has shown that by the time of '*Liberté-Égalité*' (a recently published manuscript from 1951 which discusses the influence of the Reformation and Jansenism on modernity) Sartre was intimately familiar with seventeenth-century theological debates, citing Molina, Jansen, and others. But this should not come as a surprise since, as Olivier Donneau writes, 'He had to familiarize himself with their polemical exchanges, which were so closely linked to the development of the classical literature he studied.'[8] Donneau's view is supported by Sartre's own statements in *What Is Literature?* (published in 1948), where Sartre characterizes this epoch as one which 'constantly pondered two historical facts: original sin and redemption'.[9]

Even earlier in Sartre's corpus—in the *Carnets Midy*, for example, written in 1924–5, we find Jansenist themes: in addition to the above-mentioned citations from the *Pensées*, we find entries on the elusiveness of *le vrai moi* and the human need for a witness.[10] When we read Sartre theologically, therefore, it is not adequate to consider the theologians (e.g. Pascal) or philosophers (e.g. Descartes) as the only sources of his theological formation. We must also look to literature—the religion in which Sartre was a self-proclaimed priest.[11]

---

[6] Sellier 2000, vol. 2: 30. NB Sellier prefers 'Port-Royal' or 'le groupe de Port Royal' over Jansenisme (2000: 72).

[7] Sellier 2000, vol. 2: 74. Sellier cites Baudelaire's *Les Fleurs du mal* as a paramount example, which is worth noting given Sartre's choice of Baudelaire as the subject for one of his existential biographies.

[8] Donneau 2010: 62.   [9] WL 67.

[10] 'Moi: J'ai cherché mon moi: je l'ai vu se manifester dans ses rapports avec mes amis, avec la nature, avec les femmes que j'ai aimées. . . . Mai mon moi proprement dit, hors des hommes et des choses, mon vrai moi, inconditionné, je ne l'ai pas trouvé' (CM 472).

'Hommes: Tous les hommes ont besoin d'un témoin. Sans doute nécessité socio-logique. Les uns inventent alors Dieu, les autres la conscience (personifiée), les autres paraissent dans le monde, ne peuvent penser sans dire ce qu'ils pensent, les autres enfin déraisonnent, imaginant obscurément de belles femmes qui les regardent' (CM 454).

[11] See W 39: 'I had found my religion: nothing seemed more important to me than a book' (and *passim*).

One cannot look to literature with the expectation of examining everything Sartre read, of course. The aim of this chapter is, necessarily, much more modest. It seeks to demonstrate some of the most relevant literary expressions of Jansenism for readers less familiar with this tradition, focusing on three important iterations of Jansenist–Augustinian sin in French literature: in Racine's Jansenist tragedy, in Voltaire's satire, and in Hugo's arch-romantic novel *Les Misérables*. All of these works were known to Sartre, and in each of them the problem of evil plays a prominent role, as does the absence of God and the human need for a witness. We then focus briefly on the contemporary literary climate of the pre-phenomenological Sartre— a climate with vibrant literary expressions of sin—for it was this climate into which Kierkegaard was first received in France in the 1920s. The chapter ends with a presentation of what I will call 'Kierkegaard *à la française*', concluding the historical part of this book.

This chapter's survey, partial though it is, demonstrates that Sartre's intellectual formation prior to the writing of *Being and Nothingness* did indeed include theological elements. And we will see in Part III how attending to these theological themes brings new aspects of the text to light.

RACINE

Given Racine's place in the French literary canon it is no surprise that Sartre read him. Sartre refers to him several times in *What Is Literature?* and other works,[12] writing that his 'genius' was 'his series of tragedies'.[13]

Racine was raised by and 'immensely indebted to'[14] Jansenists, and the question of the extent to which he waxed and waned in that tradition has spent much scholarly ink. After all, Arnauld and Nicole, the chief Jansenist spokesmen after Saint-Cyran, generally advocated detachment from the worldly pursuit of letters and luxury, and Racine wrote theatre—*divertissement*. Whether or not all of Racine's

---

[12] For direct references to Racine in Sartre's works see, e.g., WL 17, 72 (where *Phèdre* is cited), 97, 115 (where Sartre explicitly refers to the role of 'Jansenist ideology' in the invention of Racine's art); EH 37.
[13] EH 37.   [14] Lewis 1994: 320.

plays are Jansenist tragedies, as Lucien Goldmann argues[15]—this section will focus on one play in particular, *Phèdre*, because it is widely taken to be not only a masterpiece of French Classicism[16]—or, in Voltaire's words, a 'masterpiece of the human mind'[17]—but also a clear dramatic depiction of the Jansenist *juste pécheur,* the 'just sinner'.

The play—a five-act drama in alexandrine verse—is a retelling of a story from Greek mythology.[18] When the play opens, Phèdre is

> dying from a hidden malady
> Eternal discord reigns within her mind.   (I.ii.146–7)[19]

She is a divided self: 'all her wishes war among themselves!' (I.iii.162). The combatants are competing desires: for a forbidden man, on the one hand, and to do no wrong, on the other. She is the wife of Theseus, but suffers a guilt-ridden and overwhelming passion for his son (of a former marriage) Hippolytus. Near death's door on account of her torment, Phèdre's nurse, Oenone, urges her to reveal the source of her suffering. Phèdre has hardly uttered the words of her confession to the nurse when news is delivered that Theseus is dead.

Now liberated from the infidelity of her love, the nurse encourages the queen to see Hippolytus, at the very least in order to defend her own son's rights to the throne. But when Phèdre sees him she involuntarily confesses her passion, and immediately regrets it. For Theseus, far from being dead, has just returned to Troezen. Phèdre is guilt-stricken by the news, filled with regret at having been 'seduced' by hope, with its 'glimpses of a sinless love' (III.i.768, 772):

> Thanks be to Heaven, my hands have done no wrong.
> Would God my heart were innocent as they!   (I.iii.221–2)

What follows is a masterful sequence of lies and revelations: Phèdre is concerned that Hippolytus will betray her indiscretion to Theseus, and allows herself to be persuaded by Oenone that the best course of action is for the nurse to accuse Hippolytus of doing violence to the queen in his absence. 'All I need is your silence to succeed,' Oenone says (III.iii.894). Once Theseus has been thus misinformed he confronts Hippolytus, who attempts to justify himself by revealing that

---

[15] Goldmann 1964: 317, 376ff.   [16] See, e.g., Racine 1963: 141.
[17] Cited in Racine 1963: 129.
[18] Treated by Euripides in *Hippolytus* and Seneca in *Phaedra*.
[19] The translation cited here and in what follows is Racine 1963.

his affections lie elsewhere, with another forbidden object, Alicia. But Theseus does not believe his confession, and curses him with Neptune's vengeance. When Phèdre learns of Hippolytus' confession she is consumed by jealousy, and plays the silent witness as he goes to meet his death. Consumed by guilt, her own death follows swiftly after: Phèdre takes poison, confesses the truth, and dies.

The Jansenist reading of *Phèdre* has a long provenance. On this reading, she is a sinner from whom grace has been withdrawn—in Arnauld's words, 'one of the just to whom grace was not vouchsafed'.[20] As one translator puts it, 'she writhes in the nets of passion and circumstance',[21] and is guilty not because of what she *does* but on account of what she *is*.

On Goldmann's reading, Racine's Jansenist tragedy offers a 'tragic vision' of God, the world, and man. The centre of this vision, on Goldmann's reading, is that God is 'always absent and always present'.[22] He is a *Deus absconditus*, but he is not merely absent: for God is still a 'witness' to the world. As Lukàcs wrote, such a God is 'nothing more than a spectator, and he never intervenes, either by word or deed, in what the actors are doing'.[23]

Literary representations of Jansenism frequently evoke the problem of evil. How can such a spectator God be just? When Phèdre confesses her love to Hippolytus she takes little solace in having the gods as her witness. For after all, it is the gods who are to blame for her sin:

> The gods are witness, they who in my breast
> Have lit the fire fatal to all my line
> Those gods whose cruel glory it has been
> To lead astray a feeble mortal's heart. (II.5.679–82)

Several of Racine's plays include human victims confronting divine 'justice',[24] and in *Phèdre* the 'farthest-reaching Jansenist motif' is not

---

[20] According to the poet's son, Louis Racine (see Racine 1963: 133).
[21] Racine 1963: 136.   [22] Goldmann 1964: 37.
[23] Lukàcs, *The Metaphysics of Tragedy*, 1908, cited in Goldmann 1964: xii.
[24] In his first play, *La Thébaïde*, for example, we read:

> Voilà de ces grands dieux la suprême justice,
> Jusques au bord du crime ils conduisent nos pas,
> Ils nous le font commettre, et ne l'excusent pas.
> Prennent-ils donc plaisir à faire des coupables,
> Afin d'en faire après d'illustres misérables?
> Et ne peuvent-ils point quand ils sont en courroux,
> Chercher des criminels à qui le crime est doux? (III.ii.608ff.)

just 'the heroine's tortured conscience' but rather the anguished realization that divinity is receding from the world.[25]

As we saw in Chapter 2, Pascal approaches this tragedy in his depiction of fallen humanity and the hidden deity, but his concept of grace leaves room for hope (for those who receive it). For the Jansenist Phèdre, by contrast, 'hope is doomed to disillusion'.[26] It is a 'tragedy of refusal', to borrow Goldmann's phrase: Phèdre refuses the possibility of redemption, because it is the gods who 'smite the evildoer with their bolt' (IV.vi.1305). And perhaps victims of the fall—even when they strive to be just—are 'doomed to die, without grace, in unremitted sin'.[27] This is the defining characteristic of Jansenist tragedy: that it is, in Goldmann's words, 'without peripeteia and without recognition'.[28] There is no transformative moment; no vision of resolution.

VOLTAIRE

Jansenism was not only to be personified on stage; it was also to take literary lashings from one of France's sharpest satirical wits: Voltaire.[29] Voltaire intentionally set out to vex the Jansenists, whom, Roger Pearson tells us, 'he regarded at best as po-faced killjoys (like his father) and at worst as dangerous and inhumane fanatics (like his brother)'.[30]

And he succeeded in his intentions—several times and in diverse literary forms. We find derision of the Jansenist refusal of the world in the poem 'Le Mondain (ou l'Apologie du luxe')' ['The Man of the World (or An Apology for Luxury)'] (1736), where Adam is mockingly asked:

> Mon cher Adam, mon gourmand, mon bon père,
> Que faisais-tu dans les jardins d'Eden?

---

[25] See Lewis 1994: 326.   [26] Goldmann 1964: 376.   [27] Lewis 1994: 321.
[28] Goldmann 1964: 376.
[29] Like Racine, given Voltaire's prominence it is little wonder that Sartre read him. Fabrice Thumerel writes that Voltaire was, for Sartre, the 'symbol of the engaged intellectual' (Noudelmann and Philippe 2013: 517).
[30] Both relatives were Jansenist. See Pearson 2006: xxvi; Quinones 2007: 116.

The Jansenists (following Augustine) thought that all men sought their own happiness.[31] But, Voltaire says, these zealots forbid them from finding it where it is: in the world, in this 'earthly paradise'. And after all, Voltaire goads, Jansenists cannot forgo all the pleasures of this earth.

Candide, or Optimism—though better known for its parody of Leibnizian theodicy[32] in the ridiculous optimism of Dr Pangloss— also disparages the Jansenists. The 'religious convulsions crowd', Jansenist fanatics who went into convulsions in public spaces between 1729 and 1732,[33] feature in Martin's account of his travels in Europe. And the Catholic opposition to Jansenism also appears: on Candide's arrival in Paris, when he falls ill, the priest who visits him politely asks if he has 'a confessional note payable to a bearer in another world',[34] which refers to a practice common in the 1750s, whereby one could not receive last rites unless one had a note attesting to one's orthodoxy—insofar as that was measured by attesting to the Papal Bull *Unigenitus*, of 1713, condemning 'heretical' aspects of Jansenism.

Both Jansenists and their defenders, *Candide* implies, perpetuate the evils of the world (and make a mockery of Leibnizian optimism). When Candide asks his 'learned gentleman' in Paris whether he thinks this world is the best, he replies:

> I find that everything in our world is amiss, that nobody knows his place or responsibility or what he's doing or what he should do, and that, except for supper parties, which are quite jolly and where people seem to get on reasonably well, the rest of the time is spent in pointless quarrelling: Jansenists with Molinists, lawyers with churchmen, men with letters with men of letters, courtiers with courtiers, financiers with the general public, wives with husbands, relatives with relatives. It's one battle after another.[35]

But Candide's answer is simple: 'Those are just the shadows in a beautiful painting'.[36] By the Principle of Sufficient Reason, *freedom* is a great enough good that this world is the best of all possible ones. Throughout the play its characters endure a catalogue of horrors:

---

[31] See Brémond on the 'panhedonism' of Port-Royal: as Goldmann glosses it, all of the 'disciples of Saint Augustine' agreed that 'all men sought happiness' (1964: 260).
[32] Leibniz's *Essais de théodicée*—the only work published in his lifetime—were written in French and published in 1710.
[33] See Voltaire 2006: 54, and Pearson 2006: 289, n. 54.
[34] Voltaire 2006: 56.   [35] Voltaire 2006: 61.   [36] Voltaire 2006: 61.

rape, conquest, murder, massacre, cannibalism, torture, hanging, storm, shipwrecks, earthquake, illness, prostitution—not to mention Candide's regularly being fleeced on account of his wealth. By chapter 13 Candide begins to question Pangloss's optimism, which is finally renounced in the nineteenth chapter.

Divine providence and human suffering are themes that recur in Voltaire's corpus. Like Pascal and Racine, Voltaire's works often treat the problem of divine hiddenness: but he is more concerned with its moral than epistemic aspect. In addition to *Candide* the problem of evil plays a prominent role in *Zadig*, and the *Poème sur le désastre de Lisbonne* (written after the Lisbon earthquake of 1 November 1755), and *The Ingenu*. But though Leibnizean optimism did not command reasonable assent, neither did Jansenist pessimism. In Voltaire's 25th *Lettre philosophique*—originally published in 1728 and now widely known as the 'Anti-Pascal'—he offers some 'Remarks on the *Pensées* of M. Pascal', in which he intends to 'take the part of humanity against this sublime misanthrope'. For even if things are not as good as Leibniz would have us believe; neither are they as bad as bemoaned by M. Pascal. Pascal, Voltaire writes, writes against human nature as much as against the Jesuits; describing them at their worst, painting them 'tous méchans [stet] et malheureux' ('all nasty and unhappy').[37] Pascal's book is full of 'eloquent paralogisms' and 'admirably deduced falsehoods',[38] so Voltaire offers his readers a selection of the *Pensées* with his own commentary.[39]

The 'mystery' of the transmission of original sin comes under his scrutiny: 'What a strange explication!' he writes, that 'man is inconceivable without an inconceivable mystery.'[40] The losses and gains of the wager are equally deemed worthy of ridicule: 'I have an interest, without a doubt, in there being a God; but if in your system God has only come for a few people; if the small number of the elect is so frightful; if I can never do anything at all by myself, tell me, I beg you, what interest do I have in believing you?'[41] 'Your reasoning is good for nothing but making atheists.'[42] Even the sin which is 'folie' in the eyes of Pascal is—by some manner of contradiction—claimed to be *manifest*: but '[h]ow can it be, at one and the same time, both folly

---

[37] Voltaire 1819: 269.   [38] Voltaire 1819: 270.
[39] Running to thirty-six printed pages in the first edition, with an addition of four further pages (excluded by the first editors) made in 1743.
[40] Voltaire 1819: 272.   [41] Voltaire 1819: 276.   [42] Voltaire 1819: 277.

and demonstrated by reason?'[43] With meditated mockery, Pascal's metaphysics are rejected in favour of a more *reasonable* materialism.

HUGO

The Jansenist—or perhaps, in this case, Pascalian—thread in French literature can also be traced in one of the best-known works of Victor Hugo, *Les Misérables*. There is little doubt that Hugo attracted Sartre's attention,[44] nor that *Les Misérables* in particular was significant in Sartre's early formation: he read the book at a young age[45] and later described himself as wanting to be Jean Valjean.[46] Even the title of the novel—especially its original title, *Les Misères*—points the reader to Pascal.

Although Pascal is only referred to by name three times in the novel, several scholars have noted the resemblance between Hugo's work and Pascal's.[47] Some attribute it to the coincidence of religious preoccupations;[48] while others argue that the presence of key Pascalian concepts such as 'les deux infinis' and 'le Dieu sensible au coeur' suggest that the *Pensées* is 'a more prominent intertext in *Les Misérables* than critics have previously recognized'.[49] Whatever the centrality of the *Pensées* as an intertext, there is little doubt that *Les Misérables* deliberately takes as its themes good and evil, grace and law, freedom and limit. In the narrator's own words, the book is described as being 'from one end to the other ... the march from evil to good, ... from

---

[43] Voltaire 1819: 291–2.

[44] See WL 91–2; in Sartre's assessment Hugo was one of the only nineteenth-century authors to 'leave a mark' on French literature (WL 92).

[45] See 'Sartre's Readings of Youth'; Sartre placed his first reading before the age of sixteen (possibly as young as ten, according to one folio in the Gerassi collection—see RY, n.p.).

[46] See, e.g. *Les Mots*, where Sartre writes that 'je pleurai sur Jean Valjean, sur Eviradnus, mais, le livre fermé, j'effaçais leurs noms de ma mémoire et je faisais l'appel do mon vrai régiment' (LM 94, Pléiade edn). In his notes towards *Les Mots*, published in the Pléiade edition of the *Ecrits autobiographiques*, we read something different: 'Je lus *Les Misérables*. Je sanglotais: voilà l'homme que je voulais être' (VLM 1169).

[47] See O'Neil 1999, n. 3 for a summary of those who have noted the similarity.

[48] And one might wish to add to this the 'diffuse Augustinianism' in French literature generally: both Myriel and Thénardier quote Augustine in the novel (Hugo 1887: 23 and 262, respectively); and Bérulle is also mentioned twice (Hugo 1887: 329, 362).

[49] O'Neil 1999: 335.

heaven to hell, from nothingness to God'.[50] But it is not an abstract treatise: rather, it concerns the lived experience of individuals.

In the first part of the book, in which Hugo develops the character of Bishop Myriel, we discover a man who, despite his rank, 'was the same' towards all people. 'He condemned nothing in haste and without taking circumstances into account. He said, "Examine the road over which the fault has passed."' Hugo's description seems, quite deliberately, to situate the Bishop with respect to the rigorism of Pascal and the cynicism of Voltaire. Myriel describes himself 'with a smile' as 'an ex-sinner', but the narrator elaborates that 'he had none the asperities of austerity'. The novel offers this 'summary of his doctrine':

> Man has upon him his flesh, which is at once his burden and his temptation. He drags it with him and yields to it. He must watch it, check it, repress it, and obey it only at the last extremity. There may be some fault even in this obedience; but the fault thus committed is venial; it is a fall, but a fall on the knees which may terminate in prayer.
>
> To be a saint is the exception; to be an upright man is the rule. Err, fall, sin if you will, but be upright.
>
> The least possible sin is the law of man. No sin at all is the dream of the angel. All which is terrestrial is subject to sin. Sin is a gravitation.[51]

Hugo's political concerns give prominence to a third dimension in the question of sin: sin cannot be considered solely as a matter of God and the individual, but a matter of God, the individual, and *society*. 'Society is culpable', he writes; it is 'responsible for the night which it produces'. 'This soul is full of shadow, sin is therein committed. The guilty one is not the person who has committed the sin, but the person who has created the shadow.'[52]

When the Bishop meets the cynical senator—who introduces himself as 'Monsier le Comte Néant', admirer of Diderot and Voltaire—we see how *Les Misérables* can be read not only as a tale about mercy and mercilessness, but as a contribution to this particular French Augustinian conversation about nothingness, the *libido dominandi*, and the possibility of being duped by the infinite. From the senator's point of view (that of an anti-Myriel, if you will):

> God is a nonsensical monster. I would not say that in the *Moniteur*, of course, but I may whisper it among friends. *Inter pocula*. To sacrifice the

---

[50] Hugo 1887: 816.   [51] Hugo 1887: 24–5.   [52] Hugo 1887: 25.

world to paradise is to let slip the prey for the shadow. Be the dupe of the infinite! I'm not such a fool. I am a nothingness [*néant*]. I call myself Monsieur le Comte Nothingness, senator. Did I exist before my birth? No. Shall I exist after my death? No. What am I? A little dust collected in an organism. What am I to do on this earth? The choice rests with me: suffer or enjoy. Whither will suffering lead me? To nothingness; but I shall have suffered. Whither will enjoyment lead me? To nothingness; but I shall have enjoyed myself. My choice is made. One must eat or be eaten. I shall eat. It is better to be the tooth than the grass. Such is my wisdom.[53]

You must simply 'live your life', the senator urges. 'Make use of your *I* while you have it.'[54] *Le moi* may be false and deceptive, but it is all we have so we might as well make the most of it.

On hearing this homily, the Bishop claps:

'That's talking!' he exclaimed. 'What an excellent and really marvellous thing is this materialism! Not everyone who wants it can have it. Ah! When one does have it, one is no longer a dupe...'[55]

Such 'princes', the Bishop continues, have no qualms about belief in God being the philosophy of the people, just like 'goose with chestnuts is the turkey and truffles' of the poor.[56] But though he rejects Voltaire's materialism, it should not be understood by this that Myriel is a defender of Jansenist austerity: 'the hatred of luxury is not an intelligent hatred', for it would be unwise to hate the arts. But, on his view, 'an opulent priest is a contradiction'.[57]

Voltaire's intolerance of clerical hypocrisy is shared by the Bishop in theory and in practice. Contradictions cannot be lived in good conscience, and as Myriel said, Myriel did. In Chapter 13 ('What he believed') we read that we are not to assess the Bishop 'on the score of his orthodoxy' because 'in the presence of such a soul we feel ourselves in no mood but respect'.[58]

What did he think of this dogma, or of that mystery?... The point on which we are certain is that the difficulties of faith never resolved themselves into hypocrisy in his case.... The point which we consider

---

[53] Translation adapted from Hugo 1887: 36.
[54] 'Usez de votre moi pendant que vous le tenez.' Hugo 1887: 36.
[55] Hugo 1887: 36.   [56] Hugo 1887: 36.   [57] Hugo 1887: 47.
[58] Hugo 1887: 51.

it our duty to note is, that outside of and beyond his faith, as it were, the Bishop possessed an excess of love.... He lived without disdain.[59]

In Chapter 14 ('What he thought') we read that what 'enlightened this man was his heart'. *Son coeur.* 'No systems; many works.'[60] 'The humble soul loved, that was all.'[61]

> He inclined towards all that groans and all that expiates. The universe appeared to him like an immense malady; everywhere he felt fever, everywhere he heard the sound of suffering, and without seeking to solve the enigma, he strove to dress the wound.[62]

Long before the twentieth century, when Levinas proclaimed the 'end of theodicy',[63] we find in Myriel a character who did not think it fruitful to pursue theoretical 'questions why', as Marilyn McCord Adams puts it.[64] Instead, he cultivated kindness.

> Universal misery was his mine. That sadness reigned everywhere was but an excuse for unfailing kindness. Love each other; he declared this to be complete, desired nothing further, and that was the whole of his doctrine. One day, that man who believed himself to be a "philosopher", the senator who has already been alluded to, said to the bishop: "Just survey the spectacle of the world: all war against all; the strongest has the most wit. Your love each other is nonsense."—"Well," replied Monseigneur Welcome, without contesting the point, "if it is nonsense, the soul should shut itself up in it, as the pearl in the oyster." Thus he shut himself up, he lived there, he was absolutely satisfied with it, leaving on one side the prodigious questions which attract and terrify, the fathomless perspectives of abstraction, the precipices of metaphysics— all those profundities which converge, for the apostle in God, for the atheist in nothingness; destiny, good and evil, the war of being against being, the conscience of man, the thoughtful somnambulism of the animal, the transformation in death, the recapitulation of existences which the tomb contains, the incomprehensible grafting of successive loves on the persistent *I*, the essence, the substance, the Nil and the Ens [*le néant et l'être*], the soul, nature, freedom, necessity, perpendicular problems, sinister obscurities, where lean the gigantic archangels of the human mind.[65]

---

[59] Hugo 1887: 51. [60] Hugo 1887: 53. [61] Hugo 1887: 54.
[62] Hugo 1887: 54. [63] See Levinas 1988. [64] See McCord Adams 2000.
[65] Hugo 1887: 54.

Such mysterious questions were 'noticed' by Monseigneur Bienvenu, but he did not 'scrutinize them' or 'let them trouble his spirit'; rather, he simply 'had in his soul a grave respect for the shadow'.[66] He did not flippantly dismiss them in argument, like the young Candide, as 'just the shadows in a beautiful painting'.[67] Rather, he met them in situations as wounds to be dressed. This 'unfailing kindness' is what moves Jean Valjean to his first tears in nineteen years—because under the loving gaze of Monseigneur Bienvenu he sees his wretchedness: 'Je suis un misérable!'[68]

Being seen—whether the gaze is God's, another's, or one's own—is a leitmotif in the novel. Early on, we read that 'True or false, that which is said of men often occupies as important a place in their lives, and above all in their destinies, as that which they do.'[69] After Valjean sees Javert, for the first time after his escape, he is sitting alone in his bolted room, wondering what he is trying to keep out.

> It seemed to him as though he might be seen.
> By whom?
> Alas! That on which he desired to close the door had already entered; that which he desired to blind was staring him in the face—his conscience.
> His conscience; that is to say, God.[70]

Valjean is forced to decide between 'virtue without and abomination within, or holiness within and infamy without'.[71]

The problem is that the eyes of God and the eyes of men see differently. Valjean, remembering the moment in which he was transformed by His Grace, reflects that men only behold his 'mask', but the Bishop saw his face; 'men saw his life, but... the Bishop beheld his conscience. So he must go to Arras, deliver the false Jean Valjean, and denounce the real one. Alas! That was the greatest of sacrifices, the most poignant of victories, the last step to take; but it must be done. Sad fate! He would enter into sanctity in the eyes of God when he returned to infamy in the eyes of men.'[72]

In the parallel scene in which Javert feels the gaze of God, he is described as discovering a new chief: 'he became unexpectedly

---

[66] Hugo 1887: 54.   [67] Voltaire 2006: 61.   [68] Hugo 1887: 90.
[69] Hugo 1887: 17.   [70] Hugo 1887: 161.   [71] Hugo 1887: 166.
[72] Hugo 1887: 164.

conscious of' and 'embarrassed' by him. 'This unforeseen presence threw him off his bearings and he did not know what to do with this superior.'[73] For Javert's ideal was 'not to be human, to be great'—and it is worth recalling here that Pascalian polarity, *misère* and *grandeur*—rather, his ideal was to be 'irreproachable'.[74]

Although the law that Javert represents is not the Law of Christian tradition, his rigorism looks much like that for which Jansenism was famous. Mère Angelique and her nuns were once described by the Archbishop of Paris as being 'pure as angels and proud as devils', and it is precisely when Javert recognizes the impossibility of proud, irreproachable purity that he is undone. He is stuck between two crimes—'the crime of allowing a man to escape and the crime of arresting him!'[75]—and the only way out is to hand in his resignation. The God of *Les Misérables*, like the God of Pascal, 'is not responsible to men':[76] and for Javert his inscrutable ways are intolerable.

Bradley Stephens's recent work has highlighted 'overlooked parallels' between Hugo's romantic and Sartre's existentialist visions of freedom. Both, he thinks, offer 'philosophies of dramatic tension': Hugo and Sartre are both committed to a human freedom that is a 'flight towards being' or a 'dynamics of becoming'.[77] This flight is a constantly unrealized process, however, which is also a burden and a condemnation. But behind this dramatic tension, I shall argue in Part III, we find a *fallen* freedom: a tensive state of indeterminacy between being and nothingness.

BOURGEOIS SINNERS
AND BOURGEOIS PHILISTINES

There are later literary figures of demonstrable formative importance to Sartre who portray individuals in similar tensive situations, in which freedom is both liberating and a liability: some within the French tradition (e.g. Stendhal, Baudelaire, and Gide) and some without (e.g. Dostoevsky). Although there is not space to explore them in great detail here, a final historical point must be made before we turn to the final thinker to be considered in this historical section.

---

[73] Hugo 1887: 868.   [74] Hugo 1887: 867.   [75] Hugo 1887: 869.
[76] Hugo 1887: 922.   [77] Stephens 2011: 8, 9.

In the 1920s, there was a resurgence of Catholic writing in France—
'a cluster of aesthetic masterpieces' that sought to redress 'the great
sin of the modern world':[78] namely, not believing in sin. 'The Catholic
writers of the interwar years, François Mauriac, Georges Bernanos,
and Paul Claudel, took up the challenge to concretize sin and expose
it beneath the surface of modern materialism and scepticism.'[79]

Mauriac provoked controversy among Catholics because the God
in his novels was terrifyingly absent: he was raised Jansenist, wrote
biographies of Racine and Pascal, and 'saw sin everywhere'.[80] Bernanos's
works revived a view of the devil as an active, personal agent of evil in
the spiritual life of every human, challenging 'the modern belief
that evil is a purely psychological phenomenon and not a metaphysical reality'.[81] And Claudel, after experiencing a mystical conversion,
conveyed a more hopeful message about the world's shadows: that
God will make things right. As David O'Connell writes, his works
embody the Portuguese proverb that 'God writes straight, but with
crooked lines.'[82] It was in this literary context—with representatives
of Jansenism, dualism, and mysticism—that the teenage Sartre grew
to adulthood.[83] And it was into this context that the writings of a
certain Danish philosopher were first published in France.

KIERKEGAARD *À LA FRANÇAISE*

Kierkegaard's the 'Seducer's Diary' (extracted from *Either/Or*) was
published in France in 1929. Six years later, in 1935, *Le Concept de
l'angoisse* appeared.[84] In a letter dated 1 December 1939, Sartre
requested a copy of *Le Concept de l'angoisse* from Beauvoir to read
while on military service.[85] In the same month Sartre read it carefully,
making extensive notes—including line-by-line quotations—in his

---

[78] O'Connell 1994: 855.   [79] O'Connell 1994: 856.

[80] See O'Connell 1994: 856. The biographies are *Vie de Jean Racine* and *Blaise Pascal et sa soeur Jacqueline*.

[81] O'Connell 1994: 858.   [82] O'Connell 1994: 860.

[83] See Kirkpatrick 2017: 76–82 for a discussion of Sartre's readings of and reactions to Mauriac, Bernanos, and Claudel.

[84] Kierkegaard 1935, 1929. For more on Kierkegaard's reception in France, see Teboul 2005; Lafarge 2009.

[85] Sartre to Beauvoir, 1 December 1939 (WML 378).

notebooks.[86] On 18 December, for example, he notes the extent to which Heidegger borrowed from Kierkegaard in his account of anxiety—such as the precise use of the phrase 'the dread of nothing', and reflects on the different meanings 'nothing' had for these two predecessors.[87]

Three days later, in a letter to Beauvoir, he writes that he 'found a theory of nothingness while reading Kierkegaard'.[88] His enthusiasm was contagious; the next year Beauvoir's own letters express that she has 'heaps of books by Kierkegaard', and Jean Wahl's essays on him, which 'really interest me'.[89] Sartre also read and respected Wahl's *Études kierkegaardiennes*; he cites them several times in *Being and Nothingness* and in *A New Mystic*.[90]

Jon Stewart has provided an outline of the evidence of Sartre's direct reading of Kierkegaard, and particularly for the formation of the ideas expressed in *Being and Nothingness*, concluding that the work 'clearly bears the stamp of some of Kierkegaard's thoughts'.[91] In *Being and Nothingness*, *The Concept of Anxiety* is explicitly acknowledged in Sartre's discussion of *l'angoisse*, where we read:

> Kierkegaard describing [anxiety] before the sin characterizes it as [anxiety] in the face of freedom. But Heidegger, whom we know to have been greatly influenced by Kierkegaard, considers [anxiety] instead

[86] For more on Kierkegaard's influence on Sartre's thinking at this time, see CG 329, 334, 342, 352, 626; WD 131–4; LS Tome 1: 491, 495, 500; LS Tome 2, 264.

[87] WD 131–4.

[88] WML 421. See Chapter 4: Sartre had already written about *néant* in the 1930s.

[89] Beauvoir 1990: letters 219, 220, pp. 213–14; Beauvoir 1991: 355–7.

[90] BN 53, where the reference is to the appendix 'Kierkegaard et Heidegger'; NM 275. It is impossible to know to what extent Sartre engaged directly with Kierkegaard and to what extent he received him second-hand through the works of Wahl and other contemporaries; but given that we know Sartre read (and received professional encouragement) from Wahl (see WML 386, n. 2)—and that Wahl dedicates the seventh chapter of his *Études* to a sustained analysis of *Le Concept de l'angoisse*, complete with notes relating it to other Kierkegaard texts—the importance of such indirect influences should not be underestimated. Indeed, Manuela Hackel suggests that 'it is mainly due to Wahl's efforts that Kierkegaard attracted Sartre's attention' (Hackel 2011: 330).

[91] Stewart 2009: 436. Sartre also mentions Kierkegaard in EH, where he demonstrates familiarity with Kierkegaard's analysis of 'the anxiety of Abraham' in *Fear and Trembling*. Though the early Sartre's indebtedness to Kierkegaard has received greater attention than his later philosophy—so much so that some scholars call it 'commonplace' (McBride 1995: 19)—his later works, including the UNESCO lecture of 1963, indicate that Kierkegaard continued to exert a significant influence. See Stewart 2009, McBride 1995, and Hackel 2011 for further explorations of this influence.

as the apprehension of nothingness. These two descriptions of [anxiety] do not appear to us contradictory; on the contrary the one implies the other.[92]

Sartre's own list of formative reading, 'Readings of Youth', lists Kierkegaard along with Heidegger under the heading [19]39–45, specifying in parentheses *Le Concept de l'angoisse* and Abraham.[93]

But Sartre and Kierkegaard make an odd couple. As Stewart writes, 'It is interesting that such a profoundly secular thinker as Sartre could be so keenly interested in the thought of such a profoundly religious thinker as Kierkegaard. Indeed, it is telling that Sartre effectively ignores the context of Kierkegaard's account of freedom, namely, an analysis of the concept of sin.'[94] The 'obvious disparity between the admitted and the actual Kierkegaard influence'[95] has led scholars such as Roger Poole to comment that 'Sartre never ceased trying to evade the issue of his debt to Kierkegaard.'[96] But the most plausible explanation of this disparity, it seems to this author, is that Sartre was trying to evade a larger debt to the concept of *sin*. On this reading, Kierkegaard was a single creditor in the tradition from which he borrowed. But before defending this assertion, in Part III, we will consider the relevant aspects of Kierkegaard's account of sin and its consequences.

The Concept of Anxiety

In a journal entry from 1842 Kierkegaard writes that 'The nature of original sin has often been explained, and still a primary category has been lacking—it is anxiety (*Angst*); this is the essential determinant.'[97] Indeed, Kierkegaard's analysis of anxiety 'as the psychological pre-condition of original or hereditary sin (*Arvesynd*)' is taken by many to be one of his 'most original and most notable contributions to Christian thought'.[98] Kierkegaard's analysis also, as we shall see in Chapter 4, made a notable contribution to Sartre's account of human freedom.[99]

---

[92] BN 53; this is the passage that includes Sartre's citation of Wahl's essay (see n. 90).
[93] RY n.p.   [94] Stewart 2009: 440.   [95] Hackel 2011: 324.
[96] Poole 1998: 54.   [97] JP i.94, cited in Wahl 1938: 223.
[98] Walsh 2009: 80; she cites Tillich, Niebuhr, and Brunner as examples.
[99] See WD 131ff., especially p. 132, where Sartre discusses the relations of negation, freedom, and nothingness, and imagination. Later in WD Sartre writes that 'men

In the English-language secondary literature, *The Concept of Anxiety* has been granted the distinction of being 'possibly the most difficult of Kierkegaard's works',[100] with most commentators agreeing—if not stating explicitly—that 'the concept [of anxiety] that emerges is by no means clear cut'.[101] Like many of Kierkegaard's pseudonymous works, it is concerned with existence as the pursuit of self-realization, or existential wholeness—which, in his own terms, is to achieve a synthesis of the psychical and physical in and through spirit. For Kierkegaard, this can only be accomplished in Christian existence: '[I]n relating itself to itself and in willing to be itself, the self rests transparently in the power that established it'[102]—that is, it rests in God.

The work's subtitle describes it as 'a simple psychologically orienting deliberation on the dogmatic issue of hereditary sin'. Before lifting the cover, therefore, the reader is advised that this is not a theological treatise but a psychological examination. A few pages in, Vigilius Haufniensis[103] tells us that this analysis of anxiety 'constantly keeps in mind and before its eye the dogma of hereditary sin'.[104] The reason for this is that sin eludes scientific study, where such study is intended to produce rational explanations of their subjects. As Walsh writes, 'sin is an actuality that should be dealt with in a personal or existential manner, not in a scholarly context, which alters the true concept of sin by subjecting it to "the nonessential refraction of reflection"'.[105] It should be overcome in individuals' lives, rather than parsed in an abstract analysis.

Psychology is no more able to explain *why* sin comes into the world than theology or any other science. But given its subject matter—the human psyche—the question of *how* sin comes into existence, or of the possibility of sin, is of the utmost interest.[106] Walsh notes that Haufniensis does not use the term in the empirical sense in which it is usually understood today, but rather as 'rational psychology', 'whose aim is to give a rational explanation of the theoretical and practical, mental and physical aspects of the human psyche'. As such, psychology

deserve war', explaining that 'It's like the sin of Adam that each individual, according to Kierkegaard, freely adopts as his own' (WD 164).

[100] Kierkegaard 1980: xii.   [101] Macquarrie 1973: 167.
[102] See *The Concept of Anxiety*, xvii; Kierkegaard 1983: 13–14.
[103] The 'vigilant watchman of Copenhagen'. See Dunning 1985: 11.
[104] Kierkegaard 1980: 14.   [105] Walsh 2009: 81.
[106] Kierkegaard 1980: 21–2.

should work with theology, with psychology explaining sin as something real—as an actual possibility—in order for dogmatics to explain the conceptual possibility of sin through the concept of hereditary sin.[107]

Haufniensis begins his analysis with the story of the fall as presented in Genesis, exploring what he perceived as the structural similarities between the origin of *sin* and that of *freedom*. In the reflections that follow, some commentators take him to reject the orthodox doctrine of hereditary sin altogether; others see him as attempting to correct the errors that evolved in both Catholic and Protestant doctrines—to find 'the middle course between Augustine and Pelagius'.[108]

In examining the origins of sin Haufniensis offers his own interpretation of the Adam story, saying that 'sin came into the world by a sin'.[109] Sin came into the world through Adam's first sin and it comes into the world in precisely the same manner in all subsequent generations—each person commits a first sin which is a qualitative leap.[110] As Walsh puts it, 'The first sin of later individuals is not caused by Adam's sin or by the quantitative build-up of sinfulness in the world after the Fall, as this would mean that sinfulness precedes sin, which is a contradiction.'[111] We must be innocent in order to be truly guilty of sin.[112]

But this leads to the central question: how could the innocence of Eden be lost? The only plausible answer must be psychological. Because science cannot explain sin—and the qualitative leap by which it enters the world—psychology must concern itself with the preconditions that lead to (but which nonetheless do not necessitate or explain) the leap. Previous attempts to explain the fall—whether focusing on prohibition, temptation, or concupiscence—have failed to capture one of its most important components: anxiety.[113] This neglected category is eventually defined as 'a sympathetic antipathy and an antipathetic sympathy',[114] a feeling of attraction and repulsion. It is a tensive state, always already ambiguous.

---

[107] Kierkegaard 1980: 23. See Wahl 1938: 218 on 'l'impuissance de psychologie' in this regard; Wahl's reading of *angoisse* does not ignore its religious dimension.
[108] Walsh 2009: 86.　　　　[109] Kierkegaard 1980: 32.
[110] Kierkegaard 1980: 32, 36.　　　[111] Walsh 2009: 87.
[112] Kierkegaard 1980: 35.　　　[113] Kierkegaard 1980: 39–42.
[114] Kierkegaard 1980: 42.

Of the reflections that follow, most pertinent for our purposes are the following four theses (which are by no means exhaustive):

1. *Anxiety is a distinctively human characteristic because the human being is a synthesis.* Anxiety's role as a defining characteristic of humanity is of such importance that Haufniensis calls it 'the pivot upon which everything turns'.[115] Animals cannot be anxious. Only human beings are qualified by spirit, and 'for this reason, anxiety is not found in the beast, precisely because by nature the beast is not qualified as spirit'.[116] The extent to which anxiety is defining, however, is somewhat startling: 'If a human being were a beast or an angel, he could not be in anxiety. Because he is a synthesis, he can be in anxiety; and the more profoundly he is in anxiety, the greater is the man.'[117] Haufniensis clarifies that we are syntheses of body and psyche, temporal and eternal. In sin, the equilibria of these syntheses are disrupted. In the case of body and psyche, spirit forms a third party in the synthesis,[118] and when sensuousness becomes sin, spirit 'feels itself a foreigner', a stranger.[119] As soon as sin is posited, sensuality and temporality signify sinfulness,[120] the sensual becomes disordered, and time divisive.

2. *Anxiety is not the same as fear.* It is 'almost never treated in psychology', and 'altogether different from fear and similar concepts that refer to something definite'.[121]

3. *Anxiety does not have an object. Or, the object of anxiety is nothing.* 'If we ask more particularly what the object of anxiety is, then the answer, here as elsewhere, must be that it is nothing.'[122]

4. *Anxiety reveals 'freedom's possibility'.* In Haufniensis's own words, 'anxiety is freedom's actuality as the possibility of possibility'.[123] Haufniensis distinguishes between objective and subjective anxiety. The former denotes the anxiety felt by innocence; this is the anxiety that reveals the possibility of freedom. Subjective anxiety, by contrast, is a consequence of sin. It is 'the dizziness [or vertigo] of freedom, which emerges when the spirit wants

[115] Kierkegaard 1980: 43.   [116] Kierkegaard 1980: 42.
[117] Kierkegaard 1980: 155.   [118] Kierkegaard 1980: 85.
[119] Kierkegaard 1980: 76, 69, 71; see 68ff.   [120] Kierkegaard 1980: 92.
[121] Kierkegaard 1980: 42.   [122] Kierkegaard 1980: 96.
[123] Kierkegaard 1980: 42, 155.

to posit the synthesis and freedom looks down into its own possibility, laying hold of finiteness to support itself.'[124] While such anxiety is dangerous if misunderstood, it has the potential to educate to faith; through faith, it is 'absolutely educative, because it consumes all finite ends and discovers all their deceptiveness'.[125]

For Kierkegaard, there is no explanation of the fall; it constitutes a 'qualitative leap'.[126] But if sin happened by necessity, 'there can be no anxiety'.[127] Sin thus comes into existence in every individual *as it did in Adam* through a first sin: 'a qualitative leap from innocence to guilt as a result of becoming anxious about the possibility of freedom'.[128]

As Jean Wahl summarizes it, 'Pour chaque homme, comme pour Adam, Kierkegaard conçoit un état pré-Adamique.'[129] This pre-Adamic state is a dynamic inaugurated by freedom: 'La tentation naît; la liberté s'éveille, pouvoir qui est et qui n'est pas, qu'Adam fuit et aime. C'est l'angoisse; elle est le vertige de la liberté.'[130] But however unsettling the vertiginous experience of anxiety may be, it can be a force for the good—'Whoever has learned to be anxious in the right way has learned the ultimate,'[131] Haufniensis writes, because '[w]ith the help of faith, anxiety brings up the individuality to rest in providence'.[132]

The Sickness unto Death

The Sickness unto Death was published in French as *Le Traité du déséspoir* in 1932—and it is worth remembering another Pascalian polarity with reference to the French publishers' choice of title: pride and despair.[133] Whether or not Sartre read the work directly, there is good reason to think he would have been familiar with the ideas it expressed.[134] *La Maladie jusqu'àla mort* is mentioned numerous times in Wahl's *Études kierkegaardiennes*, which includes passages

---

[124] Kierkegaard 1980: 61.   [125] Kierkegaard 1980: 155.
[126] Kierkegaard 1980: 48.   [127] Kierkegaard 1980: 49.
[128] Walsh 2009: 92.   [129] Wahl 1938: 219.   [130] Wahl 1938: 220.
[131] Kierkegaard 1980: 155.   [132] Kierkegaard 1980: 161.
[133] See Wahl 1938: 739; NB Wahl uses the alternative title *La Maladie jusqu'à la mort*.
[134] We do not have the same evidence of Sartre's direct engagement with *The Sickness unto Death*, though Stewart suggests that Sartre's footnote in *Being and Nothingness*—referring to the 'ambiguous realities' of Kierkegaard—taken in conjunction with a diary entry from the war period (17 December 1939) indicates that Sartre may have been familiar with this work. (See Stewart 2009: 446ff.; and Wahl 1938: 141 on ambiguity in Kierkegaard.) On Bernard Sève's reading, Sartre shared the

on despair in the essay on the *stade esthétique*, discussions of the dialectical nature of the human—necessity and possibility, finite and infinite, temporal and eternal, etc.[135] Wahl does not shy away from 'sin' in discussing Kierkegaard's thought, but on the contrary sees it as furnishing a response to some of his greatest questions,[136] as well as playing a central role in Kierkegaard's critique of Hegel.[137] For those still in the aesthetic sphere, Wahl writes, Kierkegaard gives two commandments: 'Despair!' and 'Choose yourself.'[138]

The work was published pseudonymously in 1849 by Anti-Climacus,[139] and the sickness it describes is a relational disease that affects the relation of the self to itself and to God. Where anxiety is the precondition and consequence of human freedom, despair is the manifestation of the mis-relation of the human being to itself. Following Hegel,[140] Anti-Climacus famously defines the self as 'a relation that relates itself to itself'.[141] Hegel's relational definition marked a departure from classical conceptions of self as a static, fixed substance that persists despite any changes to its accidental properties. But Anti-Climacus's definition of the self does not end there; in addition to being 'a relation that relates itself to itself', 'in relating

---

Heideggerian and Kierkegaardian conception of a 'possibility for death' (*possibilité pour la mort*)—for which the relevant text in Kierkegaard is the third chapter of Part I of *The Sickness unto Death* (Sève 1996: 92). Michael Theunissen suggests that, although Sartre does not draw on *The Sickness unto Death* as openly as on *The Concept of Anxiety*, the former is the lens through which Sartre critically read (and corrected) Heidegger (Theunissen 2005: 30).

[135] See, for example, Wahl 1938: 69–86, 198, 244, 255, n. 1. Of particular note, perhaps, is his description of the despair of defiance and the despair of weakness:

> Parfois [l'homme] veut être si pleinement soi qu'il fait de soi un horrible Dieu. Dans la fureur démoniaque, l'homme veut, par haine de l'existence, par haine de soi-même, être soi-même dans toute son horreur et protester par ce tourment contre tout l'être. Parfois, il sort de lui-même, il va vers l'extrême divertissement et ne veut plus se reconnaître. Dans les deux cas, qu'il se cherche ou se fuie, c'est qu'il ne se possède pas; les deux formes du désespoir souvent ne peuvent être distinguées l'une de l'autre, plus exactement encore, elles ne sont que deux aspects du même phénomène de la mésentente du moi avec lui-même. La faiblesse et le défi, le refus de soi et la délectation volontaire en soi viennent se mêler l'un à l'autre. (1938: 70)

[136] Wahl 1938: 390.   [137] Wahl 1938: 134.

[138] And later: 'Le désespoir est son remède à lui-même. Quand l'homme désespère absolument, il se remet à Dieu, il se fonde sur lui, il devient transparent. Il acquiert la simplicité, l'authenticité' (Wahl 1938: 83–4).

[139] For the significance of these two works being published under different pseudonyms, see Walsh 2009: 96.

[140] Hegel 1977: 83–4.   [141] Kierkegaard 1983: 13.

itself to itself it relates itself to another', namely *God*. That is why there are two forms of despair: human beings do not establish themselves. If we did, there could only be one form of despair: *not to will to be* oneself. But not being our own foundation—'the inability of the self to arrive at or to be in equilibrium and rest by itself'— means that we may also despairingly *will to be* ourselves.[142]

Like anxiety, despair is distinctively human, demonstrating that we are of a different order to animals in that we are not simply physical beings but also—and essentially—constituted of 'spirit'. Unlike anxiety, which is anxiety of nothing in particular, despair has an object. But its object is often not what it appears to be—despair over this or that thing, in actuality, is despair over *oneself*.[143] This 'most dangerous of illnesses' affects everyone: 'there is not one single living human being who does not despair a little, who does not secretly harbour an unrest, an inner strife, a disharmony, an anxiety... about himself'.[144] Whether or not it is recognized as such, it is a universal condition.

'The self is freedom,' Anti-Climacus writes. 'But freedom is the dialectical aspect of the categories of possibility and necessity.'[145] Because the self is made of dialectical constituents, despair can take several forms. The self is a synthesis of the temporal and the eternal, finitude and infinitude, necessity and possibility. Anti-Climacus focuses mainly on the latter two pairs,[146] the first having been introduced in the *Concept of Anxiety*. An effect of this dialectical nature of the self is that despair—in any of its forms—cannot be defined directly, but 'only by reflecting on its opposite'.[147]

Finitude is limiting; infinitude is extending. Infinitude's despair, therefore, 'is the fantastic, the unlimited, for the self is healthy and free from despair only when, precisely by having despaired, it rests transparently in God'. As a general rule, we read, imagination is the medium for infinitizing despair; '[imagination] is not a capacity, as are the others—if one wishes to speak in those terms, it is the capacity *instar omnium* [for all capacities]... The self is reflection, and the imagination is reflection, is the rendition of the self as the self's possibility.'[148] But imagination can carry one further and further away from the true selfhood one lacks.

---

[142] Kierkegaard 1983: 14.   [143] Kierkegaard 1983: 19.
[144] Kierkegaard 1983: 22.   [145] Kierkegaard 1983: 29.
[146] Kierkegaard 1983: 29–42.   [147] Kierkegaard 1983: 30.
[148] Kierkegaard 1983: 30–1.

Despair is not always visible to the naked eye. Indeed, as Kierkegaard writes, outward appearances may give no indication of lacking a self:

> Such things do not create much of a stir in the world, for a self is the last thing the world cares about and the most dangerous thing of all for a person to show signs of having. The greatest hazard of all, losing the self, can occur very quietly in the world, as if it were nothing at all. No other loss can occur so quietly; any other loss—an arm, a leg, five dollars, a wife, etc.—is surely to be noticed.[149]

When, on the other hand, one lacks infinitude, the self is swallowed up by the finite, tricked out of itself by 'the others'.

> Surrounded by hordes of men, absorbed in all sorts of secular matters, more and more shrewd about the ways of the world—such a person forgets himself, forgets his name divinely understood, does not dare to believe in himself, finds it too hazardous to be himself and far easier and safer to be like the others, to become a copy, a number, a mass man.[150]

A further tension exists between possibility (freedom) and necessity (limit). Both are 'equally essential' to becoming a self, but an imbalance of the two results in despair.[151]

In addition to exploring despair as the manifestation of these dialectics, Anti-Climacus also distinguishes between forms of despair in terms of the despairing person's *consciousness* of being a self-in-despair. At the lowest and most common level we find unconscious despair—a lack of awareness of despair or even the possession of an eternal self (what *The Concept of Anxiety* identifies as spiritlessness). Comparing the human to a house with a basement and two storeys, Anti-Climacus writes that 'all too regrettably the sad and ludicrous truth about the majority of people is that in their own house they prefer to live in the basement'.[152] That is to say, we would prefer to remain in our physical senses in the dark rather than occupy all of the floors, the entirety of the psychical-physical-*and spiritual* habitat that is truly human.

Though we may be dimly aware of our state, this preference to remain in blissful ignorance is so strong that we employ all manner of self-deceptions to avoid realizing the alternative. Indeed, the resemblance of Kierkegaard's descriptions of the flight from despair to

[149] Kierkegaard 1983: 32–3.   [150] Kierkegaard 1983: 33–4.
[151] Kierkegaard 1983: 35–6.   [152] Kierkegaard 1983: 43.

Pascal's account of *divertissement* has not been overlooked,[153] with Wahl himself writing that although Kierkegaard did not cite Pascal frequently, 'there must be a relationship between their thought'.[154] Although contemporary scholarship does not assign much weight to the influence of Pascal on Kierkegaard, the influence of Pascal on Kierkegaard's French reception is another matter—and one which has not received the attention it deserves.

At the conscious level, we find two forms of despair: 'despairingly not to will to be oneself' (the despair of weakness) and 'despairingly to will to be oneself' (the despair of defiance). This distinction, however, is 'only relative', because both defiance and weakness are present in all despair.[155] The despair of weakness can manifest in two ways: as 'despair over the earthly or over something earthly' or 'despair over the eternal or over oneself'.[156] Defiant despair involves a greater consciousness of the self, in the sense that one 'wills to be oneself'. But the self one wills to be is not the self God wills. In Anti-Climacus's words, 'the self in despair wants to be master of itself or to create itself, to make his self into the self he wants to be, to determine what he will have or not have in his concrete self'.[157] As Walsh puts it, 'Flouting and rebelling against all existence, the defiant self does not want to be helped temporally by the eternal but demonically prefers to be itself "with all the agonies of hell".'[158]

This taxonomy of despair, however, is but the psychological groundwork. The edifice that Anti-Climacus wants to build on it is a theological examination of sin which can *edify* the individual. In the opening paragraphs of *The Sickness unto Death* despair is introduced as a relational disease infecting the relations of the self to itself and to another. This latter dimension—relatedness to the other—comes into prominence in the second part of the work, where we learn that, quite simply, 'despair is sin' and 'sin is: before God'.[159] Unlike the pagan conception of sin as vice (whose opposite is virtue), the Christian conception of sin has as its opposite *faith*.

---

[153] See, e.g., 'diversionary means' described in *The Sickness unto Death* 48; Kierkegaard owned three editions of the *Pensées* (Landkildehus 2009: 130); see also Patrick 1947.

[154] Wahl 1938: 416; translation mine. Šajda 2009 shows the influence of Fénelon on Kierkegaard.

[155] Kierkegaard 1983: 49.   [156] Kierkegaard 1983: 50ff.
[157] Kierkegaard 1983: 68.   [158] Walsh 2009: 103.
[159] Kierkegaard 1983: 77.

And faith is this: 'that the self in being itself and in willing to be itself rests transparently in God'.[160] Anti-Climacus deems this 'one of the most decisive definitions for all Christianity—that the opposite of sin is not virtue but faith'.[161]

On Anti-Climacus' view, we are far from knowing how fallen we are. For sin to be sin, it must be revealed for what it is by God, namely, 'before God in despair not to will to be oneself or in despair to will to be oneself'.[162] But this definition results in a rather strange conclusion: if followed strictly, the lives of most people—the majority being basement-dwellers despite the fact that 'no one is born devoid of spirit'[163]—are too spiritless to be called sinful.

But for sinners who are conscious of sin, sin has the potential to grow and intensify such that it becomes a new sin: despair over sin itself. In despair over sin 'there may be a new intensification, a demonic closing up'; it is 'an effort to give stability and interest to sin as a power by deciding once and for all that one will refuse to hear anything about repentance and grace'.[164]

SINNERS IN SITUATIONS

In both Jansenist pessimism and Kierkegaardian despair, therefore, we find a tragic refusal. This chapter has shown that the French revival of Augustinianism—in particular in its Jansenist, Pascalian forms—left a literary legacy with which Sartre was familiar. In philosophy, too, questions of sin did not belong exclusively to the past: in the period of Sartre's ascendancy Georges Bataille gave a famous lecture—'Discussion on Sin' (1944)—which directly responded to Sartre and raised the question of whether sin and grace can coexist.[165] In Part III I argue that Sartre unifies the Augustinian notion of nothingnesss with a Kierkegaardian emphasis on the individual—on

---

[160] Kierkegaard 1983: 82.   [161] Kierkegaard 1983: 82.
[162] Kierkegaard 1983: 96.   [163] Kierkegaard 1983: 102.
[164] Kierkegaard 1983: 110.
[165] The same year that *Being and Nothingness* was published, in NM (1943) Sartre had argued that Bataille's celebration of inner experience was in bad faith; the death of God was not something to be mourned. See Kirkpatrick 2013 for further discussion of NM. See Surya 2002: 335ff. on Sartre's response to Bataille's 'Discussion on Sin'.

the *subjective* experience of sin. In doing so he draws not only on philosophers and theologians, but on literature: for universal themes such as sin and salvation are not best approached in abstraction, but in *situation*. Literary depiction engages us affectively, drawing readers into the lives of individuals and the ambiguity of particular situations. Being, Sartre writes in *Being and Nothingness*, 'is an individual venture' (BN 639); and so is nothingness.

Part III

A Phenomenology of Sin

4

Problems of Nothingness

Identity, Anxiety, and Bad Faith

[E]ach time that we approach the study of human reality from a new point of view we rediscover that indissoluble dyad, Being and Nothingness.[1]

This chapter is the first of four dedicated to the textual and conceptual analysis of *Being and Nothingness*.[2] It focuses on BN Part I ('The Problem of Nothingness'), arguing that *le néant* in Sartre's text has been influenced by the theological concepts of nothingness (*qua* original sin) introduced in Part II of this book. Moreover, the theological account of nothingness undergirds Sartre's conceptual divergences from Hegel, Husserl, and Heidegger.[3] My argument is supported by and illuminates the logic behind the structure of BN Part I: for after introducing his metaphysical claims about nothingness and consciousness, Sartre goes on to introduce problems which are cognates of nothingness (*qua* original sin) in the theological thinkers from whom he drew: with respect to personal identity, anxiety, and bad faith. The lived experience of nothingness, on Sartre's account, is characterized by self-estrangement and self-deception.

In Chapter 2 we saw, very briefly, that the sceptical project of Descartes's *Meditations* is rooted in the concept of the fall. To read it as an exploration of philosophical error alone is to miss its account of the noetic effects of sin, its epistemological theodicy. In the fourth

---

[1] BN 143.

[2] As stated in the introduction, the chapters in this part (like the parts of *Being and Nothingness*) must be taken together as stages in a reflection.

[3] Sartre's treatment of the German phenomenologists are often dismissed as 'misleading interpretations and inadequate assessments' (Schroeder 1984: 1).

meditation, as has already been noted, we find the words believed to have inspired the title of Sartre's *L'Être et le néant*:[4]

> I am, as it were, an intermediary between God and nothingness, or between supreme being and non-being: my nature is such that insofar as I was created by the supreme being, there is nothing in me to enable me to go wrong or lead me astray; but insofar as I participate in nothingness or non-being, that is, in so far as I am not myself the supreme being and am lacking in countless respects, it is no wonder that I make mistakes. I understand, then, that error as such is not something real which depends on God, but merely a defect.[5]

For the Descartes of the fourth meditation, it is only 'myself and God' whose existence can be known with certainty; these things and these alone are impervious to the doubts induced by *le néant*. God cannot be the source of error, so the problem, Descartes reasons, must lie in the thinking thing. More specifically, 'the scope of the will is wider than that of the intellect; but instead of restricting it within the same limits, I extend its use to matters which I do not understand'.[6] This 'privation' on my part 'does not require the concurrence of God, since it is not a thing; indeed, when it is referred to God as its cause, it should be called not a privation but simply a negation'.[7]

As Richmond notes, Sartre's interest in phenomenology 'co-existed with and was an instrument for his wish to demonstrate the existence of human freedom, and his sense that the way to do this was by establishing an essential connection of consciousness with nothingness'.[8] For Descartes, nothingness has epistemological consequences. In Sartre, the emphasis shifts: the consequences of nothingness are existential—which is to say, *lived* experiences. So it is to Sartre's concept of nothingness that I now turn.

IDENTITY AND NOTHINGNESS

Before examining *Being and Nothingness* itself we must briefly consider an earlier work. In *The Transcendence of the Ego* (1936),[9]

---

[4] See Morris 2008: 9; Sartre's indebtedness to Descartes has been widely noted, not least by Sartre himself (BN 98; 109). See Catalano 1985: 1ff. on 'Descartes and Sartre'.
[5] Descartes 1988: 99–100.   [6] Descartes 1988: 102.
[7] Descartes 1988: 104.   [8] Richmond 2013: 94.
[9] Written in 1934, published in 1937. Cf. Contat and Rybalka 1974, vol. 1: 47ff.

Sartre addresses a problem he perceives in Husserl's interpretation of Kant's transcendental unity of apperception. On Sartre's view, there is no 'transcendental ego in the sense of an *a priori* structure of consciousness that predetermines the unity of beliefs and perceptions'.[10] Sartre does not deny the existence of an ego (or self) altogether, but he does deny that there is an ego which is *behind* (or part of) consciousness as a subject. But as Christian Onaf notes, Sartre's *The Transcendence of the Ego* does more than reject the transcendental ego. It introduces a different form of consciousness: *reflective* consciousness.[11] Sartre takes Husserl's observation that the psychological ego was constituted by the subject[12] and argues that the same reflective constitution applies to the transcendental ego. In Sartre's own words, 'the consciousness which says "I think" is precisely not the consciousness which thinks' (TE 45): the 'I' of the cogito is not discovered but created. Moreover, 'the problems of the relations between the *I* and consciousness are . . . existential problems' (TE 4). Sartre rereads Kant to make an existential point.

To give a concrete example: when I am engaged in my daily activities there is no ego involved. If I am writing a chapter, I am aware of the words I combine and the feel of the keyboard as I type them, even the sound the keys make in response, but no 'I' can be said to *inhabit* this consciousness (TE 47, 48). The 'I' only comes into it when I reflect on the activity and see it as mine—for example by saying to my husband, 'I worked on Chapter 4 today.' With that step, the ego comes into existence as the intentional object of consciousness. The ego (as self-*known*) presupposes consciousness (as self-*knowing*).

This distinction between self-known and self-knowing is important because, on Aristotle's classic definition, identity is 'the fact that a thing is itself'.[13] But what does it mean for me to be 'myself'? Human beings are free and do many different things, leading us to question *why*? What explains my doing this, or your saying that? Most answers to such questions resort to 'motives' or 'reasons' or 'causes' as the explanatory antecedents of action.[14] Frequently these answers fit into one of two categories: situational or personal.[15] In the first category you might find explanations like 'I got out of bed because I need to write my book'. In the second category, 'he kept my secret because he

---

[10] Catalano 1990: 682.　　[11] Onaf 2013: 34–5.　　[12] Moran 2000: 169–71.
[13] Aristotle 1979: VII.17.　　[14] Wang 2009: 23.
[15] In Sartre's words, 'the situation as acting on the man or the man as acting on the situation' (BN 53).

is trustworthy'. Human action, likewise, is often understood as a response to circumstantial demands or an expression of personal identity (or, in a different idiom, *essence*).

But Sartre finds both of these ways of thinking dissatisfying and backwards. On his view, it is *by* acting that we establish an identity and allow external demands to shape our action. We call someone trustworthy *because* they have kept our secrets. And getting out of bed implies a prior choice to assign value to writing books. In the slogan form, Sartre wrote that: 'existence precedes essence'.[16] But the kind of 'essence' (or 'identity') that follows existence is ambiguous and insecure. Consequently the Socratic injunction—the famous imperative to *know thyself!*—is an impossible ideal.

In the Introduction to *Being and Nothingness* Sartre revisits this problematic disjunction between consciousness and the ego. There, he defines consciousness as 'the knowing being in so far as he is, not in so far as he is known' (BN 7), reiterating that 'there is a pre-reflective cogito which is the condition of the Cartesian cogito' (BN 9). 'As it is known', the 'ego is a perpetually deceptive mirage' (TE 38–9); 'It is that which escapes, that which offers itself only in fleeting and successive profiles' (BN 17).

Sartre's 'dense and intricate'[17] Introduction contains strong metaphysical theses about consciousness and its objects, which, as Sebastian Gardner writes, 'prove essential for nearly all of the major claims Sartre is going to make in [*Being and Nothingness*]: the most striking theses of B&N, in particular concerning human freedom, are to a large extent either amplifications or direct developments of metaphysical propositions laid down in the introduction'.[18] Indeed, Gardner is not alone in thinking that the entire book can be seen to clarify claims made in the Introduction.[19]

One of its most important theses is that Cartesian epistemology does not do justice to the lived experience of consciousness.[20] It is in the context of this discussion that Sartre revises Heidegger's *Dasein*, offering a new description of the phenomenological subject. Consciousness, for the Sartre of *Being and Nothingness*, '*is a being such*

---

[16] EH 49.   [17] Gardner 2009: 38.

[18] Gardner 2009: 38. Although Sartre would likely reject the label 'metaphysical' on the basis that he is concerned not with the question of why there is something rather than nothing, but with fundamental descriptions of being (see Catalano 1985: 15).

[19] See Catalano 1985: 19.

[20] See the section of Chapter 5 entitled 'I think therefore I was'.

that in its being, its being is in question in so far as this being implies a being other than itself (BN 18; italics original).[21] Unlike being—which 'is itself so completely that the perpetual reflection which constitutes the self is dissolved in an identity' (BN 21), 'the being of the for-itself is defined, on the contrary, as being what it is not and not being what it is' (BN 21). Being 'knows no otherness' (BN 22). But such identity perpetually eludes consciousness, which is contingent and incomplete.

It is worth saying at this point that Sartre's position vis-à-vis epistemology is ambiguous. Gardner argues that Sartre's turn to ontology is not, as in Heidegger, 'a turning away from epistemological issues as ill-formed or *nonsensical*'.[22] Rather, Sartre 'uses the inability of other philosophical accounts to solve epistemological problems as an argument for his own ontology'.[23] In other words, the failures of 'epistemology', on Sartre's view, are taken to support his metaphysics of *nothingness* (*le néant*).

On Sartre's view, consciousness 'anthropomorphically expresses' its lack of being by saying that being is *superfluous* (*de trop*). It cannot derive being from anything: Sartre is explicit that consciousness is 'uncreated' and 'without reason for being' (BN 22). The problem is nothingness:

> We set upon our pursuit of being, and it seemed to us that the series of our questions had led us to the heart of being. But behold, at the moment when we thought we were arriving at the goal, a glance cast on the question itself has revealed to us suddenly that we are encompassed with nothingness. The permanent possibility of non-being, outside us and within us, conditions our questions about being. (BN 29)

In BN Chapter 1 Sartre states that this is so because negation is the 'original basis of a relation of man to the world' (BN 31). In characteristically dramatic language, he describes negation as 'a refusal of existence. By means of it a being (or a way of being) is posited, and then thrown back into nothingness' (BN 35). I may refuse the existence of this chapter, for example, by deciding not to write it. Moreover, this

---

[21] It is important to note that this discussion of being shows dependence not only to Heidegger. Sartre treats logical problems arising from the notion of created being, demonstrates knowledge of 'perpetual creation' (BN 20), and writes, for a further example, that the Cartesian doctrine of substance logically culminates in the work of Spinoza (BN 14).

[22] Gardner 2009: 59.   [23] Gardner 2009: 60.

capacity to refuse is distinctively human: 'Man is the only being by whom a destruction can be accomplished' (BN 32).

Mary Warnock writes that 'it is impossible to exaggerate the importance which Sartre attaches to the power of denial, of negation, of asserting not only what is but what is not the case'.[24] For Sartre this separates humanity from the unthinking world: *being-for-itself* from *being-in-itself*. He characterizes humanity as 'the Being by which Nothingness arrives in the world' (BN 47, 48). The psychological ability to negate in this way, for Sartre, is dependent on an underlying ontology. 'The necessary condition for our saying not is that non-being be a perpetual presence in us and outside of us, that nothingness *haunt* being' (BN 35).[25]

Sartre situates this discussion in the thinking of all three of 'les trois Hs', which detailed historical narrative, as Richmond argues, demonstrates the pivotal role of the concept.[26] Having restated his problem with the Husserlian ego, he then turns to Hegel and Heidegger.

> When Hegel writes '(Being and nothingness) are empty abstractions, and the one is as empty as the other,' he forgets that emptiness is emptiness of something. Being is empty *of* all other determination than identity with itself, but that non-being is empty *of being*. In a word, we must recall here against Hegel that being *is* and that nothingness *is not*. (BN 39)[27]

Heidegger's conception of nothingness is closer to the mark, Sartre writes, because 'For "Dasein" there is even a permanent possibility of finding oneself "face to face" with nothingness and discovering it as a phenomenon: this possibility is [anxiety]' (BN 41). But though his account of anxiety is illuminating (as we shall see later in this chapter), Heidegger's view of nothingness is also dismissed (BN 42–3).[28] As Christina Howells notes, for Sartre '[n]either Hegel nor Heidegger

---

[24] Warnock 1965: xvi.

[25] The image of nothingness 'haunting' being is recurrent in *Being and Nothingness*; Sartre uses it in the pages immediately following (BN 36, 40; and elsewhere), before switching to a more visceral image: 'nothingness lies coiled in the heart of being—like a worm' (BN 45).

[26] Richmond 2013: 94.

[27] On the difference between absence and mere non-presence, Morris 2008: 33 offers a helpful (analytically informed) account.

[28] For more on Sartre's treatments of Hegel and Heidegger see Gardner 2009; Hartmann 1966 (the latter treats Hegel's *Logic* specifically).

carries his study of negation through to its source in *le néant* of human consciousness'.[29]

On my reading, Sartre's rejection of the non-subjectivist accounts of Hegel and Heidegger reflects the influence of the thinkers considered in Part II. In human existence, Sartre goes on to say, there are several 'realities'—'like absence, change, otherness, repulsion, regret, distraction', and distance—which are not only objects of judgement, but 'which are experienced, opposed, feared, etc., by the human being and which in their inner structure are inhabited by negation'. These Sartre calls *négatités*. These negations cannot be 'thrown . . . back into an extra-mundane nothingness since they are dispersed in being, are supported by being, and are conditions of reality' (BN 45).

Previous scholarship has been divided as to whether or not Sartre's own account reifies nothingness. As Richmond writes, Sartre's concept of nothingness is 'mind-bogglingly slippery', a fact which is not made easier by *Being and Nothingness*'s being a 'rambling work, demonstrably in need of editing'; on Richmond's view, 'within its many pages Sartre is often inconsistent'.[30] Katherine Morris, by contrast, argues that Sartre is not, as A. J. Ayer claimed, making the blatantly contradictory claim that these (non-existent) *négatités* exist. On Ayer's analysis, this 'novelist-philosopher's nothing' really means 'something insubstantial and mysterious' like the 'nobody' whom the Red King's eye's couldn't spot.[31]

For Sartre, as Morris writes, absences are not present, possibilities are not actualities, and values are not facts—rather, 'For Pierre to be absent in relation to Thérèse is a particular way of his being present' (BN 302). On Morris's account there is 'a widespread intellectual prejudice against the non-existent, the non-factual, the non-actual, and the absent, as well as the non-quantifiable and the non-measureable', which she summarizes as 'the prejudice for the existent'.[32] This prejudice assumes that only the existent is *real*. When Ayer derisively likens Sartre's nothingness to the 'nobody' one cannot see, he fails to recognize (among other things) that there are many ways of being absent. A dead lover's absence is different to an absconding one's.

I have already noted that, for Sartre, nothingness—*outside* us and *within* us—conditions our questions about being (BN 29). We will see in Chapter 5 how Sartre develops and clarifies this statement in his

---

[29] Howells 1988: 15.   [30] Richmond 2013: 100–1.   [31] Ayer 1945: 19.
[32] Morris 2008: 47.

notions of external and internal relations; but first we will follow
Sartre's own structure, considering the origin of nothingness and its
effects in lived experience. For on Sartre's account nothingness does
have effects and, in Richmond's words, 'nothingness requires ontological recognition'.[33] But precisely what kind of recognition can be
given to it? On my reading, the slipperiness of Sartre's concept of
nothingness—the *is it something or isn't it?*—retains a tension present
in Augustinian treatments of original sin. Let us return to Sartre's
account to see how.

Nothingness, on Sartre's view, 'is not'. It is non-existent. But
nonetheless 'Nothingness "is made-to-be"' (BN 46). Sartre's *négatités*
(though nothing) are experienced. In waiting for a friend or mourn-
ing a lost one, a human being *makes nothingness* (as absence) *be*.
Consequently, he suggests, there must be a being which nihilates, a
'*being by which nothingness comes to things*' (BN 46; italics original).
Sartre agrees with Augustine that nothingness comes into the world
through human beings. The being 'by which Nothingness arrives
in the world is a being such that in its Being, the Nothingness of its
Being is in question. *The being by which Nothingness comes into the
world must be its own Nothingness*' (BN 47; italics original). But, Sartre
continues, 'this question immediately provokes another: What must
man be in his being in order that through him nothingness may come
to being?' (BN 48).[34]

The answer Sartre gives is that man must be free. He credits
Descartes as having named 'this possibility which human reality has
to secrete a nothingness which isolates it—it is *freedom*' (BN 48). But
this answer itself only leads to further questions: 'What is human
freedom if through it nothingness comes into the world?' (BN 48). At
this point in *Being and Nothingness*, Sartre writes that 'it is not yet
possible to deal with the problem of freedom in all its fullness'
(BN 49); that is reserved for BN Part IV, where Sartre treats the
'technical and philosophical concept of freedom' (BN 505)—to which
we, too, shall return later.[35] But at this point it is important to highlight

---

[33] Richmond 2013: 95.
[34] See also BN 47–8: 'Man presents himself at least in this instance as a being
who causes Nothingness to arise in the world, inasmuch as he himself is affected with
non-being to the end.'
[35] See Chapter 7.

that for Sartre, man is the source of nothingness in the world, and that nothingness comes 'through' human freedom.

As Gardner writes, 'If the philosophy of [*Being and Nothingness*] were to be reconstructed in the form of a system based on a single principle, that principle would be the identification of the human being with nothingness.'[36] This is what he calls Sartre's 'de-creation myth': consciousness, as *being-for-itself*, is *being-in-itself that has undergone a nihilation*:

> Only being which has itself been nihilated, Sartre argues, could itself have the power to nihilate. Human being is, Sartre therefore implies, a "fallen", negated form of being-in-itself—it is as if it had once been a thing, but had now undergone a kind of metaphysical destruction, so that it now exists on the earth in the form of consciousness as a kind of ghost or shadow, robbed of being.[37]

In the lived experience of freedom, every decision implies 'a cleavage between the immediate psychic past and the present. This cleavage is precisely nothingness' (BN 51). Before elaborating on his 'technical and philosophical concept of freedom' Sartre offers an early definition: freedom is 'the human being putting his past out of play by secreting his own nothingness' (BN 52), and consciousness 'continually experiences itself as the nihilation of its past being' (BN 52).

ANXIETY AND NOTHINGNESS

This is why, on Sartre's view, we become conscious of freedom through anxiety (*angoisse*, BN 53), which reveals freedom 'as being the possible destroyer in the present and in the future of what I am' (BN 61). We have already seen, in Chapter 3, that Sartre views Kierkegaard's and Heidegger's accounts of *angoisse*, in the face of freedom (before sin) and nothingness respectively, as complementary (BN 53). A passage in the *War Diaries* states that they are 'one and the same':

> [Anxiety] at Nothingness, with Heidegger? Dread of freedom with Kierkegaard? In my view it's one and the same thing, for freedom is the apparition of Nothingness in the world...

---

[36] Gardner 2009: 71.   [37] Gardner 2009: 68.

> So [Anxiety] is indeed the experience of Nothingness, hence it isn't a
> psychological phenomenon. It's an existential structure of human reality,
> it's simply freedom becoming conscious of itself as its own nothin-
> gness ... Thus the existential grasping of our facticity is Nausea, and the
> existential apprehension of our freedom is [Anxiety].   (WD 132–3)[38]

We also saw that in his letter to Beauvoir that he claimed to have
'found a theory of nothingness while reading Kierkegaard'.[39] This is
worth reiterating for two reasons: first, because it is clear from earlier
writings that Sartre already had a developed view of nothingness
(qua *néant*) before reading Kierkegaard in 1939;[40] and second,
because Sartre omits the language of sin from his discussion, despite
the centrality of that concept in *The Concept of Anxiety* and in Jean
Wahl's treatment of it in *Études Kierkegaardiennes*.

In his discussion of *l'angoisse* in *Being and Nothingness* Sartre
restates several of Kierkegaard's observations,[41] the first being that
anxiety must be distinguished from fear because 'fear is fear of beings
in the world whereas [anxiety] is [anxiety] before myself'. To clarify
this distinction he adds that '[a] situation provokes fear if there is a
possibility of my life being changed from without; my being provokes
[anxiety] to the extent that I distrust myself and my own reactions in
that situation' (BN 53). Sartrean anxiety, as Cabestan and Tomes
write, 'does not correspond to any object I encounter in the world
but to my own being, that is to say, to my freedom; it can thus be
defined as the consciousness of my freedom—and that even in the
most trivial of situations'.[42]

Anxiety is 'reflective apprehension of the self' (BN 54) because it
reveals the relation of the self to its possibilities:

> But a nothingness has slipped into the heart of this relation; I *am* not the
> self which I will be. First I am not that self because time separates me
> from it. Secondly, I am not that self because what I am is not the

---

[38] We will turn to consider 'nausea' at greater length in Chapter 5, alongside
Sartre's phenomenology of the body.

[39] Sartre to Beauvoir, 21 December 1939 (WML 421).

[40] He uses the concept of *néant* in several works written during the 1930s,
including I, IM, and TE.

[41] As discussed in Chapter 3, these are (1) that anxiety is a distinctively human
characteristic because the human being is a synthesis; (2) that anxiety is not the same
as fear; (3) that anxiety does not have an object, or the object of anxiety is nothing;
(4) that anxiety reveals 'freedom's possibility'.

[42] Cabestan and Tomes 2001: 8.

foundation of what I will be. Finally I am not that self because no actual existent can determine strictly what I am going to be. Yet as I am already what I will be (otherwise I would not be interested in any one being more than another), *I am the self which I will be, in the mode of not being it.*   (BN 56; italics original)

As Sartre puts it, if I am to call on a resolution (not to gamble, for example, or to refrain from wine and bread), 'I must remake it *ex nihilo* and freely' (BN 57). 'Anxiety', too, shows up the shortcomings of Cartesian epistemology: in *The Transcendence of the Ego* Sartre wrote that 'If the *I* of the "I think" is the primary structure of consciousness, this [anxiety] is impossible' (TE 49).

Consciousness, therefore, 'confronts' its past and future 'as facing a self which it is in the mode of not-being' (BN 58). Temporality, on Sartre's view, has a nihilating structure, such that we are estranged from our selves by time. Freedom, therefore, 'manifests itself through [anxiety]' and 'is characterized by a constantly renewed obligation to remake the self' (BN 58). This *lack* of perduring selfhood—the impossibility of identity at any instant or its continuity through time—arises because 'man is always separated by a nothingness from his essence' (BN 59). 'Nothing can ensure me against myself, cut off from the world and from my essence by this nothingness which *I am*' (BN 63).

Of course, problems of anchoring the perdurance of the post-Cartesian self are neither original nor exclusive to Sartre. But the explicitly ontological account Sartre gives recalls earlier, theological expressions. Consider this passage, which we have already seen in Fénelon:

> I am not, O my God, what is; alas, I am almost what is not. I see myself as an incomprehensible intermediate between nothingness and being. I am the one who has been; I am the one who will be; I am the one who is no longer what he has been; I am the one who is not yet what he will be; and, in this in-between that I am, something unknowable that cannot be held in itself, that has no consistency, that flows away like water; something unknowable that I cannot seize, that flees from my hands, that is no longer as soon as I wish to grasp or perceive it; something unknowable that finishes at the very instant in which it begins; so that I can never at any moment find myself stable and present to myself, so as to say simply that I am. Thus my duration is nothing but a perpetual failure/lack [*défaillance*] of being.[43]

---

[43] Fénelon 1880: 180.

We saw in Chapters 2 and 3 that for Christian thinkers such as Bérulle, Pascal, or Fénelon, the estranging nothingness of sin (and human lack of being) has an answer in the nothingness of grace. In Sartre, it does not: 'It is certain that we cannot overcome [anxiety], for we *are* [anxiety]' (BN 67; italics original). It is an original ontological condition: to be free is to be between being and nothingness.

The anxiety Sartre describes is, to understate the obvious, uncomfortable. So we attempt to hide it from ourselves. 'Everything takes place, in fact, as if our essential and immediate behaviour with respect to [anxiety] is flight' (BN 64). Sartre's first example of such flight is psychological determinism—'an attitude of excuse' which 'asserts that there are within us antagonistic forces whose type of existence is comparable to things'. It attempts to 'fill the void which encircles us, to re-establish the links between past and present, between present and future' (BN 64). If I am psychologically determined to be 'alcoholic', for example, my *essence* is fixed. I cannot refrain from drinking this wine; doing so is in my nature. Determinism of this kind 'provides us with a *nature* productive of our acts, and these very acts it makes transcendent; it assigns to them a foundation in something other than themselves by endowing them with an inertia and externality eminently reassuring because they constitute a permanent game of *excuses*' (BN 64).

It is easier not to be free, so we deny our transcendence, preferring to take our place in the order of things than that of freedom. In addition to resorting to determinism, we also resort to 'distraction', a 'more complete activity of flight', to conceal our anxiety (BN 65). In distraction, I detach myself from *my* possibilities by considering them abstractly.

These patterns of flight—such *divertissements*—explain why anxiety appears to be rare. The nature of consciousness itself, which accounts for freedom and nothingness, also requires that they be in question. Because we never face nothingness directly as a thing, anxiety has nothing as its object. Before going on to elaborate on our attempts to avoid anxiety Sartre gives one more illustration. He provides the example of writing a book (BN 60ff.).

I am presently engaged in writing this book. I have already dedicated years to research, and I am resolved to complete it. As long as I have continued in my project—finding sources, reading, and beginning to write, all the while without reflecting on my initial decision to do it—I do not experience anxiety. But 'in every act of this kind, there remains the possibility of putting this act into question,' for 'this work is a possibility in connection with which I can feel [anxiety]' (BN 60). Tomorrow my freedom might exercise its nihilating power, and every intention I have now—of completing my revisions, emailing the final manuscript to the publisher, and seeing the process through to the finished product—may come to nought.

Psychological determinism and distraction offer me two possible escape routes: for example, I might take refuge in thoughts like 'Kate, you are the sort of person who will get the work done'; or 'Kate, it sometimes happens that people do not finish their books'. In the former case I need not worry because the matter is already ordained: it is in my nature to finish. In the latter case, Sartre wants to differentiate 'not finishing' as a 'purely logical being', as 'thing', from recognizing this as one of *my* possibilities—as something that may become the lived experience (BN 65-7) of either failing the expectations of an earlier self or denying their value. Anxiety is '[anxiety] before *my*self'—not before an abstract possibility.

Sartre develops this notion of 'subjective possibility' in BN Part II, and we will discuss it further in Chapter 5. Before doing so, however, having discussed 'the origin of nothingness' and its anxiety-inducing relation to human reality, Sartre's next chapter outlines his most famous pattern of flight (bad faith), whereby one adopts reflective attitudes towards one's own consciousness in order to avoid anxiety. As Warnock observes, 'Sartre, who thinks we are responsible for everything, also thinks that the burden of responsibility is more than we can bear; and so we develop tricks and devices for evading it.'[44]

Sartre first reviews the conditions that lead to bad faith. In sum, 'For man to be able to question, he must be capable of being his own nothingness.' But Sartre says more than 'be capable' of being his own nothingness; he writes that the human person 'can be at the origin of non-being in being only if his being—in himself and by himself—is paralyzed with nothingness' (BN 69). 'Paralyzed' by nothingness, our state is such that 'we cannot overcome [anxiety], for we *are* [anxiety]' (BN 67).[45] This anxiety acquaints us with our freedom—'the aspect

---

[44] Warnock 1965: 52-3.
[45] Although Mishka Jambor (1990) argues that despite such explicit statements to the contrary 'the possibility of anguish [anxiety] being eliminated is not precluded' in Sartre's philosophy. Santoni (1995: 93) also argues that Sartrean anxiety is not solely negative; but the success of this argument depends on whether Sartre gives a satisfactory account of authenticity. See n.68 of this chapter for more on this question.

[of my being] which I do not wish to see', and confronts us with the fact that 'I must of necessity perpetually carry within me what I wish to flee' (BN 43).

As many scholars have noted, the importance of freedom in Sartre's philosophy is indubitable.[46] But similarly important is the wish to flee it—and by it my incompleteness. I am free but lacking, and the indeterminateness of my freedom is something to which I am, as Sartre repeatedly reiterates, 'condemned'.[47] The weight of freedom—and the desire to escape it—are recurring themes in Sartre's plays and novels, where his protagonists protest—often against the divine, however construed—that freedom is a curse. Like Racine, several of Sartre's plays retell Greek classics; and like Racine, the god(s) in Sartre's plays sound more like the *deus absconditus* of Jansenism than the revelling residents of Mount Olympus. His characters often display an internal rift which rents the self—and its relation to God and other men. In *The Flies*, for example, Orestes cites freedom in rejecting Zeus's authority and his version of events:

> ORESTES: Your whole universe is not enough to prove me wrong. You are the king of gods, king of stones and stars, king of the waves of the sea. But you are not the king of man.
>
> ZEUS: Impudent spawn! So I am not your king? Who, then, made you?
>
> ORESTES: You. But you blundered; you should not have made me free.

The sin is God's: he gave man freedom. And the gift has turned—irrevocably—against the giver. Orestes proclaims, 'I *am* my freedom. No sooner had you created me than I ceased to be yours' (F 117). Lines to similar effect occur in several of Sartre's plays: 'the world is badly made', we hear in *Dirty Hands*. In *The Trojan Women* Helen asks,

> Do you think it is right to put me to death
> When it was the Gods, not I, who sinned?   (TW 333)

In the novels, we find a similar preoccupation with fallen freedom. In July 1938, in a letter to Beauvoir, Sartre wrote that all of the sudden he had 'found the subject for [his next] novel, its proportions, and its

---

[46] E.g. Philonenko 1981: 145; Howells 1988: 1.

[47] For references to freedom as a state of condemnation, see BN 152; BN 462; BN 506; BN 530. (NB This list is not exhaustive.)

title. Just as you hoped, the subject is freedom.' The title of the planned tetralogy, which is conspicuously absent from the English translation of the Sartre–Beauvoir correspondence,[48] was *Lucifer*.[49] Sartre's literary protagonists succeed in conveying the impression that, as an article in *Libération* put it, 'en liberté, l'enfer ce n'est pas les autres; c'est soi-même' (in liberty, hell isn't other people; it's oneself).[50]

BAD FAITH AND NOTHINGNESS

If freedom is a 'nihiliating power' that separates me from my essence and bears likening to hell, it is little wonder that people attempt to flee it. Sartre clearly assigns such importance to bad faith that, having considered the origin of nothingness, the next item on the philosophical agenda is to consider the repercussions of nothingness on human evaluation—in the domain of self-knowledge.[51] He opens the chapter on bad faith with a reminder of his revision of Heidegger's *Dasein*: consciousness is 'a being such that in its being, its being is in question in so far as this being implies a being other than itself' (BN 70). But, he adds, 'now that we have examined the meaning of "the question"', there is a further way to present the matter, i.e. that 'Consciousness is a being, the nature of which is to be conscious of the nothingness of its being' (BN 70). There are many human practices of self-negation, Sartre writes—too many to include in his study. So he restricts his scope to one that he takes to be 'essential to human reality': bad faith (BN 71).

Bad faith is frequently but mistakenly identified with lying. But it has a different structure; lying implies that the liar is in possession of the truth. 'A man does not lie about what he is ignorant of; he does not lie when he spreads an error of which he himself is the dupe; he does not lie when he is mistaken' (BN 71). The liar *intends* to deceive. As such, the lie is 'a normal phenomenon of what Heidegger calls the *Mitsein*. It presupposes my existence, the existence of the *Other*, my existence *for* the Other, and the existence of the Other *for* me'

[48] See WML 172–3.
[49] This project resulted in the trilogy *Les Chemins de la liberté*.
[50] Lançon 2014: n.p.
[51] Indeed, Morris assigns this section 'a pivotal role' in *Being and Nothingness* (2008: 76).

(BN 72). In the lie, consciousness 'uses for its own profit the onto-logical duality of myself and myself in the eyes of the Other' (BN 72). The same cannot be said for bad faith, which is a lie to oneself. For though 'the one who practises bad faith is hiding a displeasing truth or presenting as truth a pleasing untruth', the appearance of lying is changed by the fact that it is from myself that I hide the truth: 'the duality of the deceiver and the deceived does not exist here' (BN 72).

Sartre is aware of the paradox of self-deception: 'if I deliberately and cynically attempt to lie to myself, I fail completely in this under-taking; the lie falls back and collapses beneath my look; it is ruined from behind by the very consciousness of lying to myself' (BN 73). One possible means of escaping the paradox is to resort to the unconscious, but Sartre views this as problematic. First because 'By the distinction between the "id" and the "ego", Freud has cut the psychic whole in two. I am the ego but I am not the id. I hold no privileged position in relation to my unconscious and psyche' (BN 74). Second, because self-knowledge therefore becomes possible only through a mediator (i.e. the psychoanalyst): 'The Other appears as being able to effect the synthesis between the unconscious thesis and the conscious antithesis. I can know myself only through the medi-ation of the Other, which means that I stand in relation to my "id," in the position of the Other' (BN 74). And finally, because, once we reject 'the language and the materialistic mythology of psychoanaly-sis, we perceive that the censor in order to apply its activity with discernment must know what it is repressing' (BN 75). The problem of how the censor can know what to repress is no advancement on the problem of how consciousness can persuade itself to believe as true something it knows to be false. At root, Sartre writes, 'The very essence of the reflexive idea of hiding something from oneself implies the unity of one and the same psychic mechanism and consequently a double activity in the heart of unity, tending on the one hand to maintain and locate the thing to be concealed and on the other hand to repress and disguise it' (BN 76).[52]

So, Sartre asks, 'What must be the being of man if he is to be capable of bad faith?' (BN 78). To answer this question he turns to

---

[52] The question of whether or not Sartre's account of Freud is fair is interesting but irrelevant to the present inquiry. Having said that, Jerome Neu's reading of Sartre's rejection of the unconscious—because 'it seems to absolve the individual from responsibility'—seems most plausible to this reader (Neu 1988: 99).

examples which have become some of the best-known vignettes of twentieth-century philosophy:[53] the woman on the date, the waiter, and the homosexual.[54] Whether in praise or disdain, English- and French-speaking commentators alike have highlighted this section as *Being and Nothingness*'s 'most famous'[55] or even as the 'most representative of Sartrean philosophy'.[56] Bad faith often follows the pattern of distraction: the woman on a date, who doesn't want to acknowledge her companion's intentions toward her, can distract her consciousness from the clear expressions of sexual desire to focus only on what is 'respectful and discreet' in his communications. She 'disarms words' of their sexual intent in order not to see the situation as it is (BN 78). Even when she hears the man state that he is attracted to her, or feels him take her hand, she does not reassess the situation, for 'the qualities thus attached to the person she is listening to are in this way fixed in a permanence like that of things' (BN 78).

Although she is 'profoundly aware of the desire which she inspires', 'the desire cruel and naked would humiliate and horrify her' (BN 78).[57] This woman 'uses various procedures' to maintain herself in bad faith. '[W]hile sensing profoundly the presence of her own body—to the degree of being disturbed, perhaps—she realizes herself as *not being* her own body, and she contemplates it as though from above as a passive object to which events can *happen* but which can neither provoke them nor avoid them because all its possibilities are outside of it' (BN 79).

The basic concept of bad faith involves 'the double property of the human being, who is at once a *facticity* and a *transcendence*' (BN 79). To be human is to be double, a duality—but to say this is not, like

---

[53] Bernasconi claims they are 'among the most memorable philosophical examples ever written', and that the waiter in particular is 'one of the most celebrated descriptions in the history of philosophy' (2006: 35).

[54] Indeed, Katherine Morris (2008: 91, n. 2) notes that the 'Bad Faith' chapter is the only text of Sartre's that is regularly read by analytic philosophers. It is frequently anthologized and Catalano notes that it is easy to take out of context because of the clarity of the language and examples. Taking the examples out of context has led to clear misreadings (e.g. D. Z. Phillips 1981, wherein waiters are seen to be particularly susceptible to bad faith!) and subsequent attempts at correction (e.g. Stevenson 1983). As Catalano writes, it must be remembered that this section is 'a progression in a reflection' (Catalano 1998: 158).

[55] Flynn 2014: 184.   [56] Philonenko 1981: 148.

[57] In this and the following examples of bad faith there is a unifying theme: being reduced to an object in the eyes of another.

Freud, to 'cut the psychic whole in two'.[58] In order to understand how, consider the meaning of the two terms in the duality in question. The human is constituted both by:

Facticity: the factual conditions such as the time, place, body, class, sex, gender, and race into which one is born;

Transcendence: choices which go beyond facts to values, freely chosen commitments in the future to interpret or surpass my factical constraints.

Sartre writes that while these aspects 'are and ought to be capable of a valid coordination', it is not in the nature of bad faith to wish to coordinate them: 'Bad faith seeks to affirm their identity while preserving their differences. It must affirm facticity as being transcendence and transcendence as being facticity, in such a way that at the instant when a person apprehends the one, he can find himself abruptly faced with the other' (BN 79).

This may seem no less paradoxical than the paradigms of lying to oneself and the Freudian unconscious. Sartre turns to sincerity, the antithesis of bad faith, in order to demonstrate why his explanation offers an advantage over these others. The reason is simple: bad faith reveals that the human being 'is what it is not and is not what it is'. In other words, bad faith takes us to the root of the problem, namely, that the human is not subject to the principle of identity.

[I]n order that the concepts of bad faith can put us under illusion at least for an instant, in order that the candor of "pure hearts" (cf. Gide, Kessel) can have validity for human reality as an ideal, the principle of identity must not represent a constitutive principle of human reality and human reality must not be necessarily what it is but must be able to be what it is not. (BN 82)

For Sartre, bad faith would not be possible if 'man is what he is'; if that were the case, candor would 'cease to be his ideal' and become his being (BN 82). But there is an element of *making* ourselves be. Before moving on, with Sartre, to consider the example of the waiter, it is worth noting that all three of the examples given in this section are interpersonal: the woman is in bad faith with respect to the man; the

---

[58] See Morris (2008: 79–81) on the different senses in which Sartre uses the word 'duality'. Since, for the purposes of this discussion, the facticity–transcendence duality is most pertinent, it is the only one to be considered here.

waiter with respect to 'the public' who expect restaurant rituals; and the homosexual with respect to the friend. The selves we *make ourselves be* are made in the knowledge that they will be beheld by others. Like the Pascalian *moi*, the self in bad faith is more concerned with *le paraître* than *l'être*.

Sartre's waiter famously 'plays at being' a waiter (BN 82); he 'realizes the demands' of the public, who expect the following of a certain ceremony in their service:

> There is the dance of the grocer, the tailor, of the auctioneer, by which they endeavour to persuade their clientele that they are nothing but a grocer, an auctioneer, a tailor. A grocer who dreams is offensive to the buyer, because such a grocer is not wholly grocer. Society demands that he limit himself to his function as a grocer, just as the soldier at attention makes himself into a soldier-thing... (BN 83)

There are many ways, many precautions taken, to 'imprison a man in what he is', Sartre writes: 'as if we lived in perpetual fear that he might escape from it' (BN 83). But waiters are not waiters in the same sense that inkwells are inkwells. Human beings are not reducible to any one of their attitudes or actions.[59] Bad faith is based on an ambiguity, in which 'I affirm here that I *am* my transcendence in the mode of being a thing' (BN 80).

The antithesis of bad faith is sincerity (BN 81), but this too is an ideal that is 'impossible to achieve' since to be sincere 'is to be what one is. That supposes that I am not originally what I am' (BN 85). Such impossibility is not hidden from consciousness, Sartre writes: 'it is the embarrassing constraint which we constantly experience; it is our very incapacity to recognize ourselves, to constitute ourselves as being what we are' (BN 86).

This incapacity provokes anxiety: the inability to 'recognize' oneself makes the project of self-knowledge, like the self, a mirage. Nothingness *conditions our questions about being*—not only at the abstract level of metaphysics, but at the intimate level of self-knowledge (BN 29). Sartre's homosexual, for example, 'frequently has an intolerable feeling of guilt, and his whole existence is determined in relation to this feeling' (BN 86). He does not want to admit his 'deeply rooted tendency', but rather sees his 'mistakes' as belonging to the past, or

---

[59] NB Sartre's example can be adapted to apply to any profession; see Manser 1983 on why Sartre is not (*contra* D. Z. Phillips) 'unfair to waiters'.

his lack of satisfaction in beautiful women. His friend, however, 'becomes irritated with this duplicity', asking the homosexual to declare frankly that he is 'a paederast' (BN 87). But who is in bad faith here, Sartre asks? Is it the homosexual or the champion of sincerity?

The homosexual does not wish to accept 'a destiny'. 'He does not wish to let himself be considered as a thing. He has an obscure but strong feeling that a homosexual is not a homosexual as this table is a table or as this red-haired man is red-haired' (BN 87). Sartre writes that this resistance of the label 'paederast' stems from a recognition of the 'irreducible character of human reality' (BN 87). The homosexual is correct to reject the label if he rejects it in the sense of 'I am not what I am' (BN 87). But there is a problematic ambiguity in the word *being*. If the homosexual said 'to the extent that my pattern of conduct conforms to the word "paederast", I am a paederast; but to the extent that human reality cannot be defined by such patterns of conduct, I am not'—then he would be correct in rejecting the label. But instead he rejects both senses of its applicability: this is his bad faith.

The 'champion of sincerity', by contrast, 'demands of the guilty one that he constitute himself as a thing, precisely in order no longer to treat him as a thing' (BN 88).

> Who can not see how offensive to the Other and how reassuring for me is a statement such as, "He's just a paederast," which removes a disturbing freedom from a trait and which aims at henceforth constituting all the acts of the Other as consequences following strictly from his essence?   (BN 88)

What the 'critic' is demanding of his 'victim' is that 'he should entrust his freedom to his friend as a fief' (BN 88). Sartre brings in Hegel's master–slave relation at this point, diagnosing this situation as a double movement where: '[a] person appeals to another and demands that in the name of his nature as consciousness he should radically destroy himself as consciousness, but while making this appeal he leads the other to hope for a rebirth beyond this destruction' (BN 88).

Bad faith is a 'game of mirrors', in which we attempt to escape either our freedom or our facticity. Sincerity, too, has the same essential structure: 'the sincere man constitutes himself as what he *is in order not to be it*' (BN 88). But sincerity, too, is an impossible ideal: in this case, the ideal of being 'what one is' (BN 93).

The true problem of bad faith, Sartre writes, is an epistemological problem. Namely, a problem of *belief*: 'if we take belief as meaning the adherence of being to its object when the object is not given or is given indistinctly, then bad faith is belief; and the essential problem of bad faith is the problem of belief' (BN 91).[60] A misleading method of thinking arises in bad faith, disordering our ability to evaluate:

> Bad faith does not hold the norms and criteria of truth as they are accepted by the critical thought of good faith. What it decides first, in fact, is the nature of truth. With bad faith a truth appears, a method of thinking, a type of being which is like that of objects; the ontological characteristic of the world of bad faith with which the subject suddenly surrounds himself is this: that here being is what it is not, and is not what it is.   (BN 91)

Bad faith does not admit evidence to the contrary; all such evidence is non-persuasive because one has already been 'spontaneously determined' not to accept it. For Sartre, belief is a house of cards: to believe is to appear, 'and to appear is to deny itself' (BN 92). Upon critical inspection, the house crumbles: 'To believe is to know that one believes, and to know that one believes is no longer to believe' (BN 92).

Morris's reading of *Being and Nothingness* is helpful in this regard. She presents Sartre as making an implicit distinction between non-positional and positional self-consciousness with respect to belief, such that '*reflection* transforms belief into non-belief'. 'Belief' is thus used in two senses in Sartre, where the former is 'unwavering firmness of belief' (e.g. 'I believe in God'), and the latter is something strictly subjective (e.g. 'Is Pierre my friend? I don't know; I believe so'). Morris suggests that this section is clearer if we label these two senses 'faith' and 'opinion', respectively.[61]

In cases where the object of faith is given indistinctly or not at all—such as cases about individual human identities, questions of self-knowledge—it becomes a matter of opinion-faith (to adapt Morris's terminology). As such, it is closed to persuasive evidence. The woman's denial of the implications of holding her pursuer's hand may provide evidence that she is a flirt; yet her transcendence—the fact that she refuses to accept the meaning her pursuer gives the gesture—may provide evidence that she is not. Once belief enters the reflective

---

[60] Fingarette takes Sartre's assumption that bad faith ends at belief to lead him into 'a dead-end paradox' (1969: 92). But he reads 'belief' one-dimensionally, without the necessary Sartrean qualifications made by Haynes-Curtis (1988) and Morris (1997, 2008).
[61] Morris 2008: 85.

plane, such cases seem to be matters of opinion-faith. And on such a plane, no evidence exists to support one claim over the other.[62]

Both good faith and bad faith are patterns of flight—the first brings my transcendence into greater relief; the latter emphasizes my facticity. Whereas the former's (impossible) ideal is 'to believe what one believes', bad faith takes refuge in 'not-believing what one believes' (BN 93). The woman on the date refuses to admit the evidence that her companion is amorous; she 'disarms' his words and distances herself from the body he touches.

Whatever pattern it follows, flight itself 'reveals to bad faith an inner disintegration at the heart of being, and it is this disintegration which bad faith wishes to be' (BN 93). Sartre again refers to the paradoxical nature of consciousness 'being what it is not and not being what it is' in his conclusion:

> If bad faith is possible, it is because it is an immediate, permanent threat to every project of the human being; it is because consciousness conceals in its being a permanent risk of bad faith. The origin of this risk is that the nature of consciousness simultaneously is to be what it is not and not to be what it is. In the light of these remarks we can now approach the ontological study of consciousness, not as the totality of the human being, but as the instantaneous nucleus of this being.   (BN 94)

The relentless repetition of this 'is-and-is-not' formula has irritated analytic philosophers such as Lesley Stevenson: 'I simply cannot decide, for example, whether Sartre repeats that self-contradictory slogan "human reality is what it is not and is not what it is" with the deliberate intention of infuriating philosophers, or whether he had deceived himself into thinking that by its very incantation he had achieved some deep insight into the nature of consciousness.'[63]

But on my reading, Sartre repeats it because he, like Pascal and Kierkegaard, thinks that to be human is to exist in tension. His metaphysics of nothingness—and his reworking of the theologically

---

[62] Flynn's analysis is also helpful in this regard; Sartre's conception of evidence is Husserlian here: 'Apodictic evidence such as that of the *cogito*, though rare, literally "forces" our assent. It faces us with the "indubitable" such that its denial would violate a basic logical or metaphysical principle. We simply "see" that it is the case and that it must be so. Sufficient evidence, on the other hand, one could say, "urges" our assent. To deny it would not be irrational but clearly unreasonable' (2014: 187).

[63] Stevenson 1983: 253.

cognate problems of identity, anxiety, and self-deception—present a portrait of human existence as a tensive state between being and nothingness, which is a recognizable descendent of what is described, in theological idiom, as being *fallen*. Reading *Being and Nothingness* as the child of a morganatic marriage—which drew from both the reputable philosophical method of phenomenology, and the disreputable, theological methods of *les mystiques* and *les moralistes* discussed in Part II—brings this understudied influence to light. We will see in the next chapter how Sartre's portrayal of human 'dualities' and the 'subjective notion of possibility' suggest a greater indebtedness to Pascal and Kierkegaard than is usually acknowledged. But before drawing this chapter to a close it is worth making two final points.

First, it should be noted at this stage that there are conceptual similarities between Anti-Climacus's claims about despair in *The Sickness unto Death* and Sartre's claims about bad faith in *Being and Nothingness*. We saw in Chapter 3 that Anti-Climacus defined the self as freedom, writing that 'freedom is the dialectical categories of possibility and necessity'.[64] For Kierkegaard, the misrelation of these categories results in despair. For the Sartre of *Being and Nothingness*, the misrelation of transcendence and facticity results in bad faith. Theunissen has noted this similarity, and suggested that *bad faith* is a successor of Kierkegaardian despair, writing that '[i]n a certain sense, Sartre even incorporates Kierkegaard's theological conception of sin'.[65]

Second, Theunissen is not alone in taking bad faith to be a manifestation of original sin. Robert Solomon and Jonathan Webber have both noted the similarities, although they have not specified which notion of sin they take Sartre's account to resemble.[66] Solomon writes that

> Sartre's notion of faith is not intended to be at all religious, of course, but I think that there is a plausible suggestion that bad faith is Sartre's secular and "ontological" version of Christian "original sin," that is, an intrinsic flaw in the human character, something that, no matter how one acts or what one does, cannot be transcended or avoided.

---

[64] Kierkegaard 1983: 29.   [65] Theunissen 2005: 31.

[66] See Webber (2009: 143), who writes that 'Sartre appears to think of bad faith in the way in which Christianity traditionally conceives of original sin.'

Like human sin in Christian theology, it is both blameworthy and unavoidable.[67]

But saying that Sartre's bad faith is an ontological version of original sin could imply that original sin was not an ontological doctrine to begin with. And as we saw in Chapter 2, for Augustine and his seventeenth-century interpreters, original sin was explicitly conceived in ontological terms: for them, humans brought nothingness into the world, and human existence takes place in an ontological hinterland between being and nothingness.[68]

---

[67] Solomon 2006: 13.

[68] It is worth noting at this stage that the final lines of Part I consist of a much-debated footnote that refers to 'authenticity', which Sartre defines here as a 'self-recovery of being which was previously corrupted'. But all we read further is that it 'has no place here' (BN 94, n. 9). Santoni 1995 and Webber 2009 have both argued that a Sartrean notion of 'authenticity' can be defended, but both appeal to works other than BN to provide textual support for their claims (Santoni to WD and *Anti-Semite and Jew*; Webber to EH). It is the view of this author that *Being and Nothingness* leaves little room for such a concept; we will return to this question in Chapter 7.

5

The Fallen Self

In Search of Lost Being

Thus I rediscover myself everywhere between myself and being
as the nothing which is not being.[1]

This chapter focuses on BN Part II, in which Sartre gives a fuller
account of *being-for-itself*, arguing that it can be read as a defence of
the view of nothingness presented in BN Part I—and in particular of
the internal implications of nothingness for human selves. After
drawing attention to Sartre's presentation of the self as 'existing for
a witness', it presents Sartre's discussions of internal relations and
possibility, contingency, facticity, and lack. On Sartre's view, philosophical prejudices for the existent and the external have prevented
an accurate understanding of these—for they are not only abstract
concepts but *lived experiences*. It is in this part of *Being and Nothingness* that we see most clearly how consciousness is in search of lost
being. But its search is futile; to be a self, for Sartre, is to exist in a state
of lack—to have '*fallen* into the midst of the world' (BN 169).

At the outset of BN Part II Sartre retraces his steps, writing that
'Negation has referred us to freedom, freedom to bad faith, and bad
faith to the being of consciousness, which is the requisite condition
for the possibility of bad faith' (BN 97). Now, he says, we must
'resume the description which we attempted in the Introduction of
this work; that is, we must return to the plane of the pre-reflective
cogito' (BN 97).[2]

---

[1] BN 240.
[2] See also BN 109: 'the study of human reality must begin with the cogito'.

The starting point in the search for the being of consciousness, he repeatedly reiterates, must not be Husserl's phenomenalism or Heidegger's *Dasein*, but the cogito (BN 98). What does it mean, he asks, 'that [consciousness] must necessarily be what it is not and not be what it is' (BN 98)? The answer is that 'the being of consciousness does not coincide with itself in full equivalence' (BN 98). The principle of identity applies to the in-itself, for 'There is not the slightest emptiness in being, not the tiniest crack through which nothingness might slip in.' In the case of consciousness, however—as we have seen—the principle of identity does not apply: it 'is impossible to define . . . as coincidence with itself' (BN 98).

Part II of *Being and Nothingness* is repetitive and disorganized. But it brings out important implications of Sartre's view of being-for-itself as a duality in unity. We have already seen that this duality (a) resembles the dual conceptions of humanity we find in Pascal and Kierkegaard; and (b) has important philosophical and psychological consequences for Sartre in bad faith.[3] However, Sartre believed that philosophical prejudices prevented the recognition of this duality and its effects in lived experience.[4]

EXISTING FOR A WITNESS

For Sartre, the word '*self* refers, but it refers precisely to the *subject*. It indicates a relation between the subject and himself, and this relation is precisely a duality' (BN 100).[5] That there is a relation between the subject and himself implies a separation, and it is to the cogito that he turns for explanation.

> Originally then the cogito includes this nullifying characteristic of existing for a witness, although the witness for which consciousness exists is itself. Thus by the sole fact that my belief is apprehended as belief, it *is no longer only belief*; that is, it is already no longer belief, it is troubled belief. Thus the ontological judgment 'belief is consciousness (of) belief' can under no circumstances be taken as a statement of

---

[3] See Chapter 4.   [4] Morris 2008: 42ff.
[5] Later in BN Sartre will reiterate that '*the for-itself is relation*' (BN 384; italics original).

identity; the subject and the attribute are radically different though still within the indissoluble unity of one and the same being. (BN 98–9)

Sartre's language of 'existing for a witness' in this passage has been taken by some Sartre scholars to express the distance between the reflected and reflecting, or the self-known and self-knowing;[6] and by others as an ill-grounded claim to justify Sartre's analysis of the cogito.[7]

But Sartre's uses of the phrase elsewhere in *Being and Nothingness* and in other works suggest that the phrase may have an overlooked hermeneutic importance. Even as early as the *Carnet Midy* we read, under the entry entitled 'Hommes': 'Tous les hommes ont besoin d'un témoin. Sans doute nécessité sociologique. Les uns inventent alors Dieu, les autres la conscience (personifiée), les autres paraissent dans le monde, ne peuvent penser sans dire ce qu'ils pensent, les autres enfin déraisonnent, imaginant obscurément de belles femmes qui les regardent.'[8] John Gillespie has noted that the theme of having a witness (*témoin*) is recurrent in Sartre's works, and often appears in contexts where Sartre is discussing the death of God.[9]

We saw in Chapters 2 and 3 that 'existing for a witness' was an important theme in the mysticism of *néant* and in Jansenism (in both its theological and literary expressions): Bérulle wrote that we can only have true self-knowledge 'par le regard pur de Dieu' (by the pure gaze of God);[10] and that seeing-and-being-seen is a leitmotif of Jansenist literature (whether the *paraître* of Pascal or the fickle god-witnessess of Racine's *Phèdre*).[11] In La Rochefoucauld's *Maximes*, to take another contemporary example that we know Sartre read, we read that 'La parfaite valeur, c'est de faire sans témoin ce qu'on serais capable de faire devant tout le monde.'[12]

---

[6] Flynn 1986: 11. As we saw in Chapter 4, in *The Transcendence of the Ego* Sartre had advanced the claim that the 'I' of the cogito is not discovered but created (TE 45).

[7] Onaf 2013: 42.   [8] CM 455.

[9] Gillespie 2016. A passage in Beauvoir's *The Prime of Life* (1962: 186) seems to support this: on the mutual admiration she and Sartre shared for Kafka she writes that 'Kafka described ourselves to us: he openly stated the problems *we* faced, in a world that was without God, yet where our salvation still remained at stake.'

[10] Bérulle 1987: 32.

[11] See Chapters 2 and 3; for Pascal, *Pensées* L806/B147; for Racine, *Phèdre* II.5.679–82.

[12] 'Perfect valour consists in doing without witnesses all we should be capable of doing in front of the whole world', *Maxime* 216.

We also saw in Chapter 3 that Kierkegaard's pseudonym Anti-Climacus famously defines the self as 'a relation that relates itself to itself'.[13] When Sartre writes of the cogito that it includes a 'nullifying characteristic of existing for a witness, although the witness for which consciousness exists is itself' (BN 98–9), and that this renders belief troubled, it is worth bearing in mind both the Jansenist and Kierkegaardian inflections of his language. We saw in Chapter 4 that the question of belief is 'the deepest root of Sartre's concept of bad faith',[14] and we will return to the language of belief later in this chapter. For now, however, the point to be made is that the self cannot be apprehended as a real existent: 'the subject can not be self, for coincidence with self, as we have seen, causes the self to disappear. But neither can it *not be* itself since the self is an indication of the subject himself' (BN 101).

The nature of consciousness 'is to be what it is not and not to be what it is' (BN 94). The *self*, consequently,

> represents an ideal distance within the immanence of the subject in relation to himself, a way of *not being his own coincidence*, of escaping identity while positing it as unity—in short, of being in a perpetually unstable equilibrium between identity as absolute cohesion without a trace of diversity and unity as a synthesis of multiplicity. This is what we shall call presence to itself. The law of being of the *for-itself*, as the ontological foundation of consciousness, is to be itself in the form of presence to itself.   (BN 101)

Writing against 'a strong prejudice prevalent among philosophers' which 'causes them to attribute to consciousness the highest rank in being' (BN 101), Sartre writes that the coincidence of identity only concerns *external relations* (BN 101).

INTERNAL RELATIONS

What is needed, therefore, is a better understanding of *internal* relations. This notion plays a very important role in Sartre's analysis of consciousness—indeed, Morris writes that it is 'arguably the single most important [notion] for understanding the writings of

---

[13] Kierkegaard 1983: 13.   [14] Flynn 1986: 11.

the phenomenologists'.[15] Put simply, if two things are internally related then neither would be what it is without the other; an internal relation is a duality in unity. Consider the figure/ground ambiguity in Figure 5.1. If either black or white were removed from the image, the man and the face would disappear: figure and ground are internally related.

Externally related things, by contrast, are what they are independently of other things. Here—again—Sartre uses the image of a witness. If things are not related internally—for example a lamp and a book—then a witness must observe them to bring them into relation with one another, to say 'the lamp is to the left of the book'.[16]

Sartre sees many things as internally related which other thinkers take to be externally related: for example, the past and present of a

Figure 5.1. Mooney Face Picture. Adapted from Le Cerveau à tous les niveaux.

---

[15] Morris 2008: 43. The following description is indebted to Morris's reading in Morris 2008: Chapter 4.
[16] See Morris 2008: 44.

self. Matters are complicated by the way in which Sartre expresses the internal relatedness of past and present: within the space of a few pages, we can read that 'I am my past' and that 'I am not my past' (BN 137–46). The prejudice for external relations makes such statements look contradictory.[17] But on Sartre's view, it is as inaccurate to say that a = b (where 'a' represents the past and 'b' the present) as it is to say that a ≠ b. Each of these ways of looking at the question, in isolation, is inadequate. To understand consciousness aright, on Sartre's view, they must be taken together.

On Sartre's account 'presence to self' is possible because 'an impalpable fissure has slipped into being. . . . But if we ask ourselves at this point *what* it is which separates the subject from himself, we are forced to admit that it is *nothing*' (BN 101). The usual suspects of space, time, psychology, or other forms of what he calls 'forms of "qualified reality"' are not to blame. Only '*nothing* can separate the consciousness (of) belief from belief, since belief is *nothing other* than the consciousness (of) belief' (BN 101).

In this we can hear a refrain that is Cartesian and mystical at the same time: nothingness stands between me and my past, and between consciousness (of) belief and belief. This nothingness has effects, but it *is not*. Nothingness *est été*: 'This negative which is the nothingness of being and the nihilating power both together, is *nothingness*. Nowhere else can we grasp it in such purity. The nothingness which arises in the heart of consciousness *is not*. It is *made-to-be*' (BN 102). On Sartre's view, like that of many Augustinians before him, the human is the being through which nothingness enters the world. Moreover, his non-coincident (divided) self is based on this premise: 'Human reality is being in so far as within its being and for its being it is the unique foundation of nothingness at the heart of being' (BN 103).

We have seen that on Sartre's phenomenological cogito, 'presence to itself' is characterized by a separation from the self, a non-coincidence that we *make-to-be*. Consciousness is not its own foundation. But the cogito also reveals that consciousness is not the foundation of its 'presence to the world' (BN 103). It is worth quoting at length:

> Being apprehends itself as not being its own foundation, and this apprehension is at the basis of every cogito. In this connection it is to

---

be noted that it reveals itself immediately to the reflective cogito of Descartes. When Descartes wants to profit from this revelation, he apprehends himself as an imperfect being 'since he doubts'. But in this imperfect being, he establishes the presence of the idea of perfection. He apprehends then a cleavage between the type of being which he can conceive and the being which he is. It is this cleavage or lack of being which is at the origin of the second proof of the existence of God. In fact if we get rid of the scholastic terminology, what remains of this proof? The very clear indication that the being which possesses in itself the idea of perfection can not be its own foundation, for if it were, it would have produced itself in conformance with that idea. In other words, a *being which would be its own foundation could not suffer the slightest discrepancy between what it is and what it conceives*, for it would produce itself in conformance with its comprehension of being and could conceive only of what it is.   (BN 103–4)

Sartre's explicit dismissal of scholastic terminology may distract the reader from other elements of Descartes's theological framework: as we have already noted, for Descartes the ontological depiction of sin as nothingness has noetic repercussions for both self and world. In sin, in *hamartia*, we fall short or miss the mark. Sartre sees Descartes's 'cleavage' between 'the type of being which he can conceive and the being which he is' (BN 104) as rigorous (BN 113): in Catalano's gloss, 'an imperfect consciousness demands perfection'.[18] But for Sartre the consequences of nothingness are not only noetic but *affective*. But whereas Descartes had recourse to a God who saw truly—to a divine *witness* who creates and sustains being—on Sartre's atheist phenomenological account, by contrast, we *suffer* on account of the discrepancy between being and conceiving: 'in our own apprehension of ourselves, we appear to ourselves as having the character of an unjustifiable fact' (BN 104).

INTERNAL POSSIBILITY: 'BETWEEN BEING AND CONCEIVING'

In order to explain why we suffer in this cleavage between being and conceiving, Sartre introduces a concept of possibility that, as he presents it, has not been developed by his philosophical predecessors:

[18] Catalano 1985: 105, n. 8.

a 'subjective indication' which we will call internal possibility (BN 105). Again using the language of a witness, Sartre dismisses Leibnizean 'logical possibility' and Aristotelian 'potential' in favour of his own ontological account. He gives the example of a billiard ball: if it rolls on a table it does not

> possess the possibility of being turned from its path by a fold in the cloth; neither does the possibility of deviation belong to the cloth; it can be established only by a witness synthetically as an external relation. *But possibility can also appear to us as an ontological structure of the real. Then it belongs to certain beings as their possibility; it is the possibility which they are, which they have to be.*
>
> (BN 105; emphasis added)

Possibility, in this sense, is not just a logical category but an indeterminacy that must be *lived* by consciousness—in the anxiety-arousing ways we have already seen in the last chapter.

Consider the Leibnizean example of Adam. It is not absurd to say, Sartre writes, that '"[i]t is possible that Adam might not pick the apple." This means only that there exists by virtue of the thought of the divine understanding another system of co-possibles such that Adam figures there as having not eaten the fruit of the Tree of Knowledge' (BN 121). As the story goes, we all know, Adam chose to eat the fruit. *But*, Sartre points out: 'he did not choose to be Adam' (cf. BN 489–91). Adam, like every other human, had his particular facticity. We will return to the Leibnizean account of freedom in Chapter 7, but for now it is important to note that internal possibility cannot be fully understood without two further notions which, on Sartre's view, condition the contexts in which human choices are made: contingency and facticity.

CONTINGENCY

Internal possibility is *lived*, and as such it is concrete and particular. It is questionable, therefore, whether abstract analysis is the best means by which to approach it. Let us turn to the example of contingency to see why. The question of contingency had preoccupied Sartre for over fifteen years by the time he wrote *Being and Nothingness*, and it is widely acknowledged to be a key concept in Sartre's works.[19] As early as 1926, in a letter to Simone Jollivet, Sartre mentions that he was 'writing about contingency'.[20] According to Beauvoir, he began writing a philosophical treatise on the subject in the early 1930s, which underwent several incarnations before, at the latter Simone's suggestion, Sartre switched genres and turned his preoccupation with contingency into his first literary success: the novel *La Nausée*.[21]

In *La Nausée*, we find Sartre's Adam discovering his contingency for the first time. Published in 1938, it was first written and is set in 1932; it was his constant companion over the six years in between, during which he wrote at least three complete versions that were revised and refined under Beauvoir's scrupulous eyes.[22] *La Nausée* is written in the form of a diary, in which the protagonist, Roquentin, records his experiences of and reflections upon mundane, daily happenings, observations, and affective states. It has been called 'a seamless marriage of fiction and philosophy',[23] and Sartre used literature's scope for description and irony, its capacity to express through atmosphere rather than argument, to communicate a particular subjective experience of a general philosophical problem. It is worth dwelling at length on this novel, because the subjective indication of Sartrean accounts of possibility and contingency is best understood through particular subjective examples.

Roquentin's problem is this: he has discovered that he cannot justify his existence. It is not that he objects to the quality of his life, nor that he wonders whether life is worth living—this is no contemplation of suicide. His discovery is simply that there isn't a reason to exist at all; he is superfluous, contingent, and reminded of the fact by nausea, which haunts every dimension of his experience. We read that he arrived at this conclusion—that is, that there is no reason to exist—during some travels, after which he was prompted to return to France. But in France, he finds no solace in others—unlike the other customers in the cafés he frequents. For a while he finds some justification for his existence in his research on the Adhémar, the Marquis de Rollebon—an aristocrat who lived around the time of the French Revolution. However, soon even this distraction loses its grip

---

[19] See, e.g., Noudelmann and Philippe 2013: 107.
[20] Cited in Contat and Rybalka 1974, vol.1: 5–6.
[21] See Contat and Rybalka 1974, vol.1: 53ff.
[22] Cox 2009: 79; Bernasconi 2006: 8.   [23] Cox 2009: 80.

on him, and he comes to the conclusion that the tasks one sets oneself only serve to veil the unsightly truth: that existence is absurd.

Once unveiled, absurdity is ubiquitous. In the scenes that follow Roquentin visits the town's museum, and looking at the portraits of its leading citizens he feels his own right to exist is challenged by them—challenged by men who never questioned their own lives and privileges, pompous civilians ('bastards' [*salauds*], as he calls them) who went through the motions and acquired the trappings of justification: status, family, learning, money, etc. He observes families walking in fashionable streets on Sunday afternoon—everyone *comme il faut*, but no one knowing why.

In this respect many scenes of the book—the panorama of human self-deception, or what Sartre would later call bad faith—might be seen to express agreement with Pascal. A passage in *Pensées* describes a similar sentiment:

> there was once in man a true happiness, of which all that now remains is the empty print [*marque*] and trace . . . This he tries in vain to fill with everything around him, seeking in things that are absent the help he cannot find in those that are present, though none can help, since this infinite abyss can be filled only with an infinite and immutable object—in other words, by God himself.[24]

But for Roquentin there is no solace in such vanities and there is no God; he stands face to face with his own superfluity.

He is overwhelmingly alone. He has been described as solipsistic, but even this epithet may be optimistic, for his alienation from the world is not limited to objects and other subjects, but from previous instances of himself—he has no continuity with his own past. Certain passages seem to exhibit mental illness—he self-harms, works himself into intellectual frenzies, and exhibits anhedonic affective states. But symptoms of psychosis are invoked not to render his insights invalid, but to evoke a greater lucidity.[25]

In the famous park scene, a central passage of the novel, Roquentin's eyes are opened to a new dimension of experiencing phenomena: 'shady' and indeed 'unnameable' things are apprehended in an approach most often found in mystics: by negation, by depleting or sacrificing language which specifies what things *are not*. In the tradition

---

[24] Pascal, *Pensées*, L148/B425.
[25] Indeed, some might argue, depressive realism.

of apophaticism, Roquentin's sight of a tree's roots is a revelation: they look black but 'the root *was not black*, black was not what was on this piece of wood—it was . . . *something else*' (N 186).

> The essential thing is contingency. I mean that, by definition, existence is not necessity. To exist is simply *to be there*; what exists appears, lets itself be *encountered*, but you can never deduce it. There are people, I believe, who have understood that. Only they tried to overcome contingency by inventing a necessary, causal being. But no necessary being can explain existence: contingency is not an illusion, an appearance which can be dissipated; it is absolute, and consequently perfect gratuitousness [free gift]. Everything is gratuitous, that park, this town, and myself. When you realize that, it turns your stomach over and everything starts floating about . . . ; that is the Nausea; that is what the Bastards . . . try to hide from themselves with their idea of rights. But what a poor lie: nobody has any rights; they are entirely gratuitous, like other men, they cannot succeed in not feeling superfluous. And in themselves, secretly, they *are superfluous*, that is to say, amorphous, vague, and sad.   (N 188)

Many commentators have observed that Roquentin is a prototype of Sartre's later notion of the self.[26] Indeed, in *Being and Nothingness* Sartre himself says that the 'insipid taste' of the *en soi* is what he has elsewhere referred to as 'nausea'.[27] The explicit reference to the novel here illustrates that nausea constitutes, in Sartre's philosophy, what Simone de Beauvoir described as 'a metaphysical truth expressed in a literary form'.[28] Roquentin is a for-itself colliding with the in-itself of his environment, and he recognizes this. But self-awareness in itself offers Roquentin no freedom. This is not because, like his fellow citizens, he is perpetually creating idols, running away from his freedom, but because he has nothing to *do* with his freedom, nothing to commit it to. He cannot overcome the dreaded void and, to use an expression of Georg Lukács, 'transcendental homelessness'[29] of the modern world by becoming part of something greater and better than

---

[26] E.g. Murdoch 1999; Bernasconi 2006; Cox 2009. This view is often supported by Sartre's claim of identification in *Words*: 'I was Roquentin' (W 156); earlier in the same passage he writes that 'For a long time, writing was asking Death or Religion in disguise to tear my life away from chance.'
[27] In Chapter 6 we will see how Sartre defines 'nausea' as the affective apprehension of an absolute contingency (BN 367).
[28] Beauvoir 1960: 293.   [29] Lukács 1974: 41.

himself, but rather is stuck with his own non-identical, precarious, and isolated self.

The novel concludes with an unexpected glimmer of hope. Sitting in a café at which he was a regular before catching a train from Bouville to start life over in Paris, the waitress asks if he would like to hear his favourite song, 'Some of These Days', for one last time. He says yes— after embarking on a disdainful train of thought about the bourgeois idiocy that characterizes many appreciators of Chopin or Wagner, the idea that music offers 'consolation' or 'refreshment', that 'beauty is compassionate towards them' (N 246). Wordsworth's 'sense sublime of something far more deeply interfused',[30] for Roquentin, is nothing short of ridiculous. Beauty, all-too-alluring and all-too-respectable, can only offer empty, temporary respites. But Roquentin's song is sung by a black woman, and written by a Jew.[31] And as he listens to it, he realizes that though the author and articulator will pass away, the melody stays the same. It comes from 'beyond'—it is not, like himself, superfluous. More importantly, his thoughts start to wander in the direction of redemption: the man who wrote this tune and the woman who sings it—they who give birth to something beyond themselves—have 'cleansed themselves of the sin of existing' (N 251).[32]

Roquentin is bowled over. He had lost hope, and dares not move for fear that the feeling will go away. He feels joy, an emotion we have not encountered anywhere else in the novel. But then joy turns to intimidation. If one can justify one's existence, be cleansed of sin, the question then becomes: how? The answer is in writing a book. A novel. But this book must be more than ink and paper. There must be something 'behind the printed words, behind the pages, something which didn't exist, which was *above existence*' (N 252, my emphasis). This new book, in transcending its author, would be redemptive, such that Roquentin can 'look back on his life without repugnance' (N 252).

The book's conclusion is ambiguous and the subject of much scholarly conjecture. As Steven Churchill has noted, contingency à la Roquentin should not be confused with the young Nietzsche's

---

[30] Wordsworth, *Tintern Abbey*.

[31] Adumbrating the themes of freedom and oppression which would be considered further in 'Black Orpheus' (1948) and *The Anti-Semite and the Jew* (1946).

[32] The same formula, 'the sin of existing', appears in *Words*, too (W 139).

'illusion' of necessary states of affairs; Sartre is not advocating 'salvation' through art but, at best, 'a tentative sort of hope'[33]—a hope which Sartre later renounced as youthful folly.[34]

FACTICITY

In *Being and Nothingness* Sartre's preoccupation with contingency is still evident. In BN Part II we see further theoretical development of this notion in relation to facticity. The for-itself is contingent—'an unjustifiable fact' (BN 104). But the contingency of existence in general is accompanied by the contingency of existing as the particular for-itself I am: what Sartre calls *facticity*. 'Just as my nihilating freedom is apprehended in [anxiety], so the for-itself is conscious of its facticity. It has the feeling of its complete gratuity; it apprehends itself as being there for nothing, as being *de trop*' (BN 108).

There is no reason why I should be in general; and there is no reason why *I*, in particular, should be. Our facticities—the unchosen circumstances of our birth or conditions of our bodies—appear to have no rhyme or reason. As Catalano writes, facticities 'present themselves as simply "there"'.[35] Existence precedes essence, but with every negation the for-itself determines itself as a *lack* of being. 'What our ontological description has immediately revealed is that this being is the foundation of itself as a lack of being; that is, that it determines its being by means of a being which it is not' (BN 109–10). As we saw in Chapter 4, however, there are many ways of *not being*.

> If, for example, I say of an inkwell that it is not a bird, the inkwell and the bird remain untouched by the negation. This is an external relation which can be established only by a human reality acting as witness. By contrast, there is a type of negation which establishes an internal relation between what one denies and that concerning which the denial is made.   (BN 110)

We also saw in Chapter 4 that *lack* plays an important part in Sartre's account of consciousness. To be human is to be haunted by what one

---

[33] Churchill 2013: 52–3.
[34] See, e.g., W 156 and WL 161: the latter declares that 'we could never be saved by art'.
[35] Catalano 1985: 100.

is not. Indeed, he writes that of all internal negations lack 'penetrates most deeply into being'. 'This lack does not belong to the nature of the in-itself, which is all positivity. It appears in the world only with the upsurge of human reality. *It is only in the human world that there can be lacks*' (BN 110; emphasis added).

Sartre takes the pervasiveness of lack to be self-evident. All it takes to prove that human reality 'is a lack' is desire—because desire is not 'a being whose nature is to be what it is', on his view: rather, it is an 'incomplete circle that calls for completion' (BN 111).

> If desire is to be able to be desire to itself it must necessarily be itself transcendence; that is, it must by nature be an escape from itself toward the desired object. In other words, it must be a lack—but not an object lack, a lack undergone, created by the surpassing which it is not; it must be its own lack of—. Desire is a lack of being. It is haunted in its inmost being by the being of which it is desire. Thus it bears witness to the existence of lack in the being of human reality. (BN 112)

Consciousness, when it conceives (as we saw earlier in this chapter with respect to Descartes) or desires, comes face to face with lack. On Catalano's reading Sartre makes this move in order to show that lack is not merely subjective.[36] I agree that Sartre is presenting more than a 'subjective indication' of lack: for Sartre, lack is ontological—it is an element of the real. But it is important that this lack is not *lived* neutrally, as a brute fact among brute facts. Rather, the lived experience of lack is an experience of failure (*échec*), of missing the mark. This reading is supported by what Sartre goes on to say:

> The for-itself in its being is failure because it is the foundation only of itself as nothingness. In truth this failure is its very being, but it has meaning only if the for-itself apprehends itself as failure *in the* presence of the being which it has failed to be; that is, of the being which would be the foundation of its being and no longer merely the foundation of its nothingness—or— to put it another way, which would be its foundation as coincidence with itself. By nature the cogito refers to the lacking and to the lacked, for the cogito is haunted by being, as Descartes well realized. (BN 113)

For Sartre, consciousness is haunted by what it is not. The only 'self' in the pre-reflective cogito is 'self-lack', and consciousness suffers on this account *by nature*:

---

[36] Catalano 1985: 104.

The being of human reality is suffering because it rises in being as perpetually haunted by a totality which it is without being able to be it, precisely because it could not attain the in-itself without losing itself as for-itself. Human reality therefore is by nature an unhappy consciousness with no possibility of surpassing its unhappy state.   (BN 114)

In coming into existence we recognize that we are incomplete: we are 'haunted by' and 'thirst for' being—because we are free. 'Coincidence with self' *must be lacking* in order to be what we are.[37] The cogito is linked to being-in-itself as a lack to that which defines its lack. It is in this sense that Sartre writes, as we saw earlier, that 'the second Cartesian proof is rigorous. Imperfect being surpasses itself toward perfect being; the being which is the foundation only of its nothingness surpasses itself toward the being which is the foundation of its being.' But here Sartre takes leave of Descartes, for on his view 'the being toward which human reality surpasses itself is not a transcendent God; it is at the heart of human reality; it is only human reality itself as totality' (BN 113–14).

Removing God[38] from the cogito is one of many ways in which Sartre attempts to work out the consequences of 'a consistently atheistic point of view'.[39] But this removal leaves him with the first of several 'unrealizable ideals': self-coincidence, and with it, self-knowledge. On his phenomenological ontology, 'Consciousness in relation to [the self] stands in the mode of being this being, for this being is consciousness, but as a being which consciousness can not be. It is consciousness itself, in the heart of consciousness, and yet out of reach, as an absence, an unrealizable' (BN 115).

Moreover, without God, the only source of value is 'human reality',[40] where value is 'the self in so far as the self haunts the heart of the for-itself as that for which the for-itself *is*' (BN 117, 118). Later in this passage Sartre refers to it as 'the meaning and beyond of all surpassing': consciousness is haunted by its desire not only for being but for meaning—*to be meaningful*. Sartre's account of the for-itself as *a lack*, as I have argued already, closely resembles Augustine's description of the soul's ontological hunger.[41] But Sartre's ontological

---

[37] Indeed, Sartre describes identity as self-loss: consciousness 'does not want to lose itself in the in-itself of identity' (BN 114).

[38] And, NB, continuous creation (BN 157).   [39] EH 53.

[40] '[H]uman reality is that by which value comes to the world' (BN 117).

[41] Zum Brunn 1988: 53.

hunger is inflected by a logo-logical hunger—a *desire for meaning*—
and neither hunger corresponds to any true means of satisfaction.[42]
On Sartre's account, the search for lost being only ever results in
discoveries of lack. In the *War Diaries* Sartre writes that

> It is perhaps Christianity which has come closest to this necessary
> recognition [that human reality is 'afflicted by an existential lack'], by
> showing the human soul as 'animated' by lack of God; and the writings
> of the mystics abound in striking descriptions of this inner nothingness
> there is within the heart of man.   (WD 230)

Lest we should doubt the centrality of lack in *Being and Nothingness*,
Sartre writes that consciousness is 'always predisposed to find something lacking', and describes freedom as 'really synonymous with lack'
(BN 586; see also 109ff., 124, 222). The word 'lack' appears over three
hundred times in the text. And although the French word *manque*[43] is
usually behind the English translation of 'lack'[44] Sartre also uses the
theological idiom of Descartes and Fénelon, et al.: *défaut d'être*.[45] To be
free, in other words, is to exist in a state of perpetual knowledge of
nothingness, of falling short, of exclusion from being. Sartre explicitly
(and famously) refers to this state as one of condemnation: we are
'condemned to be free' (BN 462), and consciousness is a 'fall from'[46] or
'frustration of' being (BN 160).

> We have seen that human reality as for-itself is a lack and that what it
> lacks is a certain coincidence with itself. Concretely, each particular for-
> itself (*Erlebnis*) lacks a certain particular and concrete reality, which if
> the for-itself were synthetically assimilated with it, would transform the
> for-itself into itself. It lacks something for something else—as the
> broken disc of the moon lacks that which would be necessary to
> complete it and transform it into a full moon.   (BN 119)

---

[42] Although 'salvation' is, as we have seen, mentioned in the footnote at the end of
Part I, and Sartre may have believed in 'salvation through literature' at the time of
La Nausée (1938), no such promise is contained in *Being and Nothingness* itself.

[43] E.g., 'Le pour-soi choisit parce qu'il est manque, la liberté ne fait qu'un avec le
manque, elle est le mode d'être concret du manque d'être' (EN 610).

[44] On lack see Simont 1992: 180—'specific "lackeds" (*manqués*) have their source
in the "lacked" of the for-itself as such which Sartre calls the "self—or itself as itself"
(BN 65)'.

[45] See EN 121—'le pour-soi ne peut soutenir la néantisation sans se déterminer
comme un *défaut d'être*'—and also EN 122.

[46] Although it should be noted that the word here translated 'fall' is *défléchissement*
in French, rather than the theologically connoted *chute*, which Sartre uses elsewhere.

Like nothingness and lack, Sartre writes that 'the possible' (as the cognate of internal rather than logical possibility) can only come into the world through a being that 'is its own possibility' (BN 124). But to be in such a way is constantly to escape oneself: 'from the moment that I want to account for my immediate being simply in so far as it is what it is not and is not what it is, I am thrown outside it toward a meaning which is out of reach' (BN 124).

After having considered internal relations, possibility, contingency, and lack, Sartre says that we are better placed to consider the being of the pre-reflective cogito. Its 'self' is a lacking-self. But self is not all that is lacked: 'in all cases of lack', Sartre writes, *value* is what is lacking. In this sense Catalano's account—which attempts to show that value is not merely subjective—misses an important, subjective indication. Catalano writes that as with lack, something has value only insofar as it surpasses what it is toward what it is not. In his *Commentary* we read that:

> A book has value only as related to some end or purpose. The world has value only as viewed in relation to an end or totality. Value is, in fact, the surpassing of all surpassings. If I ask myself why I am writing, I can say to complete a book. But if I continue the questioning, I do not rest with the final answer unless I have arrived at what I consider the ultimate goal or "value" of my efforts.[47]

On Catalano's reading every exercise of freedom—every transcending or surpassing—is conditioned by value, and every nihilation of consciousness is simultaneously a 'no' and 'yes', denying and affirming value. But *Being and Nothingness* leaves more room for ambiguity— indeed, this passage includes the intriguing footnote stating that the nature of the for-itself 'approaches much nearer to the "ambiguous" realities of Kierkegaard' (BN 118). For Sartre, value 'haunts' freedom:[48]

> Value is the self in so far as the self haunts the heart of the for-itself as that for which the for-itself *is*. The supreme value toward which consciousness at every instant surpasses itself by its very being is the absolute being of the self with its characteristics of identity, of purity, of permanence, etc., and as its own foundation.   (BN 117–18)

To take Roquentin as an example once more, none of the projects he undertakes will deliver the end he desires: the sense that he has value.

---

[47] Catalano 1985: 105.   [48] See BN 118ff.

Considered together, desire and possibility show the futility of the self in search of lost being:

> What desire wishes to be is a filled emptiness but one which shapes its repletion as a mould shapes the bronze which has been poured inside it. The possible of the consciousness of thirst is the consciousness of drinking. We know moreover that coincidence with the *self* is impossible, for the for-itself attained by the realization of the Possible will make itself be as for-itself—that is, with another horizon of possibilities. Hence the constant disappointment which accompanies repletion, the famous: "Is it only this?" which is not directed at the concrete pleasure which satisfaction gives but at the evanescence of the coincidence with self. Thereby we catch a glimpse of the origin of temporality since thirst is its possible at the same time that it *is* not *its possible*. This nothingness which separates human reality from itself is at the origin of time.   (BN 126)

Indeed, Sartre writes, 'each time we approach the study of human reality from a new point of view we rediscover that indissoluble dyad, Being and Nothingness' (BN 143).

'I THINK THEREFORE I WAS'

From considerations of the relation of consciousness to possibility Sartre moves to look at consciousness in relation to death and the past—both of which might be (erroneously, on Sartre's view) considered devoid of possibility. 'The terrible thing about Death', Sartre writes, citing Malraux, 'is that it transforms life into Destiny.'[49] What we must understand by this, anticipating Sartre's account of being-for-others in Part III, is that death reduces for-itself-for-others to being merely for-others. The only life after death is life in others' minds. If Pierre dies, Sartre writes in *Being and Nothingness*, then 'Today I alone am responsible for the being of the dead Pierre, I in my freedom. Those dead who have not been able to be saved and transported to the boundaries of the concrete past of a survivor are not past; they along with their pasts are annihilated' (BN 135).

---

[49] In fact, this line is cited twice in this section (BN 135, 138), and again in Part IV (BN 563).

For those inclined to the salvific reading of *La Nausée*, this kind of immortality may have been the source of Roquentin's tentative hope.

For the living, however, 'the past' *is* as a mode of being. To return to the internal relatedness of past and present, on Sartre's analysis 'was' is a mode of being, and in that sense 'I am my past' (BN 137):

> I do not have it; I am it. A remark made by someone concerning an act which I performed yesterday or a mood which I had does not leave me indifferent; I am hurt or flattered, I protest or I let it pass; I am touched to the quick. I do not dissociate myself from my past. Of course, in time I can attempt this dissociation; I can declare that 'I am no longer what I was,' argue that there has been a change, progress. But this is a matter of a secondary reaction which is given as such. To deny my solidarity of being with my past at this or that particular point is to affirm it for the whole of my life. At my limit, at that infinitesimal instant of my death, I shall be no more than my past. It alone will define me. (BN 138)

That this view has undesirable consequences is attested to by Sartre's plays, several of which exhibit a preoccupation with death and more precisely with the fear of dying *without a witness* (for which we might as well read: living without a meaning). In *Morts sans sépulture* (1946), for example, we hear that 'To die without witnesses is real annihilation' (MWS 189–90). The character Henri describes a guilt he feels: he is 'guilty about being alive' (MWS 181). This guilt is not survivor's guilt, as one might suppose for a post-war play set in the context of torture and execution. Rather, it is metaphysical: he feels that he is superfluous (see MWS 181); that he wants (but fails) to justify his existence through his acts; and that he desires to be indispensable 'to something, or to someone' (MWS 183). Canoris reminds him, however, that: 'Each one of your actions will be judged in the light of your whole life. If you let yourself be killed now when you could still go on living, then nothing could be more stupid than your death' (MWS 225).

Without God, only death can 'reunite us with ourselves', and only others can be our witness. But possibility, at that instant, ceases to be mine.

> At the moment of death we are; that is, we are defenceless before the judgments of others. They can decide in truth what we are; ultimately we have no longer any chance of escape from what an all knowing intelligence could do. A last hour repentance is a desperate effort to crack all this being which has slowly congealed and solidified around us,

a final leap to dissociate ourselves from what we are. In vain. Death fixes this leap along with the rest; it does no more than to enter into combination with what has preceded it, as one factor among others, as one particular determination which is understood only in terms of the totality. By death the for-itself is changed forever into an in-itself in that it has slipped entirely into the past. Thus the past is the ever growing totality of the in-itself which we are. (BN 138)[50]

The past, for Sartre, is facticity: both words 'indicate one and the same thing' (BN 141), and both words are related to my contingency—'the invulnerable contingency of the in-itself which I have to be without any possibility of not being it' (BN 141). We cannot re-enter the past: it is in-itself and I am for-itself. 'The past is what I am without being able to live it. The past is substance. In this sense the Cartesian cogito ought to be formulated rather: "I think; therefore I was"' (BN 142).

Sartre's criticisms of Descartes in this regard resemble Kierkegaard's; the latter was sceptical with respect to both the Cartesian notion of freedom and its role in methodical doubt. The cogito, we read in Kierkegaard's journals, emphasizes thought at the expense of act:

> ... Descartes, who himself in one of the meditations explains the possibility of error by recalling that freedom in man is superior to thought, nevertheless has construed thought, not freedom, as the absolute. Obviously this is the position of the elder Fichte—not *cogito ergo sum*, but I act *ergo sum*, for this *cogito* is something derived or it is identical with "I act"; either the consciousness of freedom is in the action, and then it should not read *cogito ergo sum*, or it is the subsequent consciousness.[51]

But Cartesian freedom, on Kierkegaard's account, fails to recognize that 'In freedom I can emerge only from that into which I have entered in freedom.... If I am going to emerge from doubt in freedom, I must enter into doubt in freedom. (Act of Will.)'[52] For Kierkegaard Descartes's epistemological problem is an existential one: it can only be 'solved' in being *lived*.

---

[50] 'Ainsi, nous devons conclure, contre Heidegger, que loin que la mort soit ma possibilité propre, elle est un fait contingent qui, en tant que tel, m'échappe par principe et ressortit originellement à ma facticité' (EN 590).

[51] Kierkegaard, JP II 2338 (*Pap.* IV C 11).

[52] Kierkegaard, JP I 777 (*Pap.* IV B 13: 21).

In *La Liberté cartesienne*, Sartre remarks that Descartes's philosophy attempted to reconcile a rationalist metaphysics with Christian theology: 'elle traduit, dans le vocabulaire du temps, cette conscience qu'a toujours eue le savant d'être un pur néant'.[53] But though Descartes is correct to assign such importance to nothingness, Sartre too thinks that Descartes misunderstood freedom: Descartes 'perpetually oscillates between identifying freedom with negativity or the negation of being ... and the conception of free will as the simple negation of negation. In a word, he failed to conceive of negativity as productive.'[54] As we shall see in greater detail in Chapter 7, on Sartre's reading Cartesian freedom is freedom only to sin: the only choice, apart from God, is nothingness, and the only way to be creative is to deviate from divine dictat.[55]

For Sartre, like Kierkegaard, the solution to Descartes's epistemological problem must be *lived*. But for Sartre, it is only when life ceases to be lived that the problem is resolved. When living, the for-itself can never be its future except problematically: 'I am my Future in the constant perspective of the possibility of not being it. Hence that [anxiety] which we have described above which springs from the fact that I am not sufficiently that Future which I have to be and which gives its meaning to my present: it is because I am a being whose meaning is always problematic' (BN 152). The past, by contrast, 'is a fatality in reverse. The For-itself can make itself what it wishes, but it can not escape from the necessity of being irremediably—for a new For-itself—what it has wished to be' (BN 169). In being made in-itself (as past), it has '*fallen* into the midst of the world' (BN 169; emphasis added).[56]

This, then, is the first explicit reference to the for-itself as *fallen*. Descartes and Kant appealed to a 'being who escapes temporality' to anchor the 'ontological mirage of the self' (BN 156, 159). For Sartre, however, the self-known is separated from the self-knowing by nothingness—the for-itself must *be* its own nihilation (BN 176). The origin and motivation of this nihilation is that 'the for-itself is outside of itself, and in its inmost heart this being-for-itself is ecstatic *since it must look for its being elsewhere*'.

---

[53] LC 30.   [54] LC 38–9.
[55] We will return to this at greater length in Chapter 7.
[56] See also 'dans sa chute au passé, l'être de l'homme se constitue comme un être en *soi*' (EN 100).

Chapter 4 showed that, for Sartre, the human being is 'the being by which nothingness comes into the world', and that Sartre's *néant*, like that of many of his Augustinian predecessors, is intimately connected with problems of epistemology—especially self-knowledge. In this chapter we have examined Sartre's notion of the for-itself in greater depth, demonstrating the *dual* character of consciousness and the 'philosophical prejudices' that prevent the recognition of this duality. Reflection, on Sartre's view, is 'an attempt to recover being'—'it is a second effort by the for-itself to found itself; that is, to be for itself what it is' (BN 176). We are in search of lost being. But everywhere we look for it we find nothingness. And when we are no longer living, all that remains of us is our being as witnessed by others: what Pascal called our *paraître*. But this *paraître* appears to someone—to an other. So it is to Sartre's treatment of being-for-others that we shall now turn.

6

Lonely Togetherness

Shame, the Body, and Dissimilarity

My original fall is the existence of the Other.[1]

In Part III of *Being and Nothingness* Sartre turns from being-for-itself to being-for-others. His first section is entitled simply 'The Problem'. For having described human reality from the standpoints of 'negating conduct' and the cogito, Sartre is not satisfied that his work is finished. Remaining in the attitude of reflective description, there are still modes of consciousness which, he thinks, point to a radically different onto-logical structure. 'This ontological structure is *mine*; it *is* in relation to myself as subject that I am concerned about myself, and yet this concern (for-myself) reveals to me a being which is *my* being without being-for-me' (BN 245).

SHAME: MY ORIGINAL RELATION TO THE OTHER

We saw in Chapter 4 that the self-knowing (consciousness) is not the end of the story; there is also the self-known (ego), elusive and indeterminate though it is. But the ego is not the product of conscious-ness alone. On the very first page of Sartre's discussion of 'the problem' he introduces an example—a 'mode of consciousness' which has an identical structure to others Sartre has described: shame.

[1] BN 286. See also WD 110: 'There is original fall and striving for redemption—and that fall with that striving constitutes human reality.'

> It is a non-positional self-consciousness, conscious (of) itself as shame...it is a shameful apprehension *of* something and this something is *me*. I am ashamed of what I *am*. Shame therefore realizes an intimate relation of myself to myself. Through shame I have discovered an aspect of my being.   (BN 245)

Sartre is insistent that shame 'is not originally a phenomenon of reflection'. Although limit cases may appear on the reflective plane (e.g. the religious *practice* of shame), shame is always shame '*before somebody*' (BN 245; emphasis original), and it is experienced as 'an immediate shudder which runs through me from head to foot without any discursive preparation' (BN 246).

For Sartre, shame is revelatory.[2] The content of its revelation is that 'the Other is the indispensable mediator between myself and me. I am ashamed of myself *as I appear* to the Other' (BN 246). The presence of the other puts me in the position to pass judgment on myself as an object, for it is as an object that I appear to the other, and the other's gaze has the potential to be, as Ralph Waldo Emerson wrote, 'the lens through which we read our own minds'.[3] It is worth quoting at length on this subject:

> [T]his object which has appeared to the Other is not an empty image in the mind of another.... Shame is by nature *recognition*. I recognize that I *am* as the Other sees me.... Thus the Other has not only revealed to me what I was; he has established me in a new type of being which can support new qualifications. This being was not in me potentially before the appearance of the Other, for it could not have found any place in the For-itself.... But this new being which appears *for* the other does not reside *in* the Other; I am responsible for it.   (BN 246)

There is a tension between passivity and activity in the experience of shame, for though I do not will it, I am nonetheless its causal source. Existence with another involves me in 'internal relations', such that I am not what I am without that other (and vice versa).[4] In the experience of shame, Sartre summarizes:

> Thus shame is shame of oneself before the Other; these two structures are inseparable. But at the same time I need the Other in order to realize fully all the structures of my being. The For-itself refers to the

---

[2] See BN 285: 'shame reveals to me' the other's freedom.
[3] Emerson 1983: 616.
[4] See Chapter 5 and Morris 2008: 43ff. on 'internal relations'.

For-others. Therefore if we wish to grasp in its totality the relation of man's being to being-in-itself, we cannot be satisfied with the descriptions outlined in the earlier chapters of this work. We must answer two far more formidable questions: first that of the existence of the Other, then that of the relation of my being to the Other. (BN 246–7)

We will return to Sartre's notion of shame later in this chapter; but before doing so we will follow *Being and Nothingness*'s structure, considering each of these 'formidable questions' (the existence of the other, and the relation of my being to the other) in turn.

The Existence of the Other

Sartre's analysis of the existence of the other can be read merely as a philosophical treatment of the problem of other minds. He discusses proposed solutions to the problem—including realism, Berkeley's *esse est percipi*, and Kantian metaphysics—but all are found wanting.[5] Like the problem of the self, the origin of the problem of the other is nothingness. There is a nothingness which separates self and other, such that negation is 'the constitutive structure of the being-of-others'. The other is defined by negation as 'the one who is not me and the one who I am not. This *not* indicates a nothingness as a *given* element of separation between the Other and myself. [...This nothingness], as a primary absence of relation, is originally the foundation of all relation between the Other and me' (BN 254).

While the distance between consciousness and the ego arises on account of time, the distance between consciousness and the other arises on account of space: Sartre attributes the separation of consciousnesses to the separation of bodies (BN 255). We shall return to the body later in the chapter. But at this stage it is important to note that whereas the solitary consciousness experiences *lack* and alienation from it*self*, Sartre describes consciousness of others as consciousness of *absence* and relationality as a ruse.[6] In a curious choice of words, Sartre

---

[5] The other is deemed to belong 'to the category of "as if"'. The other, as a philosophical hypothesis, is 'an *a priori* hypothesis with no justification save the unity which permits it to operate in our experience, an hypothesis which can not be thought without contradiction' (BN 251).

[6] BN 320: 'my relations with the Other-as-object are essentially made up of ruses designed to make him remain an object'.

writes that the 'Other's soul' is 'an absence, a meaning; the body points to it without delivering it' (BN 247).[7]

The other's absence is such that, 'the only way that he can reveal himself to me is by appearing as an *object* to my knowledge.... the other can be for me only an *image*' (BN 255).[8] But images can be true or false: 'Only a witness external both to myself and to the Other could compare the image with the model and decide whether it is a true one.'[9] If we take the spatialized notion of the other 'it must either resort to God or fall into a probabilism which leaves the door open to solipsism' (BN 256). But Sartre is emphatic that 'God is neither necessary nor sufficient as a guarantee of the Other's existence' (BN 256).

Sartre further clarifies his position in his discussion of the shortcomings of Husserl, Hegel, and Heidegger. But where the other is concerned the cogito, too, is deficient as the starting-point for philosophy: the existence of the other is prerequisite to its possibility.[10] Most instructive, for the present purposes, however, is his dismissal of Hegel, whom Sartre charges with both epistemological and ontological optimism. Epistemologically, Hegel is overconfident about the extent of our ability to know. 'The very being of self-consciousness is such that in its being its being is in question; this means that it is pure interiority. It is perpetually a reference to a *self* which it has to be. Its being is defined by this: that it *is* this being in the mode of being what it is not and of not being what it is' (BN 265). The nature of consciousness is such that it *cannot be known* by the other; there is an *ontological separation* of consciousnesses and consequently we can neither know nor be known.[11] Ontologically, Sartre criticizes Hegel for his abstraction, which results in a 'totalitarian point of view'. On the contrary, Sartre writes, 'the being of my consciousness is strictly irreducible to knowledge' (BN 267).

Heidegger's *Mitsein*, although leading closer, also fails to reach a solution. The *Mitsein* is 'of absolutely no use to us in resolving the *psychological*, concrete problem of the recognition of the Other'

---

[7] For the other as 'absence', see also BN 252, 258.

[8] It is worth bearing in mind, when we read that 'the Other can be for me only an *image*' (BN 255), that on Sartre's view 'le mode d'*être* de l'image c'est exactement son "*paraître*"' (IM 128).

[9] BN 255; there is more on the need for a witness here and on p. 256.

[10] See BN 260–1, 275.   [11] See BN 265–7.

(BN 272).[12] For in addition to the epistemological and ontological problems of the other, there is a psychological, affective aspect: 'Human-reality at the very heart of its ekstases remains alone' (BN 274).

Sartre is critical about a philosophical 'answer' which solves the metaphysical problem of 'the existence of the other' without accounting for the existential problem of human loneliness. Whether or not his philosophical predecessors were fully understood or justly accused, Sartre's point is that on the psychological level—on the level of living—we remain alone, whether the philosophical problem is 'solved' or not.

My Being in Relation to the Other: The Look

But being alone is only part of the problem. We may be lonely, unknown, and unknowing, but the other is nevertheless there, and must be recognized as a 'limit' which 'contributes to the constitution of my being' (BN 296). On the individual level, my freedom is such that, through negation, I can choose what I want to be. But on the social level, my freedom is only one of many freedoms, and my being is subject to other powers of negation. The 'problem', therefore, of my being in relation to the other is that *I am not the only being 'by which nothingness comes to the world'* (BN 47, 48). Sartre develops this point further in 'Concrete Relations with Others', where he discusses an ontological *guilt* and describes the 'limit' of the other's freedom as an 'original situation' (BN 431).

The other as 'limit' appears to us 'in the reality of everyday life' (BN 277), where we find an 'original relation to the Other which can be constantly pointed to and which consequently can be revealed to me outside all reference to a religious or mystic unknowable' (BN 277). That 'original relation' is *le regard*, usually translated in English as 'the look' or 'the gaze'.

When the other looks at me, I can no longer see myself at the centre of the world. As Sartre puts it, the other 'steals' the world, introducing distances and unknowns: when I see an object in the

---

[12] Sartre dismisses Heidegger's 'crew' as 'mute existence in common of one member of the crew with his fellows' (BN 270); Heidegger's 'I am with ...' is 'all very well', Sartre writes, 'But with whom?' (BN 449). See also BN 434ff. on the 'experience of the we', and the discrepancy between 'grammar and thought'. Later, he emphasizes that the experience of the 'We-subject' 'remains on the ground of individual psychology and remains a simple symbol of the longed-for unity of transcendences' (BN 447).

world, I know what I see, but I cannot know what is seen by the other, and she may contest that I see truly (BN 279). Moreover, just as the other 'steals' the world, the other's freedom can 'steal' my being.[13] The gaze of another reveals that my own consciousness is not the sole arbiter of who I am—I am not the only source of the 'existence' that will determine my 'essence'.

The famous example Sartre gives is of someone 'moved by jealousy, curiosity, or vice' to look through a keyhole. As Thomas Flynn writes, this famous illustration can be considered 'a kind of "eidetic reduction", a Schelerian argument by example, a paradigm case'.[14] In that action, Sartre writes:

> I am alone and on the level of a non-thetic self-consciousness. This means first of all that there is no self to inhabit my consciousness, nothing therefore to which I can refer my acts in order to qualify them. They are in no way *known*; I *am my acts* and hence they carry in themselves their whole justification. (BN 283)

Being jealous and thinking there is something behind the door involves something Sartre calls a 'double and inverted determination', in the sense that I am motivated to look because I am jealous, and the jealousy would be nothing if there were nothing to be seen. He calls this the *situation*.[15]

This situation reflects to me at once both my facticity and my freedom; on the occasion of a certain objective structure of the world which surrounds me, it refers my freedom to me in the form of tasks to be freely done. There is no constraint here since my freedom eats into my possibles and since correlatively the potentialities of the world indicate and offer only themselves. Moreover I cannot truly define myself as *being* in a situation: first because I am not a positional consciousness of myself; second because I am my own nothingness (BN 283).

> But all of a sudden I hear footsteps in the hall. Someone is looking at me! What does this mean? It means that I am suddenly affected in my

---

[13] Though Sartre uses the imagery of theft for the world, he does not explicitly use it for 'one's being'.

[14] Flynn 2014: 207.

[15] See also BN 509, where the situation is defined as 'the common product of the contingency of the in-itself and of freedom', which is 'an ambiguous phenomenon in which it is impossible to distinguish the contribution of freedom from that of the brute existent'.

being and that essential modifications appear in my structure—
modifications which I can apprehend and fix conceptually by means
of the reflective cogito. (BN 283–4)

Only reflective consciousness has the self directly as an object (BN
284). When alone, I can see the fissure between the self-knowing and
the self-known. But in the experience of being seen we discover another
'dimension of being' from which we are 'separated by a radical nothingness': the other's freedom (BN 286).[16] The self-known is always
indeterminate, because it is always subject to the freedom of others: 'the
Other's freedom is revealed to me across the uneasy indetermination
of the being which I am for him. Thus this being is not my possible; it is
not always in question at the heart of my freedom. On the contrary it
is the limit of my freedom' (BN 285). In characteristically dramatic
language, Sartre writes that in the look there is a 'death of my possibilities' which causes me to 'experience the Other's freedom' (BN 294–5).
The negating freedom of the other 'fixes' my possibilities (BN 294).

This is why 'My original fall is the existence of the Other' (BN 286).
For my 'nature' is not of my making. It is not a divine birthright, a
God-given essence: rather, 'the very stuff of my being is the unpre-
dictable freedom of another' (BN 286). Moreover, the alienation of
my being involves an alienation of my world, which also falls beneath
the other's gaze. 'The appearance of the Other causes the appearance
in the situation of an aspect which I did not wish, of which I am not
master, and which on principle escapes me since it is *for the Other.*'
This is what Sartre, following Gide, calls 'the devil's part' (BN 289).

That Sartre should use such language requires comment. First,
a wordsmith like Sartre is unlikely to have been ignorant that the
devil's Old Testament moniker, *Satan*, meant 'accuser' or 'adversary'.

---

[16] Importantly, Sartre does not insist that an empirical observer is a necessary
component of this experience. Every 'look' is provoked by sense, but not by a
determined form, e.g. a moral agent. In this his account might be said to adumbrate
aspects of the HADD discussed in the cognitive science of religion literature. As Sartre
puts it, 'Of course what *most often* manifests a look is the convergence of two ocular
globes in my direction. But the look will be given just as well on occasion when there is
a rustling of branches, or the sound of a footstep followed by silence, or the slight
opening of a shutter, or a light movement of a curtain' (BN 281). This requires no
empirical observer, and indeed, 'if I apprehend the look, I cease to perceive the eyes'
(BN 282). 'What I apprehend immediately when I hear the branches crackling behind
me is not that *there is someone there*; it is that I am vulnerable, that I have a body
which can be hurt, that I occupy a place and that I cannot in any case escape from the
space in which I am without defense—in short, that *I am seen*' (BN 282).

Second, because the 'devilishness' of the other is a theme that recurs in Sartre's plays. In the following section, therefore, we will leave Sartre's theoretical account briefly in order to see its concrete application in a play in which this theme—the other as accuser—is particularly prominent: *La Poutain respecteuse*.

THE OTHER AS ACCUSER: PLAYING
THE DEVIL'S PART

The Respectable[17] *Prostitute* is Sartre's only American play.[18] The play opens in the room of Lizzie MacKay, who has just arrived in the Deep South with the intention of going into the oldest profession.

Her first customer (who refuses to give his name) is hiding in the bathroom when Lizzie answers the door to 'the Negro'. The Negro asks Lizzie to defend him in the face of unjust accusations—he and Lizzie had arrived on the same train the day before, and during the journey events had unfolded which led to the Negro's being accused of raping her. Knowing the society in which he lives, he pleads with Lizzie to tell the judge he is innocent.

Hurrying to get him out of the room on account of her waiting customer, Lizzie says that if they force her to testify she promises to tell the truth—and then slams the door in his face. At that moment her customer emerges from the bathroom, asking who was there. 'Nobody', Lizzie says (RP 247). She begins to vacuum the room, and when the customer protests at the noise she says she 'can't help it. The next morning I have to take a bath and run the vacuum cleaner'.

---

[17] Sometimes translated *Respectful*.

[18] It was published a year after his five-month stay in America (from January to May 1945), where he was one of several French journalists invited by the US State Department (Cox 2009: 144). Clearly, this play was powerfully shaped by its historical context—and even if Sartre's American visit is not considered an adequate stimulus, it is interesting to note that RP was published the same year as *Anti-Semite and Jew*, at a time when Sartre was exploring white supremacy in its European manifestation as anti-Semitism (as well as its American manifestation as racism). Although Sartre's handling of racism in America has been criticized on account of its 'failure to grasp the complexities of race prejudice' (Peters 1997: 21), he did wish to challenge the hypocrisy of a nation which had just—in the name of liberty and democracy—helped to defeat Nazism abroad, while simultaneously allowing prejudice, injustice, and violence on its own streets.

There follows an exchange in which the customer tells her to cover the bed since 'it smells of sin' (RP 247), and accuses her of being 'the Devil' (RP 250).

The customer—who has still not given his name—attempts to pay her, and to add insult to injury it is a measly $10 he offers. Lizzie is enraged and takes a vase in hand, intent on throwing it at him. The customer tells her not to throw it, or he'll have her 'run in' (RP 252). Lizzie questions his ability to follow through with this threat, and suddenly the customer is willing to reveal that he is, in fact, a senator's son. It becomes clear that he is very rich and very powerful, to which news Lizzie takes no objection.

Then the customer asks whether she was the one 'the n[*]gger tried to rape' (RP 254). Lizzie responds in surprise (how could he know to ask?), and the customer goes on to ask whether she arrived yesterday on the 6:00 train. She says yes, but that no one tried to rape her.

It becomes clear that her customer is not seeing her purely for 'professional' reasons. He has heard a certain version of the events of the train journey: two black men jumped on her, she called for help and some white men came. 'One of the n[*]ggers flashed his razor, and a white man shot him. The other n[*]gger got away' (RP 255). But that isn't what happened, Lizzie says:

> The two n[*]ggers kept to themselves and didn't even look at me. Then four white men got on the train, and two of them made passes at me. They had just won a football game, and they were drunk. They said that they could smell n[*]gger and wanted to throw them out of the window. The blacks fought back as well as they could, and one of the white men got punched in the eye. And that was when he pulled out a gun and fired. That was all. The other n[*]gger jumped off the train as we were coming into the station.   (RP 255)

The customer asks Lizzie whether she will tell that story if she has to testify before a judge, and she says that she'll 'tell them what she saw' (RP 255).

He reveals that 'Thomas', the man who felt her up and shot the 'n[*]gger', is his cousin. The customer offers her $500 to change her story, which would mean that a good, upstanding, Harvard-graduate citizen would be free instead of some good-for-nothing. Lizzie is livid. But before the scene reaches fever pitch the police arrive—cronies of the customer, of course—and threaten to press charges for prostitution. She says she didn't accept payment, but the customer points out

the $10 bill lying on the table. The police have a statement of events
(as Thomas recounted them), and offer Lizzie two options: sign or
face charges. She refuses to bear false witness and is mocked for doing
so: 'a $10-whore who doesn't want to lie...'?

After further drama, deception, and the lynching of an innocent
black man, Lizzie's customer returns to her. She tells him to 'get the
hell out' (RP 273), but (sending mixed messages!) then asks him
where he's been. He hears a noise in the bathroom. Out comes the
Negro, who makes a dash through the door with the customer in
pursuit, armed with a pistol. Lizzie is shouting that he's innocent
(which the customer too clearly knows, anyway). He fires two shots
and then comes back to Lizzie, who has retrieved her own revolver.
She asks whether he 'got the n[*]gger' and then threatens to shoot
him, but the customer proves himself his father's son, rhetorically
delineating what an assault it would be to America to kill a man like
him, from one of the oldest, most respectable families, destined to be
a senator. 'A girl like you can't shoot a man like me' (RP 275).

Besides, he adds: the shot he fired missed its target. And she could
come live in his keeping 'in a beautiful house, with a garden, on the
hill across the river' (RP 275), with regular visiting times, 'n[*]gger
servants and more money than you ever dreamed of' (RP 275). Lizzie
gives in, becoming his respectable prostitute.

Lizzie's character has been taken to exemplify the importance
Sartre assigned to the 'ordinary' person in the perpetuation of injustice. She means well, initially, but her conscience is clouded by wealthy
and powerful voices. As Cox puts it, 'She falls into bad faith, aspiring
to relinquish responsibility for herself in order to become a plaything
of the ruling class'.[19] But RP is not just an object lesson in class- (or
race- or sex-) based injustice. It contains passages—particularly in the
dialogue between Lizzie and the customer in the opening of the first
and closing of the last scenes—which illustrate the social nature of
original sin, the 'perpetual feeling of lack and of uneasiness' (BN 403)
concerning my relation to the other.

In the first scene, the post-coital Lizzie is compulsively vacuuming
(RP 247), because 'the next morning I have to take a bath and run
the vacuum cleaner'; it is clear that here—and at the next point where
she is seen to vacuum, after signing the senator's false statement—she

---

[19] Cox 2009: 148.

performs an action symbolizing the need for cleansing. In the exchange with the customer, he tells her to cover the bed, while she's at it, since 'it smells of sin' (RP 247). Then he proceeds to accuse her of being 'the Devil' (RP 250). It is the first of four instances of this accusation in the play (RP 250, 254, 256, 273), and this repetition points to the importance of the concept being expressed: for the customer, Lizzie is his *satan*, his accuser.

When she begins to discuss the previous night's antics, he tells her to 'shut up. What's done in the night belongs to the night. In the daytime you don't talk about it.' But Lizzie doesn't shut up. So he resorts to insisting he's 'completely forgotten' what happened. He takes hold of her neck, as if to strangle her so that 'there would be no one in the world to remember last night' (RP 251). But Lizzie doesn't understand: 'If it disgusts you to make love, why did you come here to me?' (RP 253).

Because she remembers—i.e. under her gaze—he sees himself as repugnant. At the moment when she realizes his purpose in coming to see her, she says he is the sort of gentleman she 'can do without' (RP 256), that it is unsurprising that he comes from the same family as the 'guy who kept rubbing up against me and tried to put his hand under my skirt' (RP 256). It is not just the previous night that the customer wishes to obliterate; it is the gaze of anyone who contests his self-image as the 'upstanding citizen'. He does not want the revelation his shame delivers. But Lizzie—the other—serves as his tribunal—until she becomes his accomplice.

This is only one of the many, intersecting and indeed intersectional, points the play makes: the injustices it depicts arise on account of race, class, and sex. But each of these injustices involves a common axis: the body.

THE BODY

Joseph Catalano describes the chapter on 'The Body' as 'the pivotal chapter' of *Being and Nothingness*.[20] Izumi-Shearer writes of Sartre

---

[20] Catalano 2009: 26. In addition to the second chapter of Part III of *Being and Nothingness*, entitled 'The Body', further passages in *Being in Nothingness* extend Sartre's discussion—in the sections on hunger and desire, for example, in 'Concrete Relations with Others', and at the conclusion of the book in his treatment of holes and

that 'le thème du corps constitue un des thèmes clefs de son appré-
hension existentielle de l'homme'.[21] Despite such claims for the
centrality of the body in Sartre's ontology, however, it has been a
'neglected' area in Sartre scholarship.[22] Perhaps this is because, as
Moran writes, the chapter on 'The Body' is characteristically 'dense,
difficult, and confused'—even 'tortured'. Nevertheless, it is 'a ground-
breaking and radical philosophical meditation on embodiment'.[23]

In it Sartre wished to distinguish between different *levels* of ontology because he believed that his philosophical predecessors had
misunderstood the body on account of confusing the orders of
knowing and *being*, or *le corps-vu* and *le corps-existé* (cf. BN 241,
325). For Sartre, the body is one of the 'indissoluble' structures of
human reality (BN 247), and the ontology of the body is comprised of
three levels—'different modes of manifestation'[24]—each of which is
given a sub-chapter in *Being and Nothingness*:

1) The body-for-itself (for which he also uses the term 'facticity')
   (BN 330–62);

2) The body-for-others (BN 362–75); and

3) The awkwardly entitled 'third ontological dimension of the
   body' (BN 375–82).

We will examine each of these in turn before proceeding to consider
how they might be understood to be fallen.

The Body-for-Itself

On the first level, the body is the manner in which I exist pre-
reflectively; 'the body is *lived* and not *known*' (BN 348). Sartre writes

slime in 'Doing and Having'. Taken together with Sartre's literary representations of
embodiment in his plays, novels, and short stories, there is a strong case to be made
that Sartre has retained a negative view of embodiment which preserves a Christian
notion of the body as a pre-eminent site of the effects of human fallenness. This
section focuses on III.2 of *Being and Nothingness* and on the literary example of
La Nausée's Roquentin.

[21] Izumi-Shearer 1976: 96.

[22] Boulé and O'Donohoe 2011: 3. Though recent publications have begun to
redress this neglect. In addition to Boulé and O'Donohoe 2011, see Moran 2009
and 2011; Morris 2009.

[23] Moran 2009: 41. It should also be credited with the introduction of the key
concept of 'the flesh' (*la chair*), which became important in the later Merleau-Ponty
(Moran 2011: 9).

[24] Moran 2011:13.

that 'my body as it is *for me* does not appear to me in the midst of the world' (BN 327). It isn't a thing, but rather 'a transparent medium for my experience of the world, but also as somehow *surpassed* toward the world'.[25] It is a conscious structure of consciousness, but a point of view on which I cannot have a point of view—for though I can see my eye reflected in a mirror I cannot, as Sartre puts it, 'see the seeing'. The body at this level is not something one can intuit as an object: following Marcel, Sartre is emphatic that I *am* my body (BN 342).[26]

On this level Sartre writes that the body is indistinguishable from the recognition that there is a world (BN 342), and indeed from the 'situation' of the *pour soi*, since for the *pour soi* 'to exist and to be situated are one and the same' (BN 333). But, he continues,

> a situation is not a pure contingent given. Quite the contrary, it is revealed only to the extent that the for-itself surpasses it toward itself. Consequently the body for itself is never a given which I can know. It is there everywhere as surpassed; it exists only in so far as I escape it by nihilating myself. The body is what I nihilate.... It is the fact that I am my own motivation without being my own foundation. (BN 333)

Sartre repeatedly emphasizes the given and unchosen nature of embodiment. To have a body, he writes, 'is to be the foundation of one's own nothingness and not to be the foundation of one's being' (BN 350). The body is something to be escaped by nihilation (BN 350), and the overwhelming characteristic of corporeality is that it is 'the inexpressible which one wishes to flee' (BN 357). On this first, pre-reflective level, therefore, embodiment is an encumbrance,[27] the site of self-alienation.

Each consciousness undergoes an individual fall from being when it comes into existence through the bodily process of *birth*, which he describes as 'the primary nihilation which causes me to arise from the in-itself which I am in fact without having to be it' (BN 351).[28] As such, the body in some sense *is* my contingency. Sartre writes that 'the body is the contingent form which is taken up by the necessity of my contingency. We can never apprehend this contingency as such in so

---

[25] Moran 2009: 43.

[26] See Marcel's *Metaphysical Journal* (1927) for discussions of incarnation and Mui 2009 for a discussion of Sartre's indebtedness to Marcel.

[27] On encumbrance cf. Izumi-Shearer 1976: 114.

[28] It is worth noting at this point that sex and gestation as the causal antecedents of birth are conspicuously absent from his account. Although earlier in BN we read 'Through birth a Past appears in the world' (BN 163).

far as our body is *for us*; for we are a choice, and for us, to be is to choose ourselves' (BN 352).

But though we can choose ourselves, we exist irrespective of choice. We *cannot* found our being: this is the brute fact that corporeality confronts us with. The body constitutes a *limit* to freedom. As Sartre objects later in *Being and Nothingness*: 'Adam chose to take the apple, but he did not choose to be Adam' (cf. BN 489–91).[29]

The contingent unchosenness of existence in general and one's body in particular reveals itself to consciousness through a 'dull and inescapable' nausea, which is deeply connected with the apprehension of my body as flesh (*la chair*, BN 381). We attempt to escape it by seeking pain or pleasure, but eventually such attempts at distraction prove futile, and we are left again to face facticity and contingency (BN 362).[30]

In addition to effecting this internal discomfort, the contingent unchosenness of our bodies affects our relations with others in ways beyond our control. Briefly departing from considering first-order embodiment, Sartre elaborates that birth—as a source of particularity and dissimilarity—is a source of alienation and limitation. It conditions the way in which objects appear to me and the way I appear as an object—whether in terms of race, sex, class, nationality, character, physiology, or what have you. In short, '*my past*, as everything which I have experienced is indicated as my point of view on the world by the world itself'. My body becomes 'the necessary condition of the existence of a world and . . . the contingent realization of this condition' (BN 352). We will return to the notion of facticity later in this chapter, but at this stage it is important to note that this connotes an important sense in which embodiment implies limitation: bodies are the axes of the relationship between being-for-itself and being-for-others.

The Body-for-Others

The second level Sartre expounds is the body as *seen* rather than *lived* (*le corps-vu* rather than *le corps-existé*). This is the domain of the body as utilized and known by others, studied and idealized by the

---

[29] This occurs in the second of two passages in BN devoted to Leibniz's notion of possibility—cf. BN 120–1; 489–91. We will discuss Leibniz's Adam further in Chapter 7.

[30] Sartre continues: 'We must not take the term nausea as a metaphor derived from our physiological disgust. On the contrary, we must realize that it is on the foundation of this nausea that all concrete and empirical nauseas . . . are produced' (BN 362).

'objective sciences'. I do not know from my own experience that I have a brain or endocrine glands, for example, but I learn that I have them from others. Sartre uses the imagery of tools to elucidate the distinction between this and the previous ontological order of embodiment. On the first order, the body is the centre of reference, the point of view on which I cannot have a point of view. On the second, however, my body appears as the 'tool of tools' in my instrumental engagement with the world. It appears as 'a thing' which I am.

The distinction arises because the body of another is not given to me in the same manner as my own: 'it is presented to me originally with a certain objective coefficient of utility and of adversity' (BN 364). I assess the other in terms of what help or hindrance he constitutes to my own pursuits. The other, therefore, is given in a thing-like manner, as 'the pure in-itself of his being—an in-itself among in-itselfs and one which I surpass towards my possibilities' (BN 366). The other's body appears to my consciousness as an object: it is 'given to us immediately as what the Other is' (BN 371); 'the Other's corporeality and objectivity are strictly inseparable' (BN 374).

Inherent in apprehending the other as object is that what the other experiences as 'his taste of himself' becomes for Sartre 'the *Other's flesh*'.

> The flesh is the pure contingency of presence. It is ordinarily hidden by clothes, make-up, the cut of the hair or beard, the expression, etc. But in the course of long acquaintance with a person there always comes an instant when all these disguises are thrown off and when I find myself in the presence of the pure *contingency of his presence*. In this case I achieve in the face or the other parts of a body the pure intuition of the flesh. This intuition is not only knowledge; it is the affective apprehension of an absolute contingency, and this apprehension is a particular type of *nausea*.   (BN 367)

To study the way the other's body appears to me and the way my body appears to the other are one and the same thing (BN 362). And the recognition that bodies are viewed as objects in the manner Sartre describes reveals the third and final ontological level.

The Third Ontological Dimension of the Body

On this level, embodiment entails that 'I exist for myself as a body known by the other'. We experience our bodies not only as our own, but as reflected in others' experience: 'the Other is revealed to me as the subject for whom I am an object' (BN 375). This is the level on which we experience things like shame and embarrassment. Sartre writes that 'I cannot be embarrassed by my own body as I exist it. It is my body as it may exist for the other which may embarrass me' (BN 377).

It is this dimension of the body that exposes us to the omnipresent 'gaze' of the other.[31] We are 'imprisoned' by this gaze, because the other deprives us of control over how we see our world and—more importantly—ourselves. Alone in the world I might exist as 'unqualifiable selfness which I have to be forever without relief' (BN 315).[32] But 'The Other is present to me everywhere as the one through whom I become an object' (BN 303).

Just as my own gaze reduces others to their instrumentality, the gaze of the other reduces me to the status of mere object. We experience shame, Sartre writes, not because we are this or that object in particular, but because we are *an object*.[33] In the context of discussing *shame* Sartre explicitly refers to the Genesis account and introduces the symbolism and theological idiom of sin into his phenomenology.[34] It is worth quoting this passage at length, for shame is described as a consciousness:

> of being irremediably what I always was: "in suspense"—that is, in the mode of the "not-yet" or of the "already-no-longer." Pure shame is not a feeling of being this or that guilty object but in general of being *an* object; that is, of *recognizing myself* in this degraded, fixed, and dependent being which I am for the Other. Shame is the feeling of an *original fall*, not because of the fact that I may have committed this or that particular fault but simply that I have "fallen" into the world in the midst of things and that I need the mediation of the Other in order to be what I am.   (BN 312)

> Modesty and in particular the fear of being surprised in a state of nakedness are only a symbolic specification of original shame; the body symbolizes here our defenceless state as objects. To put on clothes is to hide one's object-state; it is to claim the right of seeing without

---

[31] Although, as previously mentioned, Sartre clearly does not use the term 'omnipresent' in an empirical sense.

[32] 'I am condemned to be forever my own nihilation' (BN 322).

[33] Shame is 'a unitary apprehension with three dimensions: "I am ashamed of *myself* before the *Other*"' (BN 313).

[34] Ricoeur (1974) might suggest that this is a move into the level of hermeneutic phenomenology or interpretation.

being seen; that is, to be pure subject. That is why the Biblical symbol of the fall after the original sin is the fact that Adam and Eve "know that they are naked." The reaction to shame will consist in apprehending as an object the one who apprehended *my* own object-state.   (BN 312)

This imagery and language has not escaped the notice of commentators. Karsten Harries observes, 'How Christian the atheist Sartre here sounds, so Christian in fact that one has to wonder whether his ontology and anthropology are not unduly burdened by an all too uncritically assumed Christian inheritance.'[35]

Such a view is supported by Sartre's next step here, which is to link shame with *pride*. We read that 'it is on the ground of fundamental shame or shame of being an object that pride is built' (BN 314). Here as elsewhere Sartre prioritizes 'being seen' by others over our own 'seeing' in the project to define ourselves.[36] This is important because for Sartre the body as others encounter it—that is, the body in its social situation—is a domain of contestation and conflict: 'Conflict is the original meaning of being-for-others' (BN 386), he writes. 'The object-state of my body for the Other is not an object for me and can not constitute my body as an object; it is experienced as the flight of the body which I exist' (BN 378). But despite the struggle that existence with others entails, for Sartre, the other performs a necessary role: the other reveals something I cannot learn on my own, which is *how I really am*. It appears to us that the other can achieve something 'of which we are incapable and yet which is incumbent upon us: to *see ourselves as we are*' (BN 377).

Again we see the importance of seeing-and-being-seen—so prominent in *Being and Nothingness*. It recurs in BN III.3 ('Concrete Relations with Others'), where Sartre introduces a concept of 'original guilt'. There we read that 'It is before the Other that I am *guilty*.... beneath the Other's look I experience my alienation and my nakedness as a fall from grace which I must assume... Thus my original sin is my upsurge in a world where there are others; and whatever may be my further relations with others, these relations will only be variations on the original theme of my guilt' (BN 431–2).

---

[35] See Harries 2004: 28. He specifies similarities to Augustine. Barnes (1958: xxxii) writes that 'rather surprisingly in a non-theistic philosophy we find also a concept of existential guilt, an inescapable guilt, a species of Original Sin'.

[36] Moran 2009: 53.

Sartre's account marks a pronounced departure from Pascal in this regard. In a fragment Sartre copied into the *Carnet Midy* we read the following from Pascal's *Pensées*:

> We are not content with the life we have in ourselves and with our own being. We want to lead an imaginary life in the eyes of others, and we try hard to get it noticed. We work incessantly to embellish and conserve this imaginary being and neglect the true one.   (L806/B146)[37]

For Sartre the first two sentences hold. But the third does not: there is no *true* being to be neglected. There is no *vrai moi*, as he wrote elsewhere in the *Carnet Midy*.[38] In *Being and Nothingness* the absence of God is taken to its conclusion: without a divine witness, and without the perdurance of my own witness to myself, only the other can see me. My *être* is ultimately reducible to my *paraître*.

Whether or not the other succeeds in seeing us *as we are* is a question we shall return to in Chapter 8. But there is a final point to make before concluding this section. We have seen that Sartre's account of 'the problem' of the other—the absence and loneliness that characterize human relations—is not an epistemological enquiry. It is not concerned with 'knowledge' of other minds but with the lived experience of other freedoms—*fallen* freedoms.

The experience of fallen freedom, as Sartre depicts it, is an experience of feeling unjustified (contingent) and unjustifiably condemned (in *shame*, by being reduced to the object seen in the other's gaze). But both of these are emphatically *embodied* experiences: both nausea and shame palpably change human physiology and awareness of the world. The other experiences nausea as the apprehension of his own contingency (BN 366), as do I. And the other's apprehension of my contingency demands that I give a justification of myself.

As Katherine Morris notes, it is not generally Sartre's style to acknowledge his intellectual predecessors.[39] But Descartes and Heidegger

---

[37] Cited in CM 477.   [38] CM 471–2.

[39] Morris 2009: 10. This is partly because the French educational system allowed Sartre to presume knowledge on behalf of his (French) readers. Where the body in particular is concerned, Moran (2011: 11–12) provides a sketch of likely and known influences from both the French and German traditions. The former includes the works of Descartes, Condillac, Maine de Biran, Comte, Bergson, Brunschwicg, Pradines, and Marcel, among others. The latter includes the works of Max Scheler, Heidegger's *Being and Time*, and Husserl's then-published works (*Logical Investigations, Ideas I, Formal and Transcendental Logic,* and *Cartesian Meditations*). He may

loom large in Sartre's account of embodiment, dividing the second-ary scholarship on this subject into two camps. On the first, Sartre is seen to espouse a descendant of Cartesianism which, as Catalano puts it, 'is precariously close to what Merleau-Ponty... identifies as the intellec-tualist view of the self and the world'.[40] On the second reading, he is 'resolutely anti-dualist'[41] or seen to accept 'the fundamental Heideggerian critique of panoramic consciousness and all traditional dualisms'.[42]

There are proof texts for both views, leading other scholars such as Izumi-Shearer to emphasize that while there is no rupture between body and consciousness, Sartre's account is not straightforward: it is ambiguous and dialectical.[43] On my reading, however, such ambigu-ity reflects not just 'confusion', as Moran writes, but something about the experience of embodiment itself. Fallen bodies are lived in a tensive state—in which 'I am' my body, and yet it is simultaneously, as Sartre puts it, an 'inexpressible' which I wish to flee: as we shall see in the next section, it is both warrior and war zone in the fight for my identity.

Where the ambiguous nature of embodiment is concerned there is no better expositor than the protagonist from *La Nausée*, whom we met in Chapter 5.[44] Roquentin describes his life as having a 'halting, incoherent aspect' (N 14), and his diary is certainly not plot-driven in the page-turning sense. Its epistolary form lends an episodic air, which Goldthorpe argues is 'designed to demonstrate the inadequacy of the structures which men seek to impose upon the external world'.[45] But as Andrew Leak points out, if one defines plot as the 'deferred resolution of an enigma, then something resembling a plot exists in *La Nausée*, despite its deceptive formlessness'; it is a meta-physical 'who- or what-dunnit'.[46]

Roquentin is uneasy because something has changed—that is why he decides to keep his diary: 'in order to understand it'. The primary

---

also have had access to the ideas expressed in *Ideas II* through discussions with Merleau-Ponty.

[40] Catalano 2009: 27.   [41] Howells 1988: 20.

[42] Catalano 2009: 27. For a Cartesian reading see Royle 2005: 90ff.

[43] Izumi-Shearer 1976: 115.

[44] Although there are those who warn against reading Sartre's later philosophy into the novel (e.g. Bernasconi 2006: 9), there are also those who insist that even in his literary writing Sartre was always 'en classe' (e.g. Louette 2002/3).

[45] Goldthorpe 1984: 4.   [46] Leak 2006: 30.

symptom is nausea—an *embodied* experience—which occurs with
increasing frequency and usually at the provocation of the material
world: pebbles that ooze slime and hands that appear to be fat
maggots. But why? What elicits this response? At first Roquentin
locates the change in himself, in the conscious subject. Then he
attempts to locate it outside his consciousness, in objects. But finally,
after abandoning the biography of M. de Rollebon, a life-consuming
project he needed 'in order not to feel his being' (NA 143), Roquentin
undergoes an especially extreme bout of nausea. He has discovered its
source: 'a painful rumination' that

> I exist. It is I. The body lives all by itself once it is started. But when it
> comes to thought, it is I who continue it, who unwind it. I exist. I think
> I exist. Oh, how long and serpentine this feeling of existence is—and
> I unwind it, slowly... if only I could prevent myself from thinking!...
> At this very moment—this is terrible—if I exist *it is because* I hate
> existing. It is I, it is I who pull myself from the nothingness to which
> I aspire: hatred and disgust for existence are just so many ways of
> *making me* exist, of thrusting me into existence.   (NA 145)

Following this realization, Roquentin stabs himself with a pen knife,
watching the blood seep from his hand into a pool where it 'at last
stop[s] being me' (NA 146). This is one of many passages which have
prompted readers to comment that Roquentin is mentally unwell. But
psychotically induced or not, the torrent of thoughts which follows
this incident includes the realization that 'existence is a fallen fall...
existence is an imperfection' (NA 147). This is the problem: 'I exist,
that's all. And that particular trouble is so vague, so metaphysical, that
I am ashamed of it' (NA 153).

But though the problem is vague and metaphysical, it reveals itself
concretely in the physical. Geneviève Idt writes that the confusion
prompted by contingency dissolves any distinctions between the
human, animal, and vegetable.[47] But throughout the slow crescendo
which culminates in the famous scene before a chestnut tree, Sartre's
surreal metaphors change human beings into beasts or body parts—
from consciousnesses into things. The problem does not rest in the
subject alone, nor in objects alone. As Andrew Leak writes, 'If the
body is *both* an object in the world *and* the object that I exist, then
nausea must reside not at one or other pole, but in the *relation*

---

[47] Cf. Idt 1971: 44.

between the two poles of lived experience.'[48] For Sartre, the relation between consciousness and the body seems to indicate a schism in the self.

Sartre's tripartite ontology of the body may seem rather abstract—even disembodied. But in his literary works it is made concrete, applied in situations that illuminate and extend the discussion. In *La Nausée*, we find Sartre's Adam discovering his nakedness for the first time: he is contingent, limited, alienated from himself and imprisoned by others. Roquentin feels himself 'devoid of secret dimensions, limited to my body' (NA 53). His body is his only possession (NA 97), and yet he doesn't know what to do with it (NA 80), and looks at individual parts of his body with the uncertainty and distrust with which a xenophobe might regard a foreigner (NA 144). Solipsistic though Roquentin might wish to be, his body is seen by others. The judgement of the other pierces him 'like a sword'. He describes the gaze of another as 'call[ing] into question my very right to exist. And it was true, I had always realized that: I hadn't any right to exist. I had appeared by chance, I existed like a stone, a plant, a microbe' (NA 123–4).

Unlike other Sartrean characters, Roquentin resists being classed in the order of things (NA 30). For some, the objectified body is simply exploited in bad faith. In *No Exit*, for example, Estelle is entirely dependent on her body in order to feel she exists; she must be physically desired to have worth. Estelle personifies both the body-and being-for-others; as Izumi-Shearer writes, 'le besoin psychologique de se voir dans des miroirs explique que l'image de son propre corps seule peut lui faire sentir qu'elle existe'.[49] For Roquentin, by contrast, a mirror is a hole, a trap to be avoided (NA 30).

DISSIMILARITY: THE FACTICITY
OF FALLEN FLESH

On Sartre's first ontological level the body is either 'the center of reference indicated emptily by the instrumental-objects of the world or else it is the *contingency which the for-itself exists*' (BN 362). This contingency is facticity made flesh, where facticity (to recall the

---

[48] Leak 2006: 31.   [49] Izumi-Shearer 1976: 98.

discussion of the for-itself made in Chapter 5) is 'the feeling of complete gratuity; it apprehends itself as being there *for nothing*, as being *de trop* (BN 108). Facticity is 'a memory of being', a reminder of the for-itself's 'unjustifiable presence in the world' (BN 108).

Sartre's description of the contingent unchosenness of existence (in general) and my body (in particular)—which is revealed by nausea in solitude and shame with others, and which we attempt to escape by the diversions of pleasure and pain (and bad faith)—is reminiscent of the conflictual *misère* described by Augustine and Pascal, in their accounts of the human experience of nothingness qua *sin*. Man 'tries in vain to fill [this craving] with everything around him, seeking in things that are not there the help he cannot find in those that are'.[50]

But where Pascal writes that the 'infinite abyss' can be filled by an 'infinite and immutable object', Sartre does not have recourse to this solution. Instead, we must face the brute fact of embodiment and the two senses of contingency it implies: it isn't necessary that I should exist at all, let alone exist as the particular entity that I am. That I exist at all reveals that I am not the foundation of my own being.

This takes concrete shape on the second level—where the body is experienced as an object or a 'tool of tools' in its instrumental relations with the world. With the recognition that I can view my body as an object comes a recognition that I can view my body as wanting; I can compare it to other bodies and find it dissatisfactory or disadvantaged. On this level, the body can become a site of self-alienation and division from the 'thing' which I am. Shortly after writing that 'I *am* my body', Sartre refers the body as an 'it', writing that 'I am it, I who am presence to myself as the being which is its own nothingness' (BN 342). On this second level a difference arises between 'who' I am and 'what' I am. The self is divided; *res cogitans* and *res extensa* are at odds. When I view my own body as an object, it becomes more or less useful, more or less valuable, more or less something I might wish to 'have'. Moreover, as Sartre writes later in BN, 'it' does things against my will: in sexual desire, for example, the freedom of my consciousness is 'compromised'.[51] The spirit is willing,

---

[50] Pascal, *Pensées* L148/B425. See also Augustine 1961: I.20.

[51] This aspect of embodiment is explored more fully in the section on desire in 'Concrete Relations with Others'. One suspects Sartre might have agreed with Augustine that bodily desire is 'like a morass', clouding and obscuring sight (Augustine 1961: II.2).

but the flesh is weak. For Lucienne in *Intimité*, a woman who is frequently the object of—and therefore defined by—desire, having a body itself is viewed as something 'disgusting'. 'Pourquoi', she asks, 'faut-il que nous ayons des corps?' (IN 57).

'We are born into the world twice,' Catalano writes, 'once from the womb of our mothers and then again from our relation to others.'[52] And it is when we are born again—on the third ontological level— that the doors of the corporeal cell slam shut. Existing 'for myself as a body known by the other' is the ultimate limitation of my freedom: it reduces me to the status of an object. I did not choose to be, I did not choose to be what I am, and I did not choose to be seen as you see me. This is why Sartre describes the existence of the other as 'my original fall'. And as Peter Royle writes, 'si mon surgissement dans un monde où il y a l'autre est vécu comme une chute, c'est, comme pour le christianisme ou dans les philosophies de Philon et de Plotin, à cause d'un événement dont mon moi actuel n'est pas responsable'.[53]

In the absence of an omniscient God the gaze of the other becomes my tribunal.[54] And the body is on trial; not the subjective self (the who) of consciousness, but the object (the what) which is on display and beyond control. Like Adam and Eve, we are left defenceless and vulnerable. On the view Sartre outlines in *Being and Nothingness*, the body is somehow both the soldier and the battlefield in a 'battle to the death' for my identity; it is both active agent and passive site. Human relations oscillate between mastery and slavery; in the face of objectification, one can either give in (in bad faith) or fight back.

Although Hegel clearly looms large behind this motif,[55] it has a more ancient ancestry: Sartre's philosophical anthropology is indebted to theological accounts of original sin. The fallen human self 'makes itself the centre of everything', as Pascal wrote: 'it wants to assert itself over [others], for each self is the enemy, and would like to be tyrant to all

---

[52] Catalano 2010: 77.   [53] Royle 2005: 53.

[54] In *Situations IV*, Sartre states explicitly that: 'Le problème de Dieu est un problème humain qui concerne le rapport des hommes entre eux, c'est un problème total auquel chacun apporte solution par sa vie entière, et la solution qu'on lui apporte reflète l'attitude qu'on a choisie vis-à-vis autres hommes et de soi-même' (SIV 88).

[55] Most commentators take Sartre's Hegelianism to be derived from Kojève 1980, which opens with an account of the Master/Slave dialectic. But Sartre never attended Kojève's lectures and Flynn (2013) argues (on the basis of later works such as the *Notebooks for an Ethics*) that Hippolyte was more influential.

the others'.[56] 'Pride hates a fellowship of equality under God', Augustine wrote. On the Jansenist–Augustinian view of original sin, the *libido dominandi* drives human beings to objectify others, to make ourselves masters to them—or at least, to position ourselves higher up the hierarchical ladder. And facticity, as a source of dissimilarity, is a wellspring for comparison and competition. Bodies—be they black or white, female or male, ill or well, poor or rich—are the building blocks of human hierarchy, and bodily particularity a breeding ground for sin.

Sartre's view of being-for-others is notoriously bleak: underneath the other's look our reactions are fear, pride, shame, and the recognition of slavery,[57] and when we return their gaze it is with eyes full of destruction (BN 432) and hate (BN 433). Sartre, in another famous footnote, writes that his 'considerations do not exclude the possibility of an ethics of deliverance and salvation [*une morale de la délivrance et du salut*]. But this can be achieved only after a radical conversion which we cannot discuss here' (BN 434, n. 13). But, as Thomas Flynn writes, in *Being and Nothingness* as a whole Sartre 'hobbles his project of formulating a positive social theory'.[58] And on my reading, this is because in addition to the phenomenological influences that are widely acknowledged to have influenced Sartre in *Being and Nothingness*, we find a Jansenist–Augustinian pessimism. Sartre's ontology of human persons *as nothingness*—like those doctrines of sin that take humanity to be totally depraved—renders a 'positive social theory' impossible.

At this point my theological readers may be starting to wonder: What does Sartre contribute here? There is nothing new, theologically, about saying that the fall resulted in pain, suffering, and injustice. But Sartre offers a view of fallenness from a *graceless* position. And to see this more clearly we must turn to his account of freedom in BN Part IV.

---

[56] Pascal, *Pensées*, L597/B455.   [57] See BN 291ff.
[58] Flynn 2014: 205. Sebastian Gardner asks: 'Even if radical conversion is possible, and engenders ethical constraints, in what way does B&N restore intrinsic value to human existence? ... Is the for-itself's affirmation of freedom really enough to count as its *salvation*?' (2009: 197).

7

Freedom

On Being Our Own Nothingness

[F]reedom is the apparition of Nothingness in the world.[1]

Humans, since embodied, can be differentiated not only by their physical characteristics, but also by their embodied engagement with the world. We saw in Chapter 5 that to be human, as Sartre describes being-for-itself, is to crave being and to crave *meaning*, and in Chapter 6 that our embodied existence with others must be taken into account in that pursuit. In this chapter we will turn to the final part of *Being and Nothingness*, on 'Having, Doing, and Being', where Sartre further elaborates on the nature of *freedom* as a 'technical and philosophical concept' (BN 505) and on the ways in which individual freedoms seek to meet these needs. Ultimately, as Sartre famously declared, the nature of freedom is such that any search for lost being is futile: to be human is to be a 'useless passion'.

I suggested in the Introduction that attention to the theological dimensions in *Being and Nothingness* might clarify ambiguities in it: and this negative conclusion—that we are 'useless passions'—is a prime example. In this chapter, I will conclude my argument that Sartre's preoccupation with that 'critical cliché',[2] freedom, was intimately connected with problems that have always been freedom's cognates in the Christian tradition: sin and evil. We have seen already that for Sartre—as for seventeenth-century French Augustinianism in general and the Jansenist tradition in particular—freedom is intimately connected with nothingness (Chapter 4); that this nothingness has

---

[1] Sartre, WD 132–3.   [2] Howells 1988: 1.

painful psychological and epistemological consequences (Chapter 5); and that it renders our relationships with our bodies and with others conflictual (Chapter 6). In the final part of *Being and Nothingness*, Sartre offers his 'technical and philosophical' analysis of freedom. Reading his engagement with Leibniz here alongside his discussion of Descartes in *La Liberté cartesienne* (1946), I argue that Sartre's phenomenology of freedom in *Being and Nothingness* can be read as antitheodicy. Sartre rejects 'freedom' as a 'sufficient reason' for the world's ills: it is the source of too many of them.

Moreover, it will be argued that Sartre's rejection of Leibnizean optimism leaves him with a pessimism more extreme than that of his Jansenist predecessors. The for-itself is free *to the extent that it refuses* any possibility of grace. And the result is that Sartre's freedom cannot escape the determinism of nothingness.

THE 'TECHNICAL AND PHILOSOPHICAL CONCEPT OF FREEDOM'

On Sartre's existentialist view, as we have seen, the 'being of man is to be reabsorbed in the succession of his acts' (BN 453). In Part IV of *Being and Nothingness* he therefore suggests that in order to understand the concept of freedom we must turn our attention to action (BN 455). Indeed, in a characteristically rhetorical and dismissive remark, Sartre writes that 'it is strange that philosophers have been able to argue endlessly about determinism and free-will, to cite examples in favor of one or the other thesis without ever attempting first to make explicit the structures contained in the very idea of *action*' (BN 455).

In this part of *Being and Nothingness* we see further evidence of what I have already referred to as Sartre's 'morganatic marriage' of phenomenology and the 'subphilosophical' writings of *les mystiques* and *les moralistes*.[3] At the outset of his discussion of freedom, Sartre claims to be redressing the neglect of his philosophical forbears by making the phenomenological observation that actions are *intentional*,

---

[3] As previously noted there is an ambiguity in the French word *moraliste* which the English 'moralist' does not convey. See Introduction, n. 28.

which is to say that they imply as a condition 'recognition of a "desideratum"; that is, of an objective lack or again of a *negatité*' (BN 455). But, all such considerations are *negative*: 'they aim at what is not, not at what is' (BN 456).

Sartre considers himself to be redressing a misunderstanding of *motives*. Common opinion says that when we acknowledge the 'harshness of a situation' or the 'sufferings' it causes, harshness and suffering become the 'motives for conceiving of another state of affairs in which things would be better for everybody' (BN 457). But Sartre suggests that the reverse is actually the case: 'It is on the day that we can conceive of a different state of affairs that a new light falls on our troubles and our suffering and that we decide that these are unbearable' (BN 457). Suffering itself is not a motive for action; in this Sartre agrees with Hume, Kant, and others who defend a distinction between fact and value.[4] On the contrary, Sartre writes, it is only after forming the project of changing his situation that the situation takes on an intolerable cast. On Sartre's view, no factual state—political, economic, social, psychological—*motivates* any act. Rather, the act is a 'projection of the for-itself toward what it is not, and what it is can in no way determine by itself what it is not' (BN 458).

Consciousness, therefore, faces the permanent possibility of 'effecting a rupture' with its own past,

> of wrenching itself away from its past so as to be able to consider it in the light of a non-being and so as to be able to confer on it the meaning which *it has* in terms of the project of a meaning which it *does not have*. Under no circumstances can the past in any way by itself produce an act; that is, the positing of an end which turns back upon itself so as to illuminate it.   (BN 458; italics original)

In a move that arguably merits the charge of circularity, Sartre writes two pages later that 'the act is the expression of freedom', so we must describe freedom.[5] 'Freedom has no essence', but rather is 'the foundation of all essences since man reveals intra-mundane essences by surpassing the world toward his own possibilities' (BN 460).

---

[4] See Flynn 1986: 8.

[5] Sartre's philosophy of action arguably presents freedom's most positive aspect, for through action freedom can attempt to alleviate suffering. But the ekstatic temporalization of the for-itself is such that we cannot know whether our actions will result in the consequences we desire, or whether that desire will remain when the consequences are effected.

Here Sartre frames his account by directing our attention to missteps in Descartes and Husserl, writing that '[W]hat we can demand from the cogito is only that it discover for us a factual necessity.' The cogito reveals *my freedom*:

> that is, as a contingent existent but one which I *am not able* not to experience. I am indeed an existent who *learns* his freedom through his acts, but I am also an existent whose individual and unique existence temporalizes itself as freedom. As such I am necessarily a consciousness (of) freedom since nothing exists in consciousness except as the non-thetic consciousness of existing. Thus my freedom is perpetually in question in my being; it is not a quality added on or a *property* of my nature. It is very exactly the stuff of my being; and as in my being, my being is in question, I must necessarily possess a certain comprehension of freedom. It is this comprehension which we intend at present to make explicit.   (BN 460–1; italics original)

Freedom is 'the stuff of my being'; and the first step Sartre makes towards making 'this comprehension' explicit is to revisit his discussion of bad faith, reminding his readers that since human reality is its own nothingness the human person is 'condemned to exist forever beyond [his or her] essence' (BN 461). For this reason we are famously 'condemned to be free':[6] 'no limit can be found to my freedom except for freedom itself . . . we are not free to cease being free' (BN 462).

We saw in Chapters 2 and 3 how various Augustinian formulations of original sin place the human 'between being and nothingness', as Descartes wrote. But this space between 'everything' and 'nothing',[7] in Pascal's idiom, is discomfiting. We would prefer self-deception or diversion, because otherwise the human 'feels his nothingness, his abandonment, his inadequacy, his dependence, his helplessness, his emptiness. At once from the depths of his soul arises boredom, gloom, sadness, grief, vexation, despair.'[8]

The anxiety-inducing elusiveness of self-knowledge in *Being and Nothingness* has already received extensive treatment in Chapter 4; but it is significant that here, too, Sartre's treatment of freedom clearly and explicitly states of the 'coincidence' of freedom and nothingness:

---

[6] That freedom is a state of condemnation is reiterated twenty times in *Being and Nothingness*: for some of the most famous passages, see BN 152, 462, 506, 530.

[7] See *Pensées*, L199/B72.   [8] See *Pensées*, L622/B131.

freedom in its foundation coincides with the nothingness which is at the heart of man. Human reality is free because it is *not enough*. It is free because it is perpetually wrenched away from itself and because it has been separated by a nothingness from what it is and from what it will be.... Man is free because he is not himself but presence to himself. The being which is what it is can not be free. Freedom is precisely the nothingness which is *made-to-be* at the heart of man and which forces human-reality to *make itself* instead of *to be*. As we have seen, for human reality, to be is to *choose oneself*; nothing comes to it either from the outside or from within which it can *receive or accept*.

(BN 462–3; italics original)

In sum, human reality is lack and self-estrangement. It is also—as we shall see in the next sections of this chapter—auto-eklektic (self-choosing). Freedom is not a being, Sartre writes, 'it *is the being* of man—i.e. his nothingness of being'. 'Man cannot be sometimes slave and sometimes free; he is wholly and forever free or he is not free at all' (BN 463).

If we know how to use them, Sartre says, these observations will lead us to new discoveries concerning the relation of freedom and the will—and here we begin to see the theological significance of his 'technical and philosophical' freedom. Sartre is critical of the Cartesian will, which is called 'free' but nonetheless subject to the 'passions of the soul', resulting in a conception of man that is 'simultaneously free and determined' (BN 463).[9] How, he asks, can unconditioned freedom and the determined processes of the psychic life be related? The history of philosophy offers several answers: for the Stoics our passions are to be mastered: we are counselled 'to conduct ourselves with regard to affectivity as man does with respect to nature in general when he obeys it in order better to control it'. But Sartre refuses such an interpretation, offering an objection he deems too 'obvious' to 'waste time' in developing: such a 'trenchant duality is inconceivable at the heart of the psychic unity' (BN 463): 'either man is wholly determined . . . or else he is wholly free' (BN 464).

Such a dismissal looks suspiciously like Sartrean sleight of hand, particularly because, *prima facie*, it seems to directly contradict Sartre's

---

[9] Flynn writes that 'As Sartre sees it, his position rests midway between libertarianism and determinism' (1986: 8); but this is debatable: Webber, e.g., reads Sartre as an 'adamant' indeterminist (2009: 66).

claim concerning bad faith, which is only possible on his account because we are a *duality in unity*.[10] Sartre moves quickly on, saying simply that 'these observations are still not our primary concern', because we should study the will in order better to understand freedom (BN 464). But for Sartre, 'the will is nihilation' (BN 465); as such, how is it distinguishable from freedom?

The will, he writes, is not the privileged manifestation of freedom but presupposes 'the foundation of an original freedom in order to be able to constitute itself as will' (BN 465).

> [T]he will is not a privileged manifestation of freedom but . . . it is a psychic event of a peculiar structure which is constituted on the same plane as other psychic events and which is supported, neither more nor less than the others, by an original, ontological freedom. (BN 474)[11]

Sartre's account of freedom in *Being and Nothingness* is dissatisfying, in places cursory and circular, but we can nevertheless see in this move a clear departure from the Augustinian tradition: Sartre does not locate the entrance of nothingness in a defective will. Rather, the 'original, ontological freedom' is at fault.[12] Where Augustine's account of nothingness—connected as it was to his answer to the question *unde malum?*—sought to avoid laying the responsibility at God's feet, Sartre sees no need to exculpate the divine. In fact *Being and Nothingness* does quite the opposite: it shows philosophically (as his characters do theatrically[13]) that freedom is the source of suffering, guilt, and condemnation. From there it is only a short step to the sentiment of Orestes (in *Les Mouches*), Helen (in *Les Troyennes*), or Racine's Phèdre: it is God who sinned.

I will return to this point in the final section of this chapter. But first, in order to better understand this 'original, ontological freedom' it is useful to consult 'La liberté cartesienne'. In 1946 Sartre published a short anthology of Descartes's texts on freedom—a slim volume with excerpts from the *Principia*, the *Meditations*, the *Discourse*, and the *Passions*, along with excerpts from letters to Father Mesland and

---

[10] Although Morris (2008: 79–81) notes that Sartre uses the word 'duality' in different senses, so a case could be made that the resemblance is superficial.

[11] Here we find an unusual case of Sartre agreeing with Freud: 'For Freud as for us an act can not be limited to itself; it refers immediately to more profound structures' (BN 480).

[12] See Chapter 2 (and Augustine 2010: II.xv.48).   [13] See Chapter 4.

Elizabeth—with this essay as its introduction.[14] It is not long (forty-eight small pages in French), but it is nonetheless revealing: first, for showing which of Descartes's texts Sartre thought worthy of study, and second, for showing the ways in which his own use of those texts played fast and loose with them.[15]

In the fourth meditation, Descartes's analysis of the will suggests at first that its freedom, compared with God's, is something minor: 'my own nature is very weak and limited, whereas the nature of God is immense, incomprehensible, and infinite'.[16] But, when considered in itself, formally ('in the essential and strict sense'), the human will is no less free than God's:

> It is only the will, or freedom of choice, which I experience within me to be so great that the idea of any greater faculty is beyond my grasp; so much so that it is above all in virtue of the will that I understand myself to bear in some way the image and likeness of God.[17]

When we are not forced by any external power, we may or may not choose to do something; we may confirm or negate anything that the intellect proposes to us. But, Sartre suggests, Descartes did not follow his logic to its ultimate consequences—and the reason Sartre cites for this is a 'precaution' which Jedraszewski glosses as 'conformity'.[18] The 'success' of *Augustinus*, Sartre writes, 'lui avait donné des inquiétudes et il ne voulait pas risquer d'être condamné en Sorbonne' (LC 31). In other words, Descartes did not want to go the way of the Jansenists, or he would have gone the way of Sartre.[19]

Consider the world of mathematical problems. In this world, everything is already established: mathematical values and methodology are not altered by a human being solving a particular question. On Sartre's view, this is precisely the kind of world Descartes inhabited. Everything was given by God, and the human mind 'only

---

[14] Jean-Paul Sartre, *Descartes* (Les classiques de la liberté), Paris: Editions des trois collines, 1946.

[15] See Boorsch 1948 for early criticisms of Sartre's 'disdainful' treatment: 'The whole clever dialectic is as neat an exhibition of intellectual legerdemain as can be found' (91); Grimaldi 1987 is more sympathetic to Sartre's reading.

[16] Descartes 1988: 100.   [17] Descartes 1988: 101.

[18] Jedraszewski 1989: 671.

[19] Under the oppressive rule of Cardinal Richelieu, as Walter Rex (1977: 24) writes, men were *embastillés* 'over the question of how sorry to feel for one's sins'! But even so, Sartre's claims are spurious: most probably, as Boorsch writes, 'a posthumous underwriting of Sartrian [sic] Existentialism by Descartes' (1948: 92).

discovers the truth'. This being—God—was 'pure and dense, flawless [*sans faille*], without emptiness' and 'affirmed in me his own weight'. Descartes's God is 'the source of all being and all positivity, and this positivity, this plenum of existence that is a true judgment cannot have its source in me—I who am nothingness—but in him' (LC 30).

In Descartes, as we saw at the beginning of Chapter 4, the Augustinian ontology of being and nothingness has epistemological consequences, and Sartre discusses them explicitly in this essay. In particular he notes that for Descartes, just as the clear view of the Good leads to right action, the distinct vision of the truth leads to assent. 'Because the Good and the True are but one thing: to know Being' (LC 32). For Descartes, we are most free when we do the Good. But this is because, Sartre writes, he erroneously 'substitutes a definition of freedom by the *value* of the act—the freest act is the best one, the one most in conformity with the universal order—instead of defining it by autonomy' (LC 32). If we do not invent '*our* Good', if the Good 'has an independent and *a priori* existence, how could we see it without doing it?' (LC 32–3).

What we see in Descartes's account, Sartre writes, in both the search for truth and the pursuit of the Good, is 'a veritable autonomy of man'—'*but only insofar as he is a nothingness*':

> C'est par son néant et en tant qu'il a affaire au néant, au Mal, à l'Erreur, que l'homme échappe à Dieu, car Dieu qui est plénitude infinie d'être ne saurait concevoir ni régler le néant. Il a mis en moi le positif; il est l'auteur responsable de tout ce qui en moi est. Mais par ma finitude et mes limites, par ma face d'ombre, je me détourne de lui.   (LC 32–3)

It is only by turning away from God that I can be free.

On Sartre's reading, Descartes is not just attempting to align rationalist metaphysics with Christian theology, but to translate—into the vocabulary of the time—this consciousness which has always had the knowledge of being a pure nothingness (LC 30). This freedom of consciousness, for Sartre, is 'one of the most profound intuitions of Cartesian metaphysics'.[20] Sartre's language is rhetorical, even evangelistic: in his discussion of faith, where 'understanding does not provide sufficient reason for the act of faith', he is 'scandalized' to see Descartes's 'autonomous and infinite freedom' suddenly *affected*

---

[20] Grimaldi 1987: 69.

by divine grace and even *disposed* to affirm that which it does not see clearly (LC 29).[21]

But it is clear that on Sartre's view Cartesian freedom—which he explicitly equates with Christian freedom (LC 42)—we are *free only to refuse*. The only free choice is negative.

> A tous ces néants, néant moi-même, je puis dire *non*: je puis *ne pas* me décider à agir, à affirmer. Puisque l'ordre des vérités existe en dehors de moi, ce qui va me définir comme autonomie ce n'est pas l'invention créatrice, c'est le refus. C'est en refusant jusqu'à ce que nous ne puissons plus refuser que nous sommes libres.   (LC 33–4)[22]

Descartes failed to conceive of negativity as productive (LC 39), and the necessary Sartrean corrective, therefore, is that l'homme récupère cette liberté créatrice que Descartes a mise en Dieu' (LC 51). Unless we invent our own 'good', we are only nominally free. So we must refuse grace, and good, if we wish to be free truly.

Scholars have noted the various ways in which Sartre misunderstands or misrepresents Descartes in this work: in particular, Sartre introduces a concept of autonomy that is foreign to Descartes's thinking.[23] The crux of the matter, Jean Boorsch writes, it that 'there is really no common ground between a philosophy which postulates essences as Descartes' does, and a philosophy which declares that essence is ontologically posterior to existence'.[24]

But on my reading *there is a common ground here*, namely a (broadly) Augustinian anthropology of fallenness. Clearly Sartre does not assent to a historical fall (as described in Genesis or by subsequent commentators), but he nonetheless accepts the ontological account of the nothingness of humanity and the suffering-inducing consequences of that nothingness for consciousness—whether alone or with others. Some of these consequences were noetic for Descartes, for whom 'my error and sin' derives from applying my will beyond the scope of matters understood by my intellect—not because God made us poorly,

---

[21] See Descartes 1988: 102: 'Neither divine grace nor natural knowledge ever diminishes freedom; on the contrary, they increase and strengthen it.'

[22] LC 43 says even 'dans la mesure où ils sont néant, ils lui échappent'!

[23] Although those who wish to distinguish Descartes from Augustine may see more continuity between Descartes and Sartre; see, e.g., Hanby's (2003: 8ff.) criticism of Charles Taylor's 'On the way from Plato to Descartes stands Augustine'. On Sartre's use of Descartes see Boorsch 1948; Philonenko 1981.

[24] Boorsch 1948: 92.

but because of a 'privation which constitutes the essence of error'.[25] And they are noetic for Sartre, for reasons we have already seen: for the for-itself self-knowledge is an impossible ideal and 'knowing' the other is an exercise in futility, in which we incessantly oscillate between objectifying and being objectified.

To return to *Being and Nothingness*, Sartre is emphatic that 'human reality is free to the exact extent that it has to be its own nothingness' (BN 475): this is its recurring theme, on which it offers several variations. In Part IV Sartre elaborates three dimensions to this claim:

> first, by temporalizing itself—i.e., by being always at a distance from itself . . . ; second, by rising up as consciousness of something and (of) itself—i.e., by being presence to itself and not simply self, which implies that nothing exists in consciousness which is not consciousness of existing and that consequently nothing external to consciousness can motivate it; and finally, by being transcendence—i.e., not something which would first be in order subsequently to put itself into relation with this or that end, but on the contrary, a being which is originally a project—i.e., which is defined by its end.   (BN 475)

To be free, therefore, *contra* common opinion (as Sartre saw it), is to *choose oneself*. Whereas 'common opinion' called a choice free if 'it is such that it could have been other than what it is', for Sartre freedom consists in self-choice (BN 475). If we go back far enough in an individual's causal regress, we find the original choice (*choix originel*), the prime mover of her present personhood. This 'fundamental project' determines her general manner of being. Each person makes such a choice consciously but *irréfléchie*, without *being conscious* of it— which is to say, without formulating it explicitly. It can be described as a stance—for example, hard and resistant or soft and passive—which explains why my tastes, gestures, actions, and positions (political or moral, for example) have a certain coherence. As Arnaud Tomes writes, the *choix originel* is not 'a choice among possibles but it is this choice by which possibles emerge as such'.[26] Sartre likens the *choix originel* to what psychologists call 'selection', or selective perception (BN 484). Moreover, it is discoverable:

---

[25] See Descartes 1988: 102, 103.

[26] Tomes 2013: 88. Flynn similarly argues that this is not a case of criterion*less* choice (a criticism some critics have levelled against Kierkegaard), but rather a criterion-*constituting* choice (2014: 217).

by going further and further back we have reached the original relation which the for-itself chooses with its facticity and with the world. But this original relation is nothing other than the for-itself's being-in-the-world inasmuch as this being-in-the-world is a choice—that is, we have reached the original type of nihilation by which the for-itself has to be its own nothingness.   (BN 479)

CHOOSING OURSELVES: FORSAKEN AND FORLORN

Sartre admits that choosing ourselves is markedly different from 'being-chosen' (BN 486), but this theological language is not often noted by commentators. In both the Hebrew Bible and the New Testament Jews and Christians are referred to as chosen (Fr. *choisi*, Gr. ἐκλεκτός), and indeed the theological debates concerning predestination that we met in Chapters 2 and 3 concerned whom was chosen by God and whether, in light of grace, humans have any choice at all in the question of their salvation or damnation.[27]

In *Being and Nothingness*, the requirement that we choose ourselves brings with it the 'two-fold "feeling" of [anxiety] and responsibility'. It invokes a *qualitative change* in consciousness: '[Anxiety], abandonment, responsibility, whether muted or full strength, constitute the *quality* of our consciousness in so far as this is pure and simple freedom' (BN 486).

The [anxiety] which, when this possibility is revealed, manifests our freedom to our consciousness is witness of this perpetual modifiability of our initial project. In [anxiety] we do not simply apprehend the fact that the possibles which we project are perpetually eaten away by our freedom-to-come; in addition we apprehend our choice—i.e., ourselves—as *unjustifiable*. This means that we apprehend our choice as not deriving from any prior reality but rather as being about to serve as foundation for the ensemble of significations which constitute reality.

---

[27] Indeed, the Greek ἐκλεκτός can be translated in French as *choisi* or *élu*, both of which appear frequently in the debates about grace and the 'elect'. The New Testament uses *eklektos* several times: see e.g. Matthew 22:14, 24:22, 24:24, 24:31; Mark 13:20, 13:22, 13:27; Luke 18:7, 23:35; Romans 8:33, 16:13; Colossians 3:12; 1 Timothy 5:21; 2 Timothy 2:10; Titus 1:1; 1 Peter 1:2 (Gk: 1:1), 2:4, 2:6, 2:9; see also 2 John 1; 2 John 13; Revelation 17:14.

Unjustifiability is not only the subjective recognition of the absolute contingency of our being but also that of the interiorization and recovery of this contingency on our own account. (BN 486)

Much of this part of *Being and Nothingness* repeats, revisits, or refines notions developed earlier in the work, and indeed, as we have seen, the contingency Sartre expressed in novelistic form in *La Nausée*. But here we see even more clearly that Sartre's for-itself feels forsaken and forlorn on account of its freedom. We are 'perpetually threatened with choosing ourselves' and 'becoming other than we are' (BN 487).

Unlike the anxiety of Kierkegaard, which can be 'educative to faith',[28] prompting the recognition that the self can only choose itself 'from the hand of God',[29] Sartre's consciousness must choose itself again and again, without hope that its former choices will anchor its future self against the fickleness of its own freedom. Against Descartes, Sartre writes that there is no 'succession of instants separated by nothingness ... such that my choice at the instant t cannot act on my choice of the instant $t1$' (BN 487). Rather, every fundamental choice 'defines the direction of the pursued–pursuit at the same time that it temporalizes itself'. The choice, once made, is gone: there is no 'initial thrust' that makes something 'settled', such that I can draw on it in order to 'hold myself within the limits of this choice':[30]

On the contrary, the nihilation is pursued continuously, and consequently the free and continuous recovery of the choice is obligatory. This recovery, however, is not made from instant to instant while I freely reassume my choice. This is because there is no instant. The recovery is so narrowly joined to the ensemble of the process that it has no instantaneous meaning and can not have any. But precisely because it is free and perpetually recovered by freedom, my choice is limited by freedom itself; that is, it is haunted by the specter of the instant. In so far as I shall reassume my choice, the making-past of the process will be effected in perfect ontological continuity with the present. (BN 489)

[28] Kierkegaard 1980: 155.   [29] Kierkegaard 1987: 217.

[30] Neu 1988: 94 disagrees with Sartre: it is 'misleading to conclude that people always have a choice [... and] easier to be misled if one follows Sartre in thinking one is responsible for everything that it makes sense to think of oneself as "negating", where negating is simply imagining an alternative. Sartre tends to think one has a choice so long as one can imagine an alternative, but more is needed for real alternatives and real choices.'

Sartre rejects the Cartesian instant to replace it with his own notion, later citing Dostoevsky's Raskolnikov as an example of 'the [Sartrean] instant', 'the clear and most moving image of our freedom'. Such 'marvelous instants' occur 'when the prior project collapses into the past in light of a new project which rises on its ruins' (BN 498, 497). This might sound like the 'peripateia' or 'recognition' that Goldmann finds lacking in Jansenist tragedy: the moment of 'seeing' we find in the transformative experience of a Jean Valjean or Javert. But it is not; for my freedom can always contest whether the 'instant' really had the meaning I gave it at a former point in time, and the freedom of others can always give the world (and my place in it) values I do not.

It is in this context—of introducing what I will call the *auto-eklekticism* of the for-itself—that Sartre revisits Leibniz,[31] in order to clarify his own theory of freedom by comparison. Again the subject under consideration is Adam. On Leibniz's view, Sartre writes, freedom 'organizes' three different notions:

> that man is free who (1) determines himself rationally to perform an act; (2) is such that this act is understood fully by the very nature of the one who has committed it; (3) is contingent—that is, exists in such a way that other persons committing other acts in connection with the same situation would have been possible. (BN 490)

But, as we have heard already, on this account Adam cannot act otherwise; another act would require the existence of another Adam. The contingency which makes freedom possible, on Leibniz's view, is found in Adam's essence. And for Sartre, herein lies the problem: 'this essence is not chosen by himself but by God' (BN 490):

> Thus it is true that the act committed by Adam necessarily derives from Adam's essence and that it thereby depends on Adam himself and on no other, which, to be sure, is one condition of freedom. But Adam's essence is for Adam himself a given; Adam has not chosen it; he could not choose to be Adam. Consequently he does not support the responsibility for his being. Hence once he himself has been given, it is of little importance that one can attribute to him the relative responsibility for his act. (BN 490)

Clearly, for Sartre, Adam cannot be so defined: Adam's essence follows his existence. He is defined, therefore, 'by the choice of his

---

[31] As discussed in Chapters 5 and 6.

ends'—'by the upsurge of an ekstatic temporalization which has nothing in common with the logical order' (BN 490).

> Thus Adam's contingency expresses the finite choice which he has made of himself. But henceforth what makes his person known to him is the future and not the past; he chooses to learn what he is by means of ends toward which he projects himself—that is, by the totality of his tastes, his likes, his hates, etc. inasmuch as there is a thematic organization and an inherent meaning in this totality. Thus we can avoid the objection which we offered to Leibniz when we said, "To be sure, Adam chose to take the apple, but he did not choose to be Adam." For us, indeed, the problem of freedom is placed on the level of Adam's choice of himself—that is, on the determination of essence by existence.
>
> (BN 490)

Like Leibniz, Sartre affirms that another act of Adam (which implies another Adam) also implies another world. But the world that it implies is not 'a particular organization of co-possibles'; it is rather 'the revelation of another face of the world' which corresponds to another being-in-the-world of Adam. For Leibniz, Sartre writes, 'the chronological order depends on the eternal order of logic', and the possible is an abstract possible. For Sartre, however, 'the order of interpretation is strictly chronological' (BN 491), and the possibility under consideration is internal.

Leibniz's theoretical analysis does not do justice to human reality, which (Sartre says) is 'far more complex' (BN 491). In the human sphere, 'the descending hierarchy of possibles from the final and initial possible to the derived possible which we are trying to understand has nothing in common with the deductive series which goes from a principle to its consequence' (BN 491). Again Sartre returns to the notion of internal relations, because *subjective* possibilities and their relation to choice must be understood in this manner.

> The necessity of perpetually choosing myself is one with the pursued–pursuit which I am. But precisely because here we are dealing with a *choice*, this choice as it is made indicates in general other choices as possibles. The possibility of these other choices is neither made explicit nor posited, but it is lived in the feeling of unjustifiability; and it is this which is expressed by the fact of the *absurdity* of my choice and consequently of my being. Thus my freedom eats away my freedom.   (BN 502)

My existence will condition my essence. But there is no 'a priori number to the different projects which I am'. In order to understand a particular for-itself, 'it is necessary to consult each man's history' to discern how his particular projects are united in the 'global project' which he is (BN 502).[32]

This is not to say that there are no limits to one's choice. Sartre is cognizant that 'the decisive argument' of 'common sense' against freedom reminds us of our impotence:

> Far from being able to modify our situation at our whim, we seem to be unable to change ourselves. I am not 'free' either to escape the lot of my class, of my nation, of my family, or even to build up my own power or my fortune or to conquer my most insignificant appetites or habits. I am born a worker, a Frenchman, an hereditary syphilitic, or a tubercular. The history of a life, whatever it may be, is the history of a failure. The coefficient of adversity of things is such that years of patience are necessary to obtain the feeblest result.   (BN 503)

But, Sartre says, this argument has never really troubled the 'partisans of human freedom': 'Descartes, first of all, recognized both that the will is infinite and that it is necessary "to try to conquer ourselves rather than fortune"' (BN 503). And the way in which we do this, Sartre says, is by recognizing that it is *freedom* 'which constitutes the limits which it will subsequently encounter' (BN 104). The only limit to freedom is freedom itself. And freedom limits itself by *internal negation*: 'the for-itself illuminates the existents in their mutual relations by means of the ends which it posits, and it projects this end in terms of the determinations which it apprehends in the existent' (BN 505).

To be free does not mean 'to obtain what one has wished', Sartre writes, but 'by oneself to determine oneself to wish (in the broad sense of choosing)'. This is the 'technical and philosophical concept of freedom': 'the autonomy of choice' (BN 505). The Sartrean freedom is, therefore, auto-eklektic—the 'self' is ἐκλεκτός, but only by her own choosing: her being and her meaning must not come to her from without.

But there is no avoiding the matter that this fact itself is *unchosen*: 'In fact we are a freedom which chooses, but we do not choose to be free. We are condemned to freedom' (BN 506). Here Sartre revisits his notions of facticity and contingency, writing that 'the fact of not being able to be free is the *facticity* of freedom, and the fact of not

---

[32] Even 'not to choose is, in fact, to choose not to choose' (BN 503).

being able not to exist is its *contingency*' (BN 508), reminding the reader again of the many ways in which we attempt to avoid contingency (or 'justify' our existence):

> [A]mong the thousands of ways which the for-itself has of trying to wrench itself away from this original contingency, there is one which consists in trying to make oneself recognized by the Other as an existence by right. We insist on our individual rights only within the compass of a vast project which would tend to confer existence on us in terms of the function which we fulfill. This is the reason why man tries so often to identify himself with his function and seeks to see in himself only the 'Presiding Judge of the Court of Appeal,' the 'Chief Treasurer and Paymaster' etc. Each of these functions has its existence justified by its end. To be identified with one of them is to take one's own existence as saved from contingency. (BN 507)

The allure of social *divertissement*—the desire to be 'loved or feared',[33] as Augustine called it—can easily lead to bad faith, but such attempts to justify one's existence by means of the other are futile. In the absence of God who sees 'the hidden merits of our souls',[34] the matter does not end there: for 'my neighbor' can also have the effect of challenging my own 'justification' as I see it: in encountering another's freedom I encounter meanings which do not derive from my own projects (BN 530-1). For this reason, Sartre writes, we are 'haunted' by the neighbour:

> There exists, in fact, something in "my" world other than a plurality of possible meanings; there exist objective meanings which are given to me as not having been brought to light by me. I, by whom meanings come to things, I find myself engaged in an already *meaningful* world which reflects to me meanings which I have not put into it. (BN 531)

The neighbour plays an important role in the *situation*. 'The for-itself is free', Sartre writes, 'but *in condition*, and it is the relation of this condition to freedom that we are trying to define by making clear the meaning of the situation' (BN 540). In the *War Diaries* Sartre described the situation as 'the inert resistance of things, ordered in a hierarchy of motivations and a hierarchy of tools. Finally the situation is the world ordering itself as a whole in terms of the inherent possibles of consciousness' (WD 41).

---

[33] Augustine 1961: 244 (X.36).   [34] Augustine 1961: 142ff. (II. 6).

But I am not the only one who orders my possibles. In the *situation* of a given for-itself, the other brings 'a factual limit to my freedom', because by means of that other 'there appear certain determinations which *I am* without having chosen them' (BN 544). Anticipating later twentieth-century work on the 'othering' that occurs on the basis of sex, race, and age, among other things, Sartre writes:

> If my race or my physical appearance were only an image in the Other or the Other's opinion of me, we should soon have done with it; but we have seen that we are dealing with objective characteristics which define me in my being-for-others. As soon as a freedom other than mine arises confronting me, I begin to exist in a new dimension of being... (BN 545)[35]

We have to confront, on his view, the fact that 'I am something which I have not chosen to be' (BN 545).[36] Sartre is emphatic that only freedom can limit freedom; the freedom of an individual for-itself, considered in isolation, can only be limited by its own freedom; but as soon as we recognize the existence of other consciousnesses, we must recognize the existence of other limits (BN 546).

We might take this to mitigate the charges of radical voluntarism that are often levied against Sartre.[37] But his next move makes such mitigation difficult. For these limits are only *experienced* by me if 'I recover this being-for-others which I am and if I give to it a meaning in the light of the ends which I have chosen' (BN 548). The other limits my freedom only insofar, he seems to say, as I let her. For-myself, Sartre writes, I am not a professor or a prostitute, beautiful or ugly. But I may appropriate this being-for-others in my choice of meaning.

As we saw in Chapter 4, some readers of Sartre find his radical freedom inspiring and optimistic, arguing that *Being and Nothingness*

---

[35] E.g. work on internalization of oppressive gaze (e.g. Shelley 2008), performativity (e.g. Butler 1990), etc. Although the directionality of influence is a matter of debate (cf. Fullbrook and Fullbrook 2008), clearly Simone de Beauvoir's *The Second Sex* (1949) and *Old Age* (1970) both address the lived experience of the disjunction between the self as perceived by itself and another (see Kirkpatrick 2014).

[36] 'We must recognize that we have just encountered a real limit to our freedom— that is, a way of being which is imposed on us without our freedom being its foundation' (BN 545).

[37] See, e.g., Murdoch's description of Sartre's 'heady voluntarism' (1999: 21); Neu 1988: 80 on 'unconditional freedom'.

does contain a 'way out' of bad faith and anxiety. But Sartre's treatment of death in BN Part IV gives grounds for scepticism about the
optimistic reading. Again revisiting material introduced earlier in
Being and Nothingness, Sartre writes that now, after having surveyed
the nothingness of consciousness, bad faith, and being-for-others,
death can be properly understood as absurd: 'Death reveals to us
only ourselves and that from a human point of view' (BN 554). We
want to think that no one can die for us (as Heidegger says), and that
our loves, like our lives, are irreplaceable and unique. But Sartre
sounds a Pascalian note, writing that if my acts are considered from
the point of view of their 'function', 'efficacy', and 'result', 'it is certain
that the Other can always do what I do'. The Sartrean person is
vocationless.

Ultimately, all we can do is '*wait for ourselves*', Sartre writes. 'Our
life is only a long waiting'—that is the *structure of selfness*: 'to be
oneself is to come to oneself. These waitings evidently all include a
reference to a final term which would be *waited for* without waiting
for anything more' (BN 559). Christians, Sartre writes, erroneously
take death to be this final term. But the error here is analogous to
Leibniz's error concerning possibility, although this one occurs at the
other end of human existence. For Leibniz, Sartre writes, we are free
because our acts derive from our essence.

> Yet the single fact that our essence has not been chosen by us shows that
> all this freedom in particulars actually covers over a total slavery. God
> chose Adam's essence. Conversely if it is the closing of the account
> which gives our life its meaning and its value, then it is of little
> importance that all the acts of which the web of our life is made have
> been free; the very meaning of them escapes us if we do not ourselves
> choose the moment at which the account will be closed.   (BN 559)

This 'Christian' death, for Sartre, removes '*all meaning from life*' (BN 559;
italics original).

On Sartre's view, however, death is meaningful—but it is 'the
triumph of the point of view of the Other' (BN 563); it is 'the given'
(BN 567) which 'haunts me' (BN 568) because it represents 'a total
dispossession'. 'To die is to exist only through the Other' (BN 565).
Sartre is not content to say this once or twice; he repeats it in several
formulations: 'The unique characteristic of a dead life is that it is a
life of which the Other makes himself the guardian' (BN 562). We
cannot arm ourselves against death, and must consider our projects

independently of death—'not because of our blindness, as the Christian says, but on principle' (BN 568).[38]

The 'dispossession' of death is dramatically expressed in Sartre's best-known play, *No Exit*, and succinctly summarized in its best-known line, 'Hell is—other people!' (NE 45).[39] *No Exit* belongs to the pedagogical theatrical genre of *dialogues des morts* (dialogues of the dead)—a genre to which Fontanelle and Fénelon contributed in the seventeenth century, reviving Lucian. Although the vulnerability of the human subject before her earthly jury is a theme exhibited in many of Sartre's plays, *No Exit* makes this point forcefully.

The play's structure and setting are simple: one act, one scene, one room. There are three characters, each of whom is recently deceased, arriving in hell. The action begins with Joseph Garcin being shown into a Second Empire drawing room. The room is windowless and has no mirrors, with few furnishings. Garcin is surprised; he expected blazing fires, demons, and implements of torture. The valet informs him that there is nothing beyond the room but hallways and more rooms. It is impossible to sleep here, however—and it is always light, and 'one has to live with one's eyes open all the time' (NE 6).

When the second character, Inez, enters the room, she quickly makes it clear that she does not appreciate Garcin's company. He, too, would prefer to be alone, claiming that he wants to 'think things out, you know; to set my life in order, and one does that better by one's self' (NE 9). But the door is locked, and they are trapped spoiling each other's solitude, unable even to close their eyes. The door opens again, and this time Estelle enters, so the room now has a third person's gaze.

The three then share the stories of their deaths. For Estelle: pneumonia, yesterday; Inez: gas inhalation, last week; Garcin: twelve bullets in the chest, last month. It does not take long for the three of them to realize that they have very little in common, apart from

---

[38] As Flynn notes, this marks a significant departure from Heidegger: Sartre takes his distance from Heidegger throughout *Being and Nothingness*, but here 'the contrast is clearest' (2014: 219).

[39] *Huis clos* appeared less than a year after *Les Mouches*. It opened at the Théâtre du Vieux-Colombier, Paris, on 27 May 1944. *Huis clos* is the first of Sartre's plays which is not widely taken to be a direct commentary on the political situation of the time, although it does explore the theme of captivity—a theme of particular relevance to the original audience of occupied Paris, and to the recently captive Sartre. This line 'has been taken as the epitaph on the tomb of his social philosophy' (Flynn 2014: 206).

being recently dead and irritating each other intensely. But this is hell, after all, and as Inez puts it: 'people aren't damned for nothing' (NE 16). The discovery slowly dawns on them that the reason there is no 'torturer' in hell is that they will be torturers to each other: 'Hell is—other people'. In order to subvert the situation they agree to remain in silence, ignoring each other and refusing complicity in torture. But their silence is short-lived, and what follows is as an attempt—with increasing desperation—to gain attention and justification from one at the exclusion of the other.

The hell Sartre sought to portray in *No Exit* is not some other-worldly hereafter. It is a recognizable component of human life here and now—even if it is carried to paroxysm. The capacity of others to judge and condemn us—our *being-for-others*—reveals a challenge to what Nietzsche viewed as Western metaphysics' model of the subject as a 'stiff, steadfast, single individual'.[40] In *No Exit* each of the three characters becomes accuser to his or her companions—whether through words or actions, attention or ignoring, they become each other's tribunal or torment, duelling partner or *terzo incomodo*. Sartre's *troisième personne*, unlike *le tiers* of Levinas,[41] includes no transformative face-to-face encounter: for the only so-called self I can bring to meeting the other is a false one, the product of bad faith. It is the *vie imaginaire* of Pascal, the 'seeming' we project to compensate for our lost being.

Garcin's desire to 'think things out', 'to set [his] life in order' alone (NE 9), is doomed to failure. As Sartre writes in *Being and Nothingness*, being subject to the judgemental gaze of another results in being 'enslaved' by him (BN 291). The syncategorematic self that Sartre describes has no meaning or existence in isolation—and since there is no God to gaze on us with clear and complete vision, we are subject to the clouded and incomplete constructions others make of us. Whereas the Christian God 'sees not as man sees', but 'weighs hearts',[42] for Sartre, my 'heart' can never be known, and a single act (even if it is entirely 'out of character') may become the defining characteristic of my existence in the eyes of others.

On both levels of human existence, therefore—individual and relational—we are divided from ourselves. On the first we are divided from ourselves by time and the freedom of consciousness. On the

---

[40] Nietzsche 1984: 719. [41] See Levinas 1981: 56ff.
[42] See 1 Samuel 16; and, e.g., Augustine 1961: VII.6.

second, we glimpse identity, but it is the identity of the syncategorematic self—a self with no meaning in isolation, and which, given meaning by others, may be a demeaning imprisonment. A harmonious self—and harmonious relations with others—are mirages: like the fruit held just beyond Tantalus' reach.

Sartre's account of being with others, as we saw in Chapter 6, is bleak—Christina Howells calls it 'irremediably pessimistic'.[43] But theologically, it offers a realized eschatology of damnation, a phenomenology of sin from a graceless position. With no clear-sighted God, human selfhood is dependent on the fickle freedom of the other: and on the relentless, objectifying gazes that reduce us to a state of (to use Sartre's phrase) 'original shame'. This is why death is a dispossession: because the 'essence of the relations between consciousnesses is not [Heidegger's] *Mitsein* [being-with]; it is conflict' (BN 451). It is a contest of *libido dominandi*, and when I can no longer compete the enemy wins.

The auto-eklektic for-itself *is* temporalization: *it is not* but *makes* itself. But its creative endeavours are vulnerable to a conflict of interpretations. For what, then, is the for-itself responsible? The self he or she attempts to be or the self others see? In the section on 'Freedom and Responsibility' Sartre writes that his considerations are primarily of interest 'to the moralist [*moraliste*]' (BN 574), and that their 'essential consequence' is that 'man being condemned to be free carries the weight of the whole world on his shoulders; he is responsible for the world and for himself as a way of being' (BN 574).

EXISTENTIAL PSYCHOANALYSIS

Sartre's next step is perplexing. Given that he goes to such lengths to describe the ways in which we flee our freedom and fight the objectifying gaze of the other, it seems patently contradictory that *Being and Nothingness* includes the recommendation of existential psychoanalysis, a process in which we must rely on the other to gain insight into ourselves. But having studied freedom from the point of view of ontology (even if it is 'ontology for moralists'), Sartre ends up with a

---

[43] Howells 1988: 19. For more on Sartre's pessimism, see Flynn 2014: 205; and on the American reception of Sartre in particular, Fulton 1999: 29ff.

problematic freedom—a freedom which cannot save itself from its own predicament. Existential psychoanalysis, though not a 'solution' per se, can help us 'discover the past as choice rather than as conditioning',[44] thereby righting many wrongs Sartre perceives in his non-existential psychoanalytic contemporaries.[45]

Through this process Sartre thinks we can come to see that '[c]hoice and consciousness are one and the same thing' (BN 484): that is, through what Katherine Morris calls 'Sartrean therapy', to rid ourselves of intellectual prejudices and see more clearly.[46] For we not only choose ourselves, but the world through ourselves: 'We choose the world, not in its contexture as in-itself but in its meaning, by choosing ourselves' (BN 485).

Reiterating his earlier criticisms of empirical psychology, Sartre writes that the nature of human freedom is incompatible (or at least, not exhaustively discoverable) with the methods of empirical psychology because the 'objective' view of a person fails to see her in significant aspects.[47] As Christina Howells notes, in his earlier work the *Sketch for a Theory of the Emotions* Sartre plays with two meanings of the French *expérience* in developing this criticism: because phenomenological enquiry is directly concerned with the conditions of experience (*expérience*), it 'has logical and methodological precedence over psychological experiment (*expérience*)'.[48] The human, on Sartre's view, is not reducible to empirical understanding: experience requires more than experiment to be understood.[49]

---

[44] Cannon 2013: 83.

[45] See BN 74, 590ff. Given Sartre's view of death as 'dispossession', it is also intriguing that the two subjects he expresses the desire to analyse using this method (Flaubert and Dostoevsky) are both dead.

[46] See Morris 2008: Chapter 2.

[47] In *Sketch for a Theory of the Emotions* Sartre writes that psychology is concerned with facts (E 2), but to wait upon facts is to prefer 'the accident to the essential, the contingent to the necessary, disorder to order.... The psychologists do not notice, indeed, that it is just as impossible to attain the essence by heaping up the accidents as it is to arrive at unity by the indefinite addition of figures to the right of 0.99' (E 4). See also BN 578ff.

[48] Howells 1988: 8, and, e.g. BN 596: 'knowledge of man must be a totality; empirical, partial pieces of knowledge on this level lack all significance'.

[49] See BN 581. See also BN 589, where Sartre writes of existential psychoanalysis that '[i]ts point of departure is experience; its pillar of support is the fundamental, pre-ontological comprehension which man has of the human person'. He describes its task as 'hermeneutic' (BN 590), which may suggest a fruitful vein of enquiry with respect to Ricoeur's 'hermeneutics of the self' (see Ricoeur 1992: 169 and *passim*).

Human enquiry often engages in the 'ceaseless pursuit' of causes. But the 'infinite regress which has often been described as constitutive of rational research' (and which is not exclusive to empirical psychological investigations) is not a 'childish quest of a "because" which allows no further "why?"'. On the contrary, Sartre writes, it is 'a demand based on a pre-ontological comprehension of human reality and on the related refusal to consider man as capable of being analyzed and reduced to original givens, to determined desires (or "drives"), supported by the subject as properties by an object' (BN 581–2).

Appealing to *les moralistes* to illustrate his point, Sartre argues that the human cannot be reduced in this way. 'The most discerning moralists', Sartre writes, have shown that desire reaches beyond itself.

> Pascal believed that he could discover in hunting, for example, or tennis, or in a hundred other occupations, the need of being diverted. He revealed that in an activity which would be absurd if reduced to itself, there was a meaning which transcended it; that is, an indication which referred to the reality of man in general and to his condition. Similarly Stendhal in spite of his attachment to ideologists, and Proust in spite of his intellectualistic and analytical tendencies, have shown that love and jealousy can not be reduced to the strict desire of possessing a *particular* woman, but that these emotions aim at laying hold of the world in its entirety through the woman.   (BN 583)

It is worth noting that each of the writers Sartre refers to in this passage is known for his Jansenism, but Sartre doesn't explicitly invoke theological categories here, speaking rather of 'man in general' and 'his condition'.[50]

Later in the same paragraph, however, he proceeds to cite 'Catholic novelists' in defence of his view: these novelists see in carnal love its surpassing toward God.[51] He refers to Don Juan as '"the eternally unsatisfied", in sin, "the place empty of God"'. The upshot of these examples is that we must look beneath the 'partial and incomplete aspects of the subject', to rediscover 'the totality of his impulse toward

---

[50] See Chapter 2, 'Pascal' section. Stendahl's education was Jansenist and a famous chapter in Part I of *Le Rouge et le noir* contains a Jansenist education (see Imbert 1970); the writer most frequently mentioned in Proust's *In Search of Lost Time* is Racine, who (as we saw in Chapter 3) was well known for his dramatization of the Jansenist doctrine that the damned are eternally condemned by God (see Thiher 2013).

[51] See Chapter 3, 'Bourgeois Sinners' section.

being his original relationship to himself, to the world, and to the Other, in the unity of internal relations and of a fundamental project' (BN 584) because each individual's 'impulse toward being' is 'purely individual and unique' (BN 584). In successful existential psycho-analysis, when an individual approaches his or her 'fundamental choice', 'the resistance of the subject collapses suddenly and he *recognizes* the image of himself which is presented to him as if he were seeing himself in a mirror' (BN 594).

But individual and unique as each individual may be, every 'impulse toward being' is futile. The for-itself desires to be for-itself-in-itself, to be free as consciousness and reified as being. This is the 'ideal of a consciousness which would be the foundation of its own being-in-itself by the pure consciousness which it would have of itself'. We have already seen that Sartre famously, repeatedly, and explicitly refers to this state as one of condemnation: we are 'con-demned to be free':

> Freedom coincides at its roots with the non-being which is at the heart of man. For a human being, to *be* is to choose himself; nothing comes to him either from without or from within himself that he can receive or accept. He is wholly and helplessly at the mercy of the unendurable necessity to make himself be, even in the smallest details of his exist-ence. Thus freedom is not a being, it is the being of man, that is to say his non-being. ... Man cannot be at times free and at other times a slave: either he is always and entirely free or he is not free at all.[52]

Using explicitly Christian terminology for sin—the *sicut Deus* of Genesis 3:5 and Augustinian tradition—Sartre describes freedom as 'a choice of being God and all my acts, all my projects translate this choice and reflect it in a thousand and one ways' (BN 620). So central is this desire to Sartre's anthropology that he defines man as 'the being whose project is to be God'; 'To be man means to reach toward being God. Or if you prefer, man fundamentally is the desire to be God' (BN 587).[53]

---

[52] BN 463; modified translation. It is interesting to note Marcel's comment on this passage: 'one of the significant and explicit [passages] in all Sartre's work. I do not believe that in the whole history of human thought, grace, even in its most secularised forms, has ever been denied with such audacity or such impudence' (Marcel 2002: 79).

[53] On many theological accounts, this is the very essence of sin: see, e.g., Niebuhr 1937: 95, 97; Bonhoeffer 1998.

At this point Sartre anticipates his objectors, for whom such statements may sound suspiciously like a declaration of human essence.[54] What becomes of freedom if we can choose 'only to be God'? Sartre's answer is that while the meaning of every desire is 'ultimately the project of being God, the desire is never constituted by this meaning; on the contrary, it always represents a particular discovery of its ends' (BN 587). Our ends are pursued in particular empirical situations (and this pursuit constitutes our surroundings as a 'situation' in the Sartrean sense). The desire to be, our 'ontological hunger', is expressed as 'the myriads of concrete desires which constitute the web of our conscious life' (BN 588). The desire to be God can never be realized, so we divide and divert our desire[55]—into smaller, more manageable pursuits.

Several scholars have dedicated ink to Sartre's 'desire to be God', for precisely the reasons Sartre anticipated.[56] After all, as Jonathan Webber points out, if this is a necessary part of human ontology, then it seems to be incompatible with Sartre's earlier claim that human beings can radically escape bad faith. Webber suggests that the problem can be resolved by saying that only those in bad faith have 'to be God' as their fundamental project.[57] Webber draws on the final parts of BN and EH to argue that human beings can deny their desire to be God and, with it, the deception of bad faith.

It will be clear, by this point, that I share the less optimistic reading that, for the Sartre of *Being and Nothingness*, bad faith is 'our original position',[58] as Thomas Flynn puts it.[59] But even if one were to accept Webber's reading of bad faith, the portrait Sartre paints of the world we *reject* in bad faith is still heavily inflected with sin: it is a world we

---

[54] Indeed, Howells writes that for Sartre 'man's essence is defined as his liberty' (1988: 1).

[55] 'Desire', like the for-itself and consciousness, is explicitly defined by Sartre as 'a lack of being' (BN 596).

[56] See, e.g., Mulhall 2005; Morris 2008; King 1974.   [57] Webber 2009: 109.

[58] Flynn 2014: 188.

[59] In Sartre's 1961 eulogy of Merleau-Ponty, Sartre contrasted his 'eidetic of bad faith' with Merleau-Ponty's optimism concerning the outcome of the war (*Situations* IV: 196 n.). As Philonenko observes, Sartre's apology for freedom discomfits the reader—for freedom incessantly betrays itself in bad faith. It is a 'theory of masks', Philonenko writes, a *philosophie du malaise*: 'Firstly, freedom is at the root of my choice of mask. But secondly: I am not the mask. And thirdly, it seems to the Other that I am nothing but it.' If Sartrean freedom is only 'freedom-for-the-mask: this is the foundation of the philosophy of malaise' (1981: 158, 159).

fall into, and existence in it is the inescapable condition of ontological guilt and alienation.

Indeed, this theological inflection has provoked objections in the continental literature: why *God*? Why, Stathis Kouvélakis asks, speak of God at all, even if he is absent or hidden, instead of the simpler, *laïque*, 'totality'? Kouvélakis writes that it could simply be a matter of demonstrating historical provenance (in theological tradition and Christian culture). Appealing to *Questions de méthode*, he assigns Kierkegaard a leading role in a more likely explanation. For Sartre, Kierkegaard's criticisms of Hegel (in particular of totalizing, Hegelian reason) in the name of the irreducibility of lived experience and the tragedy of individual existence marked a decisive philosophical advance, which opened up the subjective dimension. Rejecting the Hegelian identity of God and Spirit, Kierkegaard offered an infinite distance between God and the world. The human is condemned to live in a world empty of divine presence, but it is on account of that very emptiness that the relationship of man to the transcendent must be a *choice*: *choose for yourself!* It must be an act of faith.[60]

We saw in Chapter 4 that Theunissen views *bad faith* as a successor of Kierkegaardian despair, wherein one 'realizes the relation to oneself [is] a misrelation' (2005: 31), and writes that 'In a certain sense, Sartre even incorporates Kierkegaard's theological conception of sin' (2005: 31). But the notion of 'sin' that Sartre incorporates is not Kierkegaard's alone. It unites the seventeenth-century French (Jansenist–Augustinian) ontology of the human person—between being and nothingness—and the Kierkegaardian emphasis on the individual.

We have seen already that '[t]he for-itself is defined ontologically as a *lack of being*', that 'freedom is really synonymous with lack', and that 'the for-itself is the being which is to itself its own lack of being' (BN 586). But it is *its* own lack of being—it misses a mark which is its alone. Sartre's idiom here is clearly Augustinian: the for-itself is defined as *privation*. 'The For-itself is not nothingness in general but a particular privation; it constitutes itself as the privation of *this being*' (BN 638; italics original).

---

[60] Kouvélakis n.d.

Being, for Sartre, 'is an individual venture' (BN 639), and so is nothingness: 'The very nothingness which I am is individual and concrete, as being *this* nihilation and not any other' (BN 619). The way I go about being *this nihilation* can be seen in my engagement with the world, which I try to appropriate through *my* knowing, having, and doing.[61] Constraints of space prevent a full consideration of each of these categories, but in each we see the way the for-itself desires to justify its existence in the face of contingency and challenge the other's gaze with respect to its facticity. Moreover, each of them can be understood in the scheme of the 'threefold concupiscence' of Jansenist Augustinianism.[62]

Very briefly, *knowing*, on Sartre's view, 'is a form of appropriation' (BN 598). Knowledge is never pursued for its own sake. In the *Carnet Midy* one of the *Pensées* Sartre cites concerns *curiosité* (the *libido sciendi*): 'Curiosité n'est que vanité. Le plus souvent on ne veut savoir que pour en parler.'[63] Sartre's analysis in *Being and Nothingness* is similarly inflected with Jansenist pessimism: When I discover a truth, 'It is through me that a facet of the world is revealed; it is to me that it reveals itself. In this sense I am creator and possessor' (BN 598). Because I want to 'possess' truths about the world by knowing them, ultimately this category can be reduced to *having*, which Sartre describes as a 'magical relation'.[64] 'I *am* these objects which I possess, but outside, so to speak, facing myself' (BN 612); 'I am what I have' (BN 612).

Moreover, knowledge and possession are not just forms of self-assertion; they are forms of self-defence: they are 'a defense against others', because 'What is mine is myself in a non-subjective form inasmuch as I am its free foundation' (BN 612–13). Like the *libido sciendi* and *libido dominandi*, Sartre's 'knowing' and 'having' play a fundamental role in the human effort to master the other. To return to *La Poutain respecteuse*, Lizzie can be her customer's accuser—contesting his *moi*, his mentally constructed 'self'—but she cannot contest his money or his status, and ultimately she is taken in by their magic.

---

[61] The French *faire* is behind the word Hazel Barnes translates here as 'doing'; it is worth noting that *faire* could also be rendered 'to make' or 'to create'.
[62] See Chapter 2.   [63] CM 478 (citing L77/B152).
[64] Sartre clearly read J. G. Frazer and uses his notion of the 'magical' here and in other works from the early period. See Anders 1950: 554 for a consideration of its use in *The Sketch for a Theory of the Emotions*.

Knowing and having demonstrate that 'the desire to have' can be reduced still further—ultimately it, too, aims at being in-itself-for-itself,[65] but *'in and through the world'*. 'It is by the appropriation of the world that the project to *have* aims at realizing the same value as the desire to be' (BN 619).[66] This is what Sartre calls *the circuit of selfness*: the world is 'inserted' 'between the for-itself and its being' (BN 619). Unlike God, human reality cannot be *ens causa sui*.

This, Sartre says, is where 'ontology abandons us': at the moment of discovering we are a 'useless passion'.

> [ontology] has merely enabled us to determine the ultimate ends of human reality, its fundamental possibilities, and the value which haunts it. Each human reality is at the same time a direct project to metamorphose its own For-itself into an In-itself-For-itself and a project of the appropriation of the world . . . Thus the passion of man is the reverse of that of Christ, for man loses himself as man in order that God may be born. But the idea of God is contradictory and we lose ourselves in vain. Man is a useless passion.   (BN 636)

But why should ontology 'abandon' us here? On my reading, it is because Sartre's for-itself is a 'fallen freedom', to borrow Gordon Michalson's words, which is 'obligated to save itself but cannot'.[67]

The conclusion of *Being and Nothingness*—for all its promises of an ethics—is bleak. The for-itself is defined there as 'a perpetual project of founding itself qua being and a perpetual failure of this project' (BN 640). In *The Ethics of Ambiguity*, Beauvoir describes Sartre's account as 'tragic', writing that 'As long as there have been men and they have lived, they have all felt this tragic ambiguity of their condition, but as long as there have been philosophers and they have thought, most of them have tried to mask it.'[68] Sartre, on her view, boldly unmasks the tragedy of existence:

> The drama of original choice is that it goes on moment by moment for an entire lifetime, that it occurs without reason, before any reason, that freedom is there as if it were present only in the form of contingency. This contingency recalls, in a way, the arbitrariness of the grace distributed

---

[65] See BN 620, 'Thus my freedom is a choice of being God and all my acts, all my projects translate this choice and reflect it in a thousand and one ways, for there is an infinity of ways of being and of ways of having'; and BN 640: 'Doing and having are both immediately or mediately reduced to the project of being.'

[66] For Sartre as for Girard 'all desire is desire to be' (Girard 1994: 28).

[67] Michalson 1990: 54.   [68] Beauvoir 2000: 7.

by God in Calvinistic doctrine. Here too there is a sort of predestination issuing not from an external tyranny but from the operation of the subject itself.[69]

Sartre's auto-eklektic 'predestination' may have the value of not being 'arbitrary': his freedom is radically egalitarian, condemning one and all.

For Sartre, the doctrine of grace is the root of many evils. Grace creates inequality: a God of election is a God of injustice, and the existence of such a God had been used to justify centuries of human suffering.[70] But though it is tragic and ambiguous, Sartre's paradigm is not as original as Beauvoir here suggests.[71] Let us revisit Pascal's criticism of Calvinism, already cited in Chapter 2:

> *Calvinists*: In creating humanity in Adam God had an absolute will, before regarding any merits and demerits, to save some and condemn others. To this end God made Adam sin, and made all of humanity sin in him, so that, all of humanity being criminal, He would be just in damning those that He had resolved to condemn at their creation, and sent Jesus Christ to save only those that He had resolved to save when He created them . . .
>
> The Calvinists' opinion is so horrible, and strikes the mind so forcefully with its image of God's cruelty, that it becomes unbearable . . .
>
> (OCM 3:766–8)

For Pascal, there are two basic truths about humanity: we are great and we are wretched. We are not 'in the state of our creation',[72] on Pascal's view, because there was a factual fall. Sartre clearly does not subscribe to this history, but he nonetheless describes human existence 'as if' it were postlapsarian:

> Everything happens as if the world, man, and man-in-the-world succeeded in realizing only a missing God. Everything happens therefore as if the in-itself and the for-itself were presented in a state of disintegration in relation to an ideal synthesis. Not that the integration has ever

---

[69] Beauvoir 2000: 40–1.   [70] See Introduction and LE, *passim*.

[71] See Ricoeur's typology of the four basic Western myths: (1) the *drama of creation*; (2) *tragic myths*; (3) the 'philosophical myth' of the *exiled soul*; and (4) the eschatological or anthropological myth of biblical history. On the tragic paradigm, no one is saved and there is no end to suffering. (Ricoeur 1967: 162–77; see Ihde 1971: 115ff. for a useful summary.)

[72] Pascal, *Pensées* L149/B430.

taken place but on the contrary precisely because it is always indicated and always impossible.   (BN 643)

Sartre's account of freedom is, indeed, tragic. But to see it as merely tragic is to miss an important component: namely, that it is an account of *refusal*, an anti-theodicy—it rejects the idea that freedom is a Sufficient Reason. There is reason to object to existence, such as it is. The for-itself 'is such that *it has the right* to turn back on itself toward its own origin' (BN 639; italics added). On Sartre's view, we *have the right* to refuse God and the good and the best of all possible worlds (with all possible Adams)—for that is what it means to be free, and that is what is required of a 'consistent atheistic point of view'.[73]

We have seen in Sartre's analysis of Descartes that we are only free in so far as we choose nothingness, and that, therefore, freedom is *refusal*.[74] Only by refusing God (or the Good, or Grace) can man claim his creative freedom. But before concluding this examination of 'the technical and philosophical concept of freedom', I will consider a final dramatic example.

BARIONA: 'THE WORLD IS AN INTERMINABLE FALL'

Bariona is Sartre's first play, written for his fellow prisoners of war in 1943. Its origins, its obscurity, and its content have drawn some scholarly comment—but surprisingly little.[75] After the war, Sartre deliberately kept it closeted, refusing to allow its performance or publication and calling it 'a bad play'.[76] As one of Sartre's closest

---

[73] EH 53.

[74] 'C'est en refusant jusqu'à ce que nous ne puissons plus refuser que nous sommes libres' (LC 33–4).

[75] During Sartre's lifetime, *Bariona* was performed only once, at Christmas 1940 in the Stalag XII D camp where he was prisoner of war, near Trèves. It was eventually published in a private printing of 500 copies in 1962 (in an *edition dactylographiée* in response to the requests of his fellow prisoners and scholars), and again privately in 1967. An English translation was published in 1970 (see de Coorebyter 2005; Contat and Rybalka 1974, vol. 1: 410–12; Esslin 1970), and it is included in the French *Pléiade* edition of *Théâtre complet*, published in 2005. Despite its availability since 1970 it receives surprisingly little comment in works dedicated to Sartre's literature, and even when it is mentioned (e.g. in Cox 2009: 218) the reference is often passing.

[76] See Contat and Rybalka 1974, vol. 1: 413.

companions in the Stalag remarked, even if the play is not 'chrétienne à proprement parler . . . se déroulerait dans un context de Noël'.[77] It stands in the tradition of medieval mysteries, with angels, shepherds, and wise men: but Sartre took pains to clarify that he was not undergoing a 'spiritual crisis' at the time of its writing.[78] Sartre's use of this myth may have just been pragmatic, simultaneously 'unifying Christians and unbelievers'[79] and building in distance which meant that in a Nazi prison camp, where an outright denunciation of fascism would not have escaped the censors, a message of resistance and hope could nonetheless be conveyed to the audience.

At Stalag XII D Sartre was on friendly terms with many priests, especially the *abbé*, whom, we hear, won Sartre over by both charm and 'the rigorous way in which he made his conduct match his beliefs'. Beauvoir described the *abbé* as having

> a keen sense of what freedom meant; in his eyes Fascism, by reducing men to bondage, was defying God's will: 'God,' he said, 'has so great a respect for liberty that He willed His creatures to be free rather than incapable of sin.' This conviction, coupled with his deep-seated humanism, endeared him to Sartre. During endless discussions, which Sartre became passionately interested in, he argued against the Jesuits in the camp that Christ had become fully man. Jesus had been born, like every child, in filth and suffering; the Virgin had not been granted a miraculous delivery. Sartre backed him up: the myth of the Incarnation lost its beauty if Christ did not take all the ills of our human condition upon him.[80]

Sartre's project—which was encouraged by the *abbé* and which grew from conception to completion in a mere six weeks—was to write something which would unify the 4,500 prisoners in his camp.[81]

The action of *Bariona* (like *Les Mouches*, *Huis clos*, and *Les Troyennes*) unfolds within the space of twenty-four hours. It opens in the home of a tax collector in Roman-occupied Palestine, who has just received the Super-Resident. The latter is travelling through this cultural backwater—a land of 'sorcerers' with a 'belly full of Messiahs' (B 40)—to collect census data and to inform Rome's local representatives of an increase in taxation. Bariona, the leader of the village of Bethaura (near Bethlehem), is a disillusioned man, whose faith in the justice of Rome has been shattered.

---

[77] Perrin 1980: 65.   [78] Contat and Rybalka 1974, vol. 1: 412.
[79] Sartre, cited in Contat and Rybalka 1974, vol. 1: 412.
[80] Beauvoir 1962: 404–5.   [81] See de Coorebyter 2005: 15.

Upon hearing the Super-Resident's message of increased taxation, he protests that Bethaura—with an aging populace and little arable land—cannot bear the weight. Bethaura is 'dying' (B 46).

The Super-Resident is unmoved by his account: the tax is what it is. Bariona responds by calling together the elders (and other residents) of the village, declaring that 'life is one long defeat . . . and the greatest folly in the world is hope' (B 47). Here we begin to see why some commentators take Bariona to be one of Sartre's earliest existential heroes, who 'repeatedly alienates those he fights for through his espousal of nihilistic, inhuman values'.[82] He proposes an unwelcome solution to the problem the Bethaurans face:

> BARIONA: [W]e should not resign ourselves to the fall, for resignation is unworthy of man. That is why I say to you: our souls must accept despair. . . . My friends, close your hearts to your sorrow, be strong and firm for the dignity of man lies in his despair. Here is my decision: we will not rebel. . . . We will pay the tax so that our wives should not suffer. But the village will entomb itself with its own hands. You'll have no more children. I have spoken.
>
> FIRST ELDER: What! No more children?
>
> BARIONA: No more children. No more sex with our wives. We do not wish to perpetuate life, to prolong the sufferings of our race. We will not beget new life. We will use up our lives in the contemplation of evil, injustice, and suffering. And then, in a quarter of a century, the last of us will be dead . . . . nothing of us will remain on this earth, nor in the minds of men. (B 47)

Moreover, there will be no one left to tax. Bariona asks them to swear 'before the God of Vengeance and Anger, before Jehovah' (B 48) that they will abstain from creating any more life, from prolonging the agony of existence (and the possibility of oppression).

Then Bariona's wife, Sarah,[83] reveals that she is pregnant. Bariona asks her to 'go to a sorcerer', but Sarah insists that even if she 'were certain that [her child] would betray me, even were he to die on the cross like a thief, cursing me, I would still give birth to him' (B 49).

---

[82] Mohanty 1974: 1097.

[83] The name 'Sarah' may be an allusion to the story of Abraham and Sarah's infertility (Gen. 11:30); prior to the action of the play Bariona and his wife had long desired children.

Bariona attempts to persuade her that nothing, no number of tears, can relieve another's suffering, and that the suffering of their child is inevitable. It isn't worth it. 'To have a child', he says,

> is to approve of the creation from the bottom of your heart, it is saying to God who torments us, 'Lord, all is well and I give thanks to you for having made the universe.' Do you really want to sing that hymn? Can you take it upon yourself to say: if the world were remade, I would make it just as it is? Let things be, my sweet Sarah, let things be. Existence is a frightful leprosy which gnaws at us all and for which our parents were guilty. (B 51)

After this exchange the villagers ask what, if anything, might change Bariona's mind. An angel, he says: a direct revelation from that vengeful God.

But when this comes to pass, and an angel delivers the message of Christ's birth to Bethauran shepherds, Bariona resists their good news. His heart, he declares, is 'thrice hardened', 'against the gods, against men, against the world'. Like Ivan Karamazov, Bariona does not wish to accept his ticket:

> BARIONA: I will not ask for mercy and I will not say thank you. I will not kneel before anyone; I will place my dignity in my hatred, I will take exact count of all my sufferings, and of those of other men. I want to be the witness and the scales of everybody's misery. I gather it and keep it in myself like a blasphemy. Like a pillar of injustice I want to set myself up against heaven; I will die alone and unreconciled, and I want my soul to take up a resounding, incensed outcry to the stars.
>
> CAIAPHUS: Take care, Bariona! God has given you a sign and you refuse to understand it.
>
> BARIONA: God will show his face between the clouds and I would still refuse to understand it, for I am a free man; and against a free man, even God can do nothing. (B 61)

He tells the shepherds and villagers to go home. 'The Messiah has not come, and if you would like to know what I think, he will never come. This world is an interminable fall, you know that only too well. The Messiah would be someone who could arrest this fall, who could suddenly change the whole course of nature and could make the world bounce like a ball' (B 62). Instead of succumbing to attractive fictions, Bariona urges his people to 'look [their] misery straight in the face, for the dignity of man is in his despair' (B 64).

But after the angel's message has been disregarded, the three wise men arrive. They are looking for Bethlehem, proclaiming the birth of the Messiah. Balthazar—the character played by Sartre in the 1940 production—addresses Bariona. The wise man enjoins him, despite his suffering, to hope. He should hope, Balthazar says, because

> [f]or you more than for anyone else Christ has come down on to the earth. For you more than for all others, because you suffer more than them. The Angel does not hope, for he rejoices in his happiness, for God has given him everything. The pebble does not hope at all, for it lives stupidly in a perpetual present. But when God fashioned the nature of man, he melted together hope and anxiety. For man, you see, is always more than he is. You see that man there, his flesh is solid, rooted to the ground by two large feet and you say, stretching out your hand to touch him: he is there. But that is not true: Wherever a man may be, Bariona, he is always elsewhere.   (B 64)

Bariona remains unconvinced, but the villagers—including his wife, Sarah—have faith and leave Bethaura in search of the Christ-child. Alone, Bariona reflects on their idiocy, and the preposterousness of the idea that God might become man.

> A God, to be changed into a man? What a fairy tale! I don't see what could possibly tempt him into our human condition. . . . A God change himself into a man? The all-powerful in the heart of his glory contemplating the lice who swarm on the old crust of the earth and pollute it with their excrement! Can you imagine him saying 'I want to be one of those vermin'? That makes me laugh.   (B 66)

And yet, if God were to become man for his sake,

> I should love him to the exclusion of all the others, it would be as if there were a blood bond between him and me, and I would not find it too much to give my life out of gratitude. Bariona is not ungrateful. But what God would be foolish enough to do that? Not ours, certainly. He has always shown himself to be proud.   (B 67)

At last Bariona decides to go to Bethlehem, to see for himself. But his 'conversion' is half-hearted; he stands outside the stable, he does not enter it. Balthazar approaches him from within, addressing his misgivings.

> Listen: Christ will suffer in the flesh because he is a man. But he is God also, with all his divinity, he is beyond that suffering. And we, the men

made in God's image, we are beyond all our suffering to the extent that we resemble God ...   (B 79)

Christ has come to redeem us; he has come to suffer and to show us how suffering should be treated. For we do not have to dwell on it, nor make it a matter of honour to suffer more than others, nor resign ourselves to suffer. . . , *It is you who give it its meaning and make it what it is.*   (B 80)

When the news of the Romans' intent to kill the infant reaches Bariona's ears, he is impassioned. He leads the effort to relocate Jesus, Mary, and Joseph so that they will escape the oppressor— even if it means sacrificing his own life, or the lives of those under his governance.

'AGAINST A FREE MAN, EVEN GOD CAN DO NOTHING'

Bariona is, as Sartre intended it to be, 'a remarkably ingenious treatment of the Nativity on two different levels, so as to appeal to both Christians and non-believers in the prison-camp audience'.[84] The problem of polyphony is obvious in this play, which leaves open politico[85]/philosophical interpretations[86] of various kinds: as his fellow prisoner Marius Perrin remarked, 'Each read what they desired' in it.[87] Perhaps it is simply anti-authoritarian, with no Saviour and no conversion; rather, Bariona stands against the Romans, which just happens to place him on the side of Christ.

What previous readings there are usually take the play's message to be proto-existentialist, citing only (or disproportionately) the lines of

[84] Weightman 1970: 31; see also Sartre's comments on the choice of the Nativity theme in Contat and Rybalka 1974, vol. 1: 412.

[85] E.g. Mohanty 1974: 1097 and Weightman 1970: 31, according to which this is a 'first draft of *Les Mouches*'. Judaken (2006: 70–4) brings out a further element in the play, reading it as a commentary on anti-Semitism which anticipates Sartre's *Anti-Semite and Jew*.

[86] E.g. Esslin's (1970: 36), according to which in embodying his philosophy in the concept of the Saviour: 'the coming of Christ stands for the irruption of *freedom* into the dreary contingency of the world. That God could become man simply means that man can transcend himself, that man is free: "You are light, Bariona. Oh, if only you knew how light man is! . . . The world and yourself . . . are a perpetual gratuitous gift to yourself."'

[87] Perrin 1980: 103.

Balthazar (the role played by Sartre himself in Stalag XII D) in their analysis.[88] But there is a theological reading to be made, too, on which a different type of anti-authoritarianism is at play. Before his 'conversion' Bariona sounds much like the contingency-obsessed Sartre of the 1930s. He sees existence as a 'defeat' and the best posture to adopt with respect to it, 'despair'. Like Roquentin in *La Nausée*, he attempts to cleanse himself from 'the sin of existing' (NA 251). But instead of adopting some project of transcendence—e.g. writing a novel for posterity—Bariona wishes to cleanse the world of sin by cutting off the line of sinners. In a reverse formation of hereditary sin, Bariona wishes to rule out evil and oppression—to halt the 'interminable fall' of the world—by contributing no one further to do the falling.

A polyphonic piece such as this, considered alone, would make a shaky foundation for my case. But taken in conjunction with Sartre's other works of the early, anti-humanist period, it can contribute to the cumulative case that Sartre was preoccupied not only with that 'critical cliché',[89] freedom, but with problems that have always been inseparable from it in the Augustinian tradition: the problem of evil and its origin in *nothingness*, or original sin.

Sartre is not a nihilist; the message of Balthazar and of the *choix originel* is that *we give and make meaning*. But for the Sartre of *Being and Nothingness*, to look freedom in the face means to see that the future will announce the ruin of my projects. This is not the best of all possible worlds. Freedom is tainted by nothingness, and it has painful psychological, epistemological, and ethical consequences—the human, as we saw in Chapter 6, exists in a state of original shame and *ontological guilt*. Sartre clearly rejects Leibnizean optimism: how could this freedom be a sufficient reason? But this results in a pessimism more thorough-going than the Jansenists': the for-itself is free *to the extent that it refuses* any possibility of grace.

For Sartre's interlocutors—Descartes and Leibniz—freedom got God off the theodical hook. But for Sartre freedom *is* the hook. Read as an anti-theodicy in this way, Sartre becomes a theologian of refusal. But in avoiding one theological determinism Sartre falls prey to another: for though he is free to refuse grace he cannot refuse nothingness.

---

[88] See, e.g., Flynn 2014: 172–4.   [89] Howells 1988: 1.

CONCLUSION OF PART III

Having completed our part-by-part examination of *Being and Nothingness*, we have now seen that after introducing 'the problem of nothingness' in his Introduction, Sartre's consideration of the lived experience of nothingness (with respect to identity, anxiety, bad faith, embodiment, and relations with others) is indebted to French theological descriptions of the lived experience of *néant* qua sin. The next chapter considers Sartre's account of love before arguing that Sartre's phenomenological ontology is a useful resource for contemporary hamartiology.

Part IV

Toward a Sartrean Hamartiology

8

Death of God, Death of Love

The Hermeneutics of Despair

> Philosophers have measured mountains,
> Fathom'd the depths of seas, of states, and kings,
> Walk'd with a staff to heaven and traced fountains:
> But there are two vast, spacious things,
> The which to measure it doth more behove:
> Yet few there are that sound them; Sin and Love.[1]

I have so far made the claim that *Being and Nothingness* can be read as (a) a phenomenology of sin; and (b) as anti-theodicy. I have also taken pains to say that Sartre refused 'le statut théologique',[2] but that attention to the theological themes in *Being and Nothingness* brings new aspects of the text to light.

In 1943, the same year that *Being and Nothingness* was published, Sartre published a review of Georges Bataille's *Inner Experience*, in which he wrote:

> There are people you might call survivors. Early on, they lost a beloved person—father, friend, or mistress—and their lives are merely the gloomy aftermath of that death. Monsieur Bataille is a survivor of the death of God. And, when one thinks about it, it would seem that our entire age is surviving that death, which he experienced, suffered, and survived. God is dead. We should not understand by that that He does not exist, nor even that he now no longer exists. He is dead: he used to speak to us and he has fallen silent, we now touch only his corpse.   (NM 234)

---

[1] George Herbert, 'Agony'.   [2] Sartre and Verstraeten 2010: 19.

Clearly, the silence of the transcendent is no new phenomenon. But for the Sartre of *Being and Nothingness*, the death of God heralds other, immanent, deaths.[3]

In the last chapter we saw that Sartre refers to sin as 'the place empty of God' (BN 584). But it is not only 'being' that escapes the for-itself when God is absent: so does love. In the history of Christian doctrine sin has been said to have many antonyms. It is often juxtaposed with 'salvation', 'atonement', and 'grace'. As nothingness it opposes being. But in the Jansenist tradition from which Sartre drew, sin as 'concupiscence' (*concupiscentia*) was juxtaposed with grace as *love* (*caritas*).[4] The Christian God, according to John's Gospel, *is* love.[5] And Sartre's account in *Being and Nothingness* presents the world without that God as loveless. We saw at the conclusion of Chapter 2 that in *What Is Literature?* Sartre wrote that '*God, if* he *existed*, would be as the *mystics* have seen him, in a situation in *relationship* [*rapport*] to man' (WL 14). But on Sartre's account, as we shall see, in the absence of such a God, human love—indeed, *relationality*—is a ruse.

In this final chapter, I argue (i) that Sartre's account of love provides further evidence of the Jansenist inflection of his pessimism. On this basis, I make the case that (ii) *Being and Nothingness* presents a 'hermeneutics of despair' (to adapt Ricoeur's phrase). I then ask (iii) whether—and if so, *how*—this reading of Sartre might usefully inform contemporary hamartiology, arguing that some theological categories (such as sin and love) cannot be known merely conceptually, but must be acknowledged personally. Finally (iv) I present the 'original optimism' of the Christian doctrine of sin, which is lacking in the situation Sartre describes.

THE RUSE OF RELATIONALITY

In a widely cited passage in *The City of God* Augustine describes the two cities as 'created by two kinds of love: the earthly city was created by self-love reaching the point of contempt for God, the Heavenly

---

[3] By 'immanent' I do not mean 'immanent in the material (or *en soi*)' in the Sartrean sense (or at least in the sense Beauvoir gives the term 'immanent' in *The Second Sex*), but rather in the sense used by Badiou, whereby theological categories such as 'grace' are reconceptualized without a divine transcendent.

[4] Thweatt 1980: 80–1.   [5] 1 John 4:8.

City by the love of God carried as far as contempt of self'.[6] Augustine uses the rhetoric of antithesis to sharpen his point: the foundations of heaven and hell consist in the objects and good order of our loves. Unlike some later Christian thinkers, Augustine is clear that *whether* one should love is not at stake. Rather, the question is *what*. 'Are you told not to love anything? Not at all! If you are to love nothing, you will be lifeless, dead, detestable, miserable. Love, but be careful what you love.'[7]

For Augustine, human love must be derived from and ordered by the love of God. If it is not, it is sin—for sin, on his view, is not only a turning away from being (as we saw in Chapter 2) but *disordered love*. To put it another way, self-love of the fallen kind prevents the love of other, whether human or divine.

For Sartre, by contrast, refusing anything that comes 'from without' (BN 463) means not only refusing grace, but refusing love. We saw in Chapter 1 that Sartre's atheism is ambiguous. 'God is dead,' he writes, 'but man has not, for all that, become atheistic. Today, as yesterday, this silence of the transcendent, combined with modern man's enduring religious need, is the great question of the age' (NM 235). Moriarty notes that his pronounced emphasis on divine hiddenness is one of Pascal's points of departure from Augustine, who spoke of 'les psaumes chantés par toute la terre' (the psalms chanted by the whole earth).[8] In the post-Cartesian world, Pascal thought, these can be heard only with the ears of faith. On Pascal's view, only Scripture can reveal that there is another way between pride and despair: the Redeemer, Jesus Christ. But purely natural arguments—without any Revelation—can establish the fact of corruption and provide rational grounds for original sin.[9]

In *Philosophical Myths of the Fall* Stephen Mulhall wrote of Nietzsche, Heidegger, and Wittgenstein that their philosophical accounts of human life include 'recognizable descendants' of the Christian doctrine of original sin,[10] on view of which human beings

---

[6] Augustine 2003: XIV.xxviii.593.
[7] *Enarr. In Ps.* 31.2.5; cited in Gilson 1961: 135. One of the 'capital themes' that Augustinian theologians would give French Classicism was *l'amour de soi* (or *l'amour propre*, in the idiom of the time).
[8] Augustine, *Confessions* IV.iv.8; cited in *Pensées* L 1/S 37/LG 1.
[9] Moriarty 2006: 125.   [10] Mulhall 2005: 11.

stand in need of redemption.[11] In each thinker he considers—as
I have argued with respect to 'nothingness' in Sartre—there is 'something deep and determining in human nature'[12] which closely resembles original sin. But, Mulhall writes, they lack 'the inherent optimism
of the original'.[13]

On Sartre's view as expressed in *Being and Nothingness*, a 'consistently atheistic point of view'[14] involves recognizing precisely this: that
the for-itself has little reason to be optimistic. We are perpetually
haunted by nothingness, and brought face to face with the unrealiz-
ability of our ideals. But encountering them piecemeal (as they occur
in *Being and Nothingness*) may obscure how *theological* Sartre's
'unrealizables' are. In addition to the unrealizable unity of being
('unity of the for-itself') (BN 102), we also find 'the beautiful' (BN
218); 'unity with the other' (BN 388); God (BN 473, 'as in-itself-for-
itself' and 'unrealizable Third'); and love (BN 388). Late in *Being and
Nothingness* Sartre writes that 'we are surrounded by an infinity of
unrealizables', but '[c]ertain among these unrealizables we feel vividly
as irritating absences' (BN 548). Some, he says, 'have impressed us
more than others' and have 'become the object of psychological
descriptions' (BN 549).

Before proceeding to examine the 'irritating absence' that is love,
on Sartre's account, we must note that Sartre's rejects the realizability
of the human desire to be *sicut Deus* in all respects but one: we saw
in Chapter 4 that self-coincidence escapes us—we cannot *be* like
Yahweh, who can say 'I am that I am.'[15] Neither can we be *ens causa
sui*—we are not our own foundations. The only realizable *locus* of
godlikeness in Sartre's account is *freedom*. As we saw in Chapter 7,
Descartes took freedom of choice to be 'above all' that by which he
understood himself 'to bear in some way the image and likeness of
God'.[16] But on Sartre's reading of Christian freedom we are *free only to
refuse* (LC 42). The only free choice is negative.

In the Christian tradition, relationships play a pivotal role in
understanding nothingness and sin as 'the urge towards relationless-
ness and dissociation'.[17] And in Sartre, behind each claim of human

---

[11] Mulhall 2005: 118.   [12] Mulhall 2005: 121.   [13] Mulhall 2005: 123.
[14] EH 53.
[15] Nor even can we accept the Apostle Paul's claim: 'By the grace of God I am what
I am' (1 Corinthians 15:10).
[16] Descartes 1988: 101.   [17] Jüngel 2001: 113.

love we find only an 'irritating absence', an ideal realizable in neither fact nor theory ('Unity with the Other ... is *in fact* unrealizable') (BN 387–8). We *cannot* love self or other, and what cannot be achieved at all cannot be ordered. We have already seen the Hegelian aspect of this part of *Being and Nothingness* in Chapter 6: 'conflict is the original meaning of being-for-others' (BN 386). But Sartre's account also exhibits themes common to the pessimism of the Jansenists and *moralistes jansenisants*, according to whom all love is ultimately reducible to *amour-propre*, the *libido dominandi* in disguise. The reason for this *original* conflict is that 'The Other holds ... the secret of what I am.' In the absence of God, *the other is my witness* and the self-known and self-knowing are irreconcilably at odds, for though 'I am responsible for my being-for-others ... I am not the foundation of it' (BN 386).

Sartre thinks that Love, therefore, is a project of recovery of being:

> Thus to the extent that I am revealed to myself as responsible for my being, I *lay claim* to this being which I am; that is, I wish to recover it, or, more exactly, I am the project of the recovery of my being. I want to stretch out my hand and grab hold of this being which is presented to me as *my being* but at a distance—like the dinner of Tantalus; I want to found it by my very freedom.   (BN 386)

But I can only do so, on Sartre's view, if I assimilate the freedom of the other. 'Thus my project of recovering myself is fundamentally a project of absorbing the Other' (BN 386–7). For Sartre, there is no room for two selves; intersubjective relationality is a ruse.

In the absence of a divine witness, we turn to the human other to justify our existence, reducing the other to a means to that end:

> To be other to oneself ... is the primary value of my relations with the Other. This means that my being-for-others is haunted by the indica-tion of an absolute-being which would be itself as other and other as itself and which by freely giving to itself its being-itself as other and its being-other as itself, would be the very being of the ontological proof—that is, God.   (BN 387)

My being can only be recovered, Sartre writes, 'if I get hold of this [the Other's] freedom and reduce it to being a freedom subject to my freedom' (BN 388).

Starting from the simple question 'Why does the lover want to be *loved*?', Sartre argues that the answer cannot simply be physical desire or desire for possession; such desires are capable of satisfaction. Rather, the lover's goal is to 'capture a "consciousness"'. Sartre dismisses simple ownership as the motivating factor, and neither can it be a question of power: 'The tyrant scorns love, he is content with fear' (BN 389). The lover's goal cannot be the beloved's enslavement, because the lover does not want to be the object of a 'passion which flows forth mechanically' (BN 389): this would make him feel that 'both his love and his being are being cheapened'. What the lover really desires is 'a special type of appropriation': 'to possess a freedom as a freedom'.

In desiring love,

> the Lover wants to be "the whole world" for the beloved. . . . He is and consents to being an *object*. But on the other hand, he wants to be the object in which the Other's freedom consents to lose itself, the object in which the Other consents to find his being and his *raison d'être* as his second facticity . . .   (BN 389)

> It is in the capacity of an end already chosen that the lover wishes to be chosen as an end.   (BN 390)

Between being and nothingness, we are haunted by our lack of completeness. Sartre agrees with Sarah Coakley and longstanding theological tradition that 'desire is the constellating category of self-hood',[18] but for Sartre, our desire is not *for God*, but to be like him—to be *sicut Deus*, as we saw in Chapter 7. And in desiring the love of another, we desire to be seen by a look that places us at the centre of the world.[19] Yet, Sartre says, we cannot escape feelings of uneasiness and shame, because

> I apprehend and experience myself in my being-for-others as that which can always be surpassed towards something else, that which is the pure object of a value judgment, a pure means, a pure tool. My uneasiness stems from the fact that I assume necessarily and freely that being which another makes me be in an absolute freedom. "God knows what I am for him! God knows what he thinks of me!" This means "God knows what he makes me be." I am haunted by this being which I fear to encounter someday at the turn of a path, this being which is so strange

---

[18] Coakley 2013: 58.

[19] '[T]o want to be loved is to want to be placed beyond the whole system of values posited by the Other and to be the condition of all valorization and the objective foundation of all values' (BN 391; see also BN 583).

to me and which is yet *my being* and which I know that I shall never encounter in spite of all my efforts to do so. (BN 390-1)

Up to this point, Sartre says, his description aligns with Hegel's master/slave dialectic: 'What the Hegelian Master is for the Slave, the lover wants to be for the beloved. But the analogy stops here, because the lover wants to be a *chosen one*' (BN 392). But this choice must not be relative and contingent: 'The lover is irritated and feels himself cheapened when he thinks that the beloved has chosen him *from among others*.' He hates the idea that another combination of circumstances may not have resulted in their togetherness: 'his love becomes one love among others and is limited by the beloved's facticity and by his own facticity as well as the contingency of encounters. . . . *Actually what the lover demands is that the beloved should make of him an absolute choice*' (BN 392, emphasis added).

We are not satisfied with being auto-eklektic, and in the absence of being chosen by God we desire another absolute. We want to be made God *by another*, for only God's being is absolute choice (BN 392). The attraction of love, Sartre writes, is that in it 'my facticity is *saved*'. The contingent and unchosen aspects of my existence are:

no longer this unthinkable and insurmountable given which I am flee-ing; it is that for which the Other freely makes himself exist; it is an end which has given to himself. . . . My existence *is* because it is required. . . . Whereas before being loved we were uneasy about that unjustified, unjustifiable protuberance which was our existence, whereas we felt ourselves "*de trop*," we now feel that our existence is taken up and willed even in its tiniest details by an absolute freedom which at the same time our existence conditions and which we ourselves will with freedom. *This is the basis for the joy of love when there is joy: we feel that our existence is justified.* (BN 393, emphasis added)

But this joy is deceptive. Even the language of love, on Sartre's view, is designed to deceive. 'Especially in seduction language does not *aim at giving to be known* but at causing to experience' (BN 395). Sartre again invokes the concept of magic to describe the workings of language: 'Thus the word is *sacred* when I employ it and *magic* when the Other hears it. Thus I do not know my language any more than I know my body for the Other. I can not hear myself speak nor see myself smile' (BN 396). In short, on Sartre's view, 'love is the demand to be loved' (BN 397); it is 'in essence the project of making oneself be loved' (BN 397). The 'true ideal of love's enterprise' is alienated freedom. 'But it is the one who wants to be loved who by the mere fact of wanting someone to love him alienates his freedom' (BN 397).

The auto-eklektic man, in short, should scorn love. It is a radical deception, in which I demand of the other that he should do what I cannot: found my being as a privileged object. But this foundation is fake and flimsy, and '[t]he problem of my being-for-others remains therefore without solution' (BN 398). All it takes to disillusion the mutual deception of lovers is the gaze of a third person. Under an outsider's gaze, lover and beloved are objectified: 'Immediately the Other is no longer for me the absolute transcendence which founds me in my being; he is a transcendence-transcended, not by me but by another.... Such is the true reason why lovers seek solitude. It is because the appearance of a third person, whoever he may be, is the destruction of their love' (BN 399).[20]

Unlike 'le tiers' of Levinas—which is 'the limit of responsibility and the birth of the question: What do I have to do with justice?'[21]— Sartre's third person is a destroyer. Love therefore, as a fundamental mode of being-for-others, contains 'the seed of its own destruction', its 'triple-destructibility'. First, it is a deception, which takes in the beloved with an illusory reference to infinity. Second, the other's 'awakening' is always possible: his love is contingent and at any stage he may make me appear as an object. Third,

> love is an absolute which is perpetually *made relative* by others. One would have to be alone in the world with the beloved in order for love to preserve its character as an absolute axis of reference—hence the lover's perpetual shame (or pride—which here amounts to the same thing). Thus it is useless for me to have tried to lose myself in objectivity; my passion will have availed me of nothing. The Other has referred me to my own unjustifiable subjectivity—either by himself or through others.
>
> (BN 399)

Clearly, the love Sartre discusses here is romantic; it is a love that seeks and fails to fulfil the lover's lack. But his critique extends to all human loves: every profession of love, on his view, is a masquerade— behind which disguise lies sadism or masochism.

---

[20] See BN 437–9 on the role of the 'third person', who, in contrast to Levinas's *le tiers*, alienates my possibilities and the other's (see Levinas 1981: 56ff.).
[21] Levinas 1981: 157.

The mask may be different in cases of non-romantic love, but it hides the same battle of *libido dominandi*, duelling *amour-propres*. Sartre is by no means the first to note that *amour-propre* masquerades not only as *eros*, but as *agape* and *philia*. In non-romantic cases, too, we can pay selective attention to our motivations, deceiving ourselves about why we profess words or perform acts of love. It is more acceptable to crowdfund an intercontinental trip in the name of humanitarian or missionary work than it is to say 'please pay for me to see the world and increase my social capital', so we hide the latter components from reflective consciousness. It is easier to justify carbon footprints made for 'the good of humankind' or 'the glory of God' if we overlook (or at least minimize) the probable byproduct that my glory and good will increase along the way. Sartre's distrust of love is evident in many of his writings, but especially in the 1955 play *Nekrassov*, which can be summarized in the line: 'Everybody means harm' (N 137). For the down-and-out character Georges, even acts of philanthropy are included in this maxim: they reduce their recipients to mere objects, cast-offs we leave behind in the wake of our own self-aggrandizement (N 176).

Sartre might thus be seen to resemble the masters of suspicion: 'Behind what professes to be love of God and neighbour they regularly find love of self, disguised beyond recognition, at least to those who perpetrate this pious fraud' (Westphal 1998: 9). But Sartre's rejection of love of God results in more than suspicion regarding the possibility of love of neighbour. The atheism of *Being and Nothingness* is not a humanism.[22] Wittingly or unwittingly, Sartre is what Leszek Kołakowski described as 'The most legitimate heirs of Pascal', because he 'display[s] to us the absurdity of a world abandoned by God'.[23] On Sartre's view, this world is loveless: I can participate in attempts to hide its lovelessness by collaborative works of bad faith, but ultimately relationality is a 'ruse'.

Sartre's treatment of love admittedly exhibits 'that peculiar taste for philosophical melodrama which has so alienated sceptical Anglo-Saxons from their excitable Continental colleagues'.[24] But it also exhibits recurring philosophical questions about the nature and possibility of

---

[22] See Introduction, n. 48. Geroulanos notes Sartre's shift from 'an antihumanist ambivalence' in *Being and Nothingness* to a minimal humanism in his postwar writing (2010: 9).
[23] Kołakowski 1995: 186.   [24] Caws 1979: 66.

love. Why should I love one person and not another or many? How can we (changing creatures) love another, whose only constant (*pace* Heraclitus) is change?[25] Is all love self-interest in disguise?

The reader's instinct may be, like mine, to protest: it is not as bad as that! But Sartre's love-scepticism, inadmissibly dark as it may seem at first sight, anticipates many of the problems that arose in twentieth-century analytic philosophy of interpersonal love. If one takes a 'union' view, like Roger Scruton, claiming that love exists 'just so soon as reciprocity becomes community: that is, just so soon as all distinction between my interests and your interests is overcome',[26] then can one ever claim to love the beloved for her own sake? Is such union desired for the good of the other or the self? To put the question in more direct, first-person language: Can I ever truly love another for their own sake? Or be loved for my own?

Robert Solomon, to take another example (and admittedly one influenced by Sartre), sees love as paradoxical: which is to say, as something about which it is difficult to formulate coherent propositions. The paradox of love is precisely that two people in love want to affirm a shared identity, even though 'this goal is impossible, unachievable, even incomprehensible'. Love, on his view is not 'a state of union but a never-ending conflict of pushing away and pulling together'.[27]

In contemporary continental philosophy, too, the idea that love is an illusion is subject to debate, with Alain Badiou challenging the pessimistic tradition of the French moralists.[28] But today, love-sceptics can choose from a wider range of reductive explanations: if not a product of the moralists' *amour-propre*, the naturalist can reduce love's illusions to ruses of nature, designed to encourage successful reproduction; and feminists can dismiss love as a pivot of oppression,[29] 'patriarchy's ideological armament',[30] or a living 'hell of mutual alienation'.[31] But despite the natural histories or genealogies of love, we keep believing in it because—as Badiou writes—'if one tried to give up love, to stop believing in it, it would be a genuine, subjective disaster and everybody knows this'.[32]

---

[25] Helm 2013.   [26] Scruton 1986: 230.   [27] Solomon 1988: 64.
[28] Badiou 2012: 34.   [29] See, e.g., Firestone 1970.   [30] Smart 2007: 60.
[31] Langford 1999: 151.   [32] Badiou 2012: 47–8.

A HERMENEUTIC OF DESPAIR

Sartre's anthropology of essenceless freedom explicitly inverts the *imago dei*, embracing instead the fallen human desire to be *sicut Deus*. But this is, as I see it, an area of his most profound insights: his psychological descriptions of unrealizables can be read as affective consequences of God's absence. Ultimately, we find in Sartre a hermeneutics not of suspicion but of *despair*.

We saw in Chapter 3 that Jean Wahl presented Kierkegaard as giving two commandments: 'Despair!' and 'Choose yourself.'[33] We also saw that where Kierkegaardian anxiety is the precondition and consequence of human freedom, despair is the manifestation of the misrelation of the human being to itself. Following Hegel,[34] Anti-Climacus famously defines the self as 'a relation that relates itself to itself'.[35] On a certain telling of the history of philosophy, Hegel's relational definition marked an unprecedented departure from classical conceptions of self as a static, fixed substance that persists despite any changes to its accidental properties. But before Hegel, in the writings of *les mystiques du néant*, the self is *relational*; it depends on *un rapport* with God.[36]

Anti-Climacus's definition of the self does not end with the 'relation that relates itself to itself'; in addition, 'in relating itself to itself it relates itself to another', namely *God*. That is why there are two forms of despair, weak and strong. Human beings do not establish themselves. If we did, there could only be one (weak) form of despair: *not to will to be oneself*. But not being our own foundation—'the inability of the self to arrive at or to be in equilibrium and rest by itself'— means that we may also despairingly *will to be* ourselves.[37] Rejecting God and a pre-existent human essence, Sartre rejects the despair of weakness. But the auto-eklekticism of his for-itself epitomizes the strong despair: the despair of defiance.

Anti-Climacus's psychological taxonomy of despair was intended to serve as the foundation for a theological examination of sin that would *edify* the individual—and this is one of the instances where the

---

[33] And later: 'Le désespoir est son remède à lui-même. Quand l'homme désespère absolument, il se remet à Dieu, il se fonde sur lui, il devient transparent. Il acquert la simplicité, l'authenticité' (Wahl 1938: 83–4).
[34] Hegel 1977: 83–4.   [35] Kierkegaard 1983: 13.
[36] See Chapter 2 on Bérulle and Fénelon, especially.
[37] Kierkegaard 1983: 14.

theological reader may read Sartre's atheism 'for edification'.[38] *The Sickness unto Death* presents despair as a relational disease infecting the relations of the self to itself and the other. This latter dimension—relatedness to the other—comes into prominence in the second part of the work, where we learn that, quite simply, 'despair is sin' and 'sin is: before God'.[39] Unlike the pagan conception of sin as vice (whose opposite is virtue), for Kierkegaard the Christian conception of sin has as its opposite *faith*. And faith is this: 'that the self in being itself and in willing to be itself rests transparently in God'.[40] Anti-Climacus deems this 'one of the most decisive definitions for all Christianity—that the opposite of sin is not virtue but faith'.[41]

On Anti-Climacus's view, we are far from knowing how fallen we are. For sin to be sin, it must be revealed for what it is by God. But, as we have already seen, this definition results in a peculiar conclusion: if followed strictly, the lives of most people are too spiritless to be called sinful. But for sinners who are conscious of sin, sin has the potential to grow and intensify such that it becomes a new sin: despair over sin itself. In despair over sin 'there may be a new intensification, a demonic closing up'; it is 'an effort to give stability and interest to sin as a power by deciding once and for all that one will refuse to hear anything about repentance and grace'.[42]

If the Jansenist temptation was to despair over grace, this is the Sartrean temptation: in despair over sin, to *refuse*. We saw in Chapter 7 that it is not only the evils without that he holds against God, but the original, onto-logical freedom which makes the human perpetuation of evils possible. Sartre's account of this freedom—and of the psychological, epistemo-logical, and ethical effects of nothingness in human life—offers us a portrait of existence as, in the words of Roquentin, 'a fallen fall' (NA 147).

It is graceless. And the absence of grace includes, on his account, the absence of love. In *Works of Love* Kierkegaard writes that 'If . . . we should believe nothing that we cannot see with our physical eyes, then we first and foremost ought to give up believing in love.'[43] For Kierke-gaard sin's opposite is faith: but, as Sharon Krishek has argued, love and faith share a common structure. Both include two conflicting forces:

---

[38] i.e., as clarified in the Introduction, as a stimulus to be reflexive and learn more about one's own position.

[39] Kierkegaard 1983: 77   [40] Kierkegaard 1983: 82

[41] Kierkegaard 1983: 82   [42] Kierkegaard 1983: 110.

[43] Kierkegaard 1998: 5.

One force is that of resignation: he is reconciled to his nothingness, he dies to the world; the other is that of affirmation: he nevertheless has his place in this world... Kierkegaard deeply wishes that these two forces could be "amicably combined".[44]

We saw in Chapter 2 that one of the disputes that took place between seventeenth-century French Augustinians concerned the weight to assign to creaturely nothingness: *néantisme* was rejected by Port-Royal as giving rise to an excessive focus on negation and to *une métaphysique douteuse*.[45] We have also seen in in Chapter 4 that Sartre's project, similarly, concentrates on negation and refusal.[46]

On Krishek's reading of Kierkegaard, love and faith are involved with one another in a way that makes it impossible to love well without faith. If faith is a relation of the self to God, and God *is* love,[47] then it follows that despair will be a misrelation of the self not only to itself but to love. Although it isn't always dressed in Kierkegaardian language, this is a common Christian claim; and more importantly, as I said at the opening of this chapter, the juxtaposition of sin and love is found in Jansen, who identified sin with concupiscence and grace with *caritas*, divine love.[48] Sartre's account of love seems to accept the Jansenist identification of grace with love—not only in its divine, transcendent form, but in any immanent, human manifestations: his hermeneutics of despair does not challenge the Kierkegaardian view that we cannot love without faith. We cannot love at all, and the auto-eklektic self should spurn the temptation to try.

ON THE POSSIBILITY OF
A SARTREAN HAMARTIOLOGY

'A genuine, subjective disaster', to borrow Badiou's phrase, is precisely what Sartre offers us in his portrait of lovelessness. He seems (tacitly) to accept the claims of Pascal that 'ethics is the consequences

---

[44] Krishek 2009: 7.   [45] Sellier 2000, vol. 2: 21.

[46] Negation, Sartre writes, appears on the 'original basis of a relation of man to the world'; it is 'a refusal of existence' (BN 31).

[47] 'It is really remarkable that while all the other attributes ascribed to God are adjectives, "Love" alone is a substantive, and it would scarcely occur to one to make the mistake of saying: "God is lovely." Thus, language itself has given expression to the substantial element that is found in this attribute' (Kierkegaard, *JP*, 1319/*Pap*, II A 418).

[48] Thweatt 1980: 80–1.

of grace in the world';[49] and with Kierkegaard that we cannot 'speak properly about love' if the 'God of love' is forgotten.[50] We saw at the opening of this chapter that Moriarty and Mulhall (although addressing different authors) take accounts of the fallenness of the world as 'validating the authority of the Judeo-Christian tradition that proclaims that belief'.[51] But can we claim the same of Sartre? Could Sartre's account contribute anything to contemporary hamartiology?

The similarity between Sartre's account of love and his Christian predecessors' accounts of unregenerate love has been noted by scholars such as Jasper Hopkins, who writes that 'if man is universally unable to sustain nonplatonic love and if love passes over psychodialectically into sadism and masochism, then the plight of man is as grave as Paul depicts in Romans 3:10–18'.[52] But Hopkins does not want to draw the consequence that Sartre's philosophy 'furnishes phenomenological support for the Pauline understanding of human reality'[53] because he does not think Sartre's philosophy rings true. Hopkins focuses on the concept of generosity; he argues that

> on the ordinary meaning of "generosity" it is empirically false that generous behavior always attempts implicitly to manipulate, transform, ensnare, control, or possess. If Sartre's description is not empirical but conceptual, then he must *justify* his conclusions instead of merely setting them forth. Sartre's account of love also fails and cannot therefore be taken as a phenomenologically valid portrayal of human reality.[54]

But this dismissal should not be accepted too hastily. Hopkins's objection stands or falls on his criteria for Sartre having *justified* his conclusions—which is to say, what criteria must be met for a phenomenology to be called *valid*. As I take it, there are two problems with his reading: first, that it associates validity with universality; and second, that it associates validity with empirical or conceptual justification. Since Sartre is, on my argument, presenting a hermeneutic phenomenology of sin *from a graceless position*, it is not incumbent upon him to provide an account with which all humans universally

---

[49] Rex 1977: 67.   [50] Kierkegaard 1998: 3.
[51] Moriarty 2006: 124. See also Mulhall 2005.   [52] Hopkins 1994: 123.
[53] Hopkins 1994: 123.   [54] Hopkins 1994: 124.

can identify unless one is committed to the claim that no humans experience grace (in any form).

Moreover, as Morris has noted, one of the intellectual prejudices against which Sartre wrote was the prejudice for knowing over living. Sartre was critical of philosophers in the grip of this prejudice, because 'our consciousness of things is by no means limited to knowledge of them. Knowledge . . . is only one of the possible forms of my consciousness "of" this tree; I can also love it, fear it, hate it' (IFI 5). The prejudice for knowing, however, can result in other forms of consciousness being excluded or devalued—particularly the lived experience of the world.[55]

The answer to the question I have posed above—whether Sartre can usefully inform hamartiology—will depend on the methodological commitments of the person asking it, and the doctrinal *locus* of their concept of sin in particular.[56] Many theologians have claimed to know what sin is, basing their knowledge of sin on the foundation of revelation, and claiming that no knowledge of it can be had without that foundation. Karl Barth provides a paradigmatic example: he draws from Sartre's account of nothingness in his own descriptions of *das Nichtige* and sin, but claims that even though Sartre is insightful, 'seeing he does not see'.[57] On the other hand, Tillich's anthropological understanding of estrangement—developed as it is to provide a 'correlated' answer to the problems posed by philosophy—admits a different kind of evidence to its consideration, including the insights

---

[55] Contemporary phenomenologists might want to extend this list of lived experience to other 'structures of consciousness' including: perception, thought, memory, imagination, emotion, desire, and volition, bodily awareness, embodied action, and social activity, including linguistic activity' (Smith 2013: n.p.).

[56] See Kelsey 1993.

[57] This is manifest in the place nothingness occupies in *Church Dogmatics* as a whole—that is, arising in the context of the doctrine of creation (where one would usually expect to find the doctrine of sin). There Barth dedicates several pages to engaging with philosophy, analysing nothingness as conceived by Heidegger and Sartre. This brings him (very close, at least) to the conclusion that knowledge of nothingness is possible outside the domain of faith. He writes that Heidegger and Sartre provide evidence that 'nothingness is really present and at work' (*CD* III.3.345); their thought is 'determined in and by real encounter with nothingness'. Barth goes so far as to claim that 'no one today can think or say anything of value without being an "existentialist" and thinking and speaking as such, i.e. without being confronted and affected by the disclosure of the presence and operation of nothingness as effected with particular impressiveness in our day' (*CD* III.3.345). He qualifies these praises, however, by insisting that 'it must be stated most emphatically that seeing they do not really see' (*CD* III.3.346).

of existentialism and depth psychology.[58] For theologians of the former stripe, it will be difficult to claim that Sartre (on my reading) can provide any useful hamartiological insights, because sin has no significance as such without the possibility of salvation in Christ.

But it is precisely on such methodological questions that I think Sartre has much to offer. Sartre's analysis of the prejudice for knowing starts by noting that knowing is connected to probability and evidence or validation/invalidation (see BN 8, 274–6, 325–6): it asks for *external proof* and excludes the ambiguities of lived experience and *internal relations* from consideration. The 'illusion of the primacy of knowledge' (BN 8) leads philosophers in the grip of such prejudice to reduce existential relationships to epistemological ones.

Husserl criticized what he called 'objective philosophy' for misunderstanding the world and the knowing subject's place in it because, as Dermot Moran glosses it, 'One cannot subtract the knowing subject from the process of knowledge, and treat the desiccated product as if it were the real world'.[59] Neither can the theologian subtract the subject's lived experience of love from the personal existential relation to God 'who is love', as if objective knowledge of God (or love) was the whole truth. In Hopkins's case, the experience of fallen love is rejected as an invalid portrayal of human reality. But the *lived experience* of human love may fall far from the objective account of love that empirical philosophy (or theology) gives it. 'Knowledge' of 'love' is only one form of consciousness one may have; but there are many other forms of consciousness of love that must be *lived* by human beings in the world.

The phenomenological method has often been dismissed, however, on the basis that 'descriptions of experience' are always descriptions of *someone's* experience, which is to say that they are subjective and therefore of limited value. Indeed, Daniel Dennett charges phenomenology in general with 'the first-person plural presumption':

---

[58] Tillich approaches sin from a diametrically opposite starting point to the (stated) Christological method of Barth, writing that it is flatly 'wrong to derive the question implied in human existence from the revelatory answer'. In fact, he asserts, it is impossible to do so, because 'the revelatory answer is meaningless if there is no question to which it is the answer. Man cannot receive an answer to a question he has not asked' (1957: 13). Tillich proposed a method of 'correlation', which 'explains the contents of the Christian Faith through existential questions and theological answers in mutual interdependence' (1953: 60).

[59] Moran 2013: 92–3.

all any phenomenologist ever talks about is the private contents of her own mind.[60]

But phenomenological reflection is not mere introspection. When a phenomenologist describes her experience—like the absence of an awaited friend, or touch of a lover, or the loneliness of being unloved—she is describing not the contents of her own mind but the *world and her consciousness of it*.[61] Her reader is supposed to recognize something in the description which provokes a relation to his or her own experience. Far from being untestable, as Morris writes, 'we might say that our recognition is a *criterion of correctness* for a phenomenological description'.[62]

Unless there is nothing recognizable in Sartre's account, therefore, to reject Sartre's phenomenology of love in such a way is to miss an opportunity for self-examination. For love is a problematic word. It is overused and ill-defined—a 'single ambiguous omnibus word'[63] with many possible (mis-)applications. It often connotes sentimentality, a lack of clear-sightedness, or—as we have seen above—delusion. It may be used to seduce and destroy. Even if it were possible to arrive at an adequate definition, as Stanley Cavell writes, 'the connection between using a word and meaning what it says is not inevitable or automatic'.[64]

And the same can be said of sin. For many, the word is worse than useless, and speaking of sin is to be avoided on account of its 'shaming, dehumanizing, and psychologically abusive effect'.[65] Sylvia Walsh (as we saw in Chapter 3) writes that sin is 'an actuality that should be dealt with in a personal or existential manner, not in a scholarly context'; because the scholarly context 'alters the true concept of sin by subjecting it to "the nonessential refraction of reflection"'.[66] Sin should, on her view, be overcome in individuals' lives, rather than parsed in an abstract analysis.

But this kind of claim may give rise to doubts, both theoretical and practical. Should we not even try to understand sin? How can we overcome something we don't understand? I would caution against a fideism of sin, insofar as such an approach would altogether silence

---

[60] Dennett 1991: 67.
[61] In fact, there is no such 'mind' as a private container of contents for the phenomenologist; instead she is conscious of that absence and that touch in the world.
[62] Morris 2008: 29.   [63] Hong and Hong 1998: xi.
[64] Cavell 1976: 270.   [65] Cooper 2003: 41.   [66] Walsh 2009: 81.

the doubts of reasoned reflection. But having made that caution, we should also take care about the form our reflection takes. Sartre's phenomenological method and observations, I argue, support the view that some theological categories—*relational* categories, fundamental to human experience—cannot be known merely by means of propositions, by reasoned reflection alone—but must be acknowledged personally. Sin and love are among them.[67]

SIN AND LOVE

Conceptually, there are several reasons one might object to the doctrine of sin. Augustine's view that 'the deliberate sin of the first man is the cause of original sin'[68] raises the spectre of paradox, or even contradiction. For if Adam did not know what sin was, prior to eating the forbidden fruit, how could he deliberately sin? And if Adam and Eve did know what sin was, in order to deliberately commit the first sin, then original sin existed before the act from which it is said to ensue. Reinhold Niebuhr writes that the orthodox view of original sin is 'self-destructive'.[69] As we saw in Chapter 3, Voltaire scoffed at Pascal's insistence on this doctrine: 'What a strange explication!' he writes, that 'man is inconceivable without an inconceivable mystery.'[70] '[H]ow can it be, at one and the same time, both folly and demonstrated by reason?'[71]

But recent work in the analytic philosophy of religion provides a helpful categorical distinction in this respect. In Eleonore Stump's *Wandering in Darkness* she argues that where God is concerned a propositional approach to knowledge is valuable but incomplete.[72] On Stump's view, there are kinds of knowledge that are irreducible to propositional knowledge.[73] Stump outlines two typologies of knowing: Dominican and Franciscan.

---

[67] This is not an exhaustive list of categories that may be so defined; it is merely constrained to the scope of this chapter. The distinction between propositional and personal, as we will see, has been developed in the recent context of analytic philosophy of religion, but it can also be found in Pascal's treatment of *savoir* and *connaître*.

[68] Augustine 1998: II.xxvi.43.   [69] Niebuhr 1937: 100.

[70] Voltaire 1819: 272.   [71] Voltaire 1819: 291–2.   [72] Stump 2010: 47.

[73] Or 'knowledge that', which tends to be the type of knowledge studied in contemporary analytic epistemology.

Metaphysics and theology, ethics and morality, can be understood and explained best, on Dominican views (typologically understood), by careful reasoning and argumentation... The ultimate foundation of reality for [the Franciscan] (typologically understood) is... personal, and for that reason knowledge of it will be a knowledge of persons.[74]

She therefore proposes narrative as a means of accessing 'knowledge of persons' because

in cases where necessary and sufficient conditions for something are hard to find or in the nature of things not available (for example, because what we are attempting to define is irreducibly vague), then Franciscan categorization or typology may in fact be more accurate, or at least more true to the phenomena, than Dominican categorization. A pretension to precision where none is available can also produce a clumsy, axe-hewn categorization, which misrepresents the thing it seeks to describe.[75]

Sartre's use of narrative—whether in philosophical examples, novels, or plays—was undergirded by a conviction that the pretension to precision concerning *individuals* can only become true precision when individuals are considered in terms of their *situated, lived* experiences. Sartrean phenomenology, too, aims to exhibit the Franciscan virtue of being 'true to the phenomena' it describes, and as such it offers a further methodological tool with which to explore personal knowledge of the kind Stump defends.

Consider, for a moment, the example of faith (as the opposite of sin). For a person of faith, if the phrase 'I believe in God' expresses not just propositional assent but a *lived experience* of relatedness, then in order to understand that faith a propositional approach will not be adequate. 'Knowledge' is only one form of consciousness; and (as Pascal would have it) 'The knowledge of God is very far from the love of him.'[76] A phenomenology of faith might strive, therefore, as Glendinning writes of phenomenology in general, 'not for new knowledge but *your acknowledgement.... [W]hat characterizes an investigation in phenomenology is a work of convincing words which, in an age dominated by science, aims to cultivate and develop your capacity faithfully to retrieve (for) yourself (as from the inside) a radically re-vis(ion)ed understanding of yourself and your place in the world and with others.'[77]

---

[74] Stump 2010: 46.   [75] Stump 2010: 47.   [76] *Pensées* L77/B280.
[77] Glendinning 2007: 27.

And so might a phenomenology of *sin*—where 'sin' is 'the place empty of God': the aim of such a phenomenology is not the empirical or conceptual establishment of *knowledge* but the phenomenological eliciting of *acknowledgement*. When Hopkins writes that 'Sartre's understanding of man' is 'of no serious use to the theologian', because his account is not 'independently plausible',[78] therefore, he has missed an opportunity not to *know* love, but to *acknowledge* the lived experience of its absence.

As Cavell writes,

> [The sceptic] says that the other alone knows, not that the other alone can acknowledge. But what is the difference? It isn't as if being in a position to acknowledge something is weaker than being in a position to know it. On the contrary: from my acknowledging that I am late it follows that I know I'm late (which is what my words say); but from my knowing I am late, it does not follow that I acknowledge I'm late—otherwise, human relationships would be altogether other than they are. One could say: Acknowledgement goes beyond knowledge. (Goes beyond not, so to speak, in the order of knowledge, but in its requirement that I do something or reveal something on the basis of that knowledge.)[79]

'Believing in sin' is not just a matter of believing propositions—whether they be historical claims about a factual fall, or doctrinal claims put forward by subsequent interpreters of the Genesis myth. As Cavell continues, with respect to knowing and acknowledging suffering,

> [Y]our suffering makes a *claim* upon me. It is not enough that I *know* (am certain) that you suffer—I must do or reveal something (whatever can be done). In a word, I must *acknowledge* it, otherwise I do not know what "(your or his) being in pain" means. Is.[80]

It is one thing to say that 'the world is fallen' or that someone else is 'sinful'. It is quite another to acknowledge the ways in which I contribute to the falling of the world—'and do or reveal something on the basis of that knowledge'.[81] It is one thing to ask, on the level of knowledge, how I could possibly be responsible for a situation that is not the direct result of my agency. It is another to acknowledge my complicity in its perpetuation.

To return to *Being and Nothingness*, we find there a notion which concerns precisely this gap between knowing and acknowledging: the

---

[78] Hopkins 1994: 125.   [79] Cavell 1976: 256–7.
[80] Cavell 1976: 264.   [81] Cavell 1976: 257.

unrealizable. Sartre writes that unrealizables must be distinguished from 'the imaginary':

> We have to do with perfectly real existences; but those for which these characteristics are really *given* are not these characteristics, and I who am them can not realize them. If I am told that I am vulgar, for example, I have often grasped by intuition as regards others the nature of vulgarity; thus I can apply the word 'vulgar' to my person. But I can not join the meaning of this word to my person. There is here exactly the indication of a connection to be effected but one which could be made only by an interiorization and a subjectivizing of the vulgarity or by the objectivizing of the person—two operations which involve the immediate collapse of the reality in question. (BN 548)

This gap between the exterior and the interior, on Sartre's account, explains why people so often deserve reproach for applying double standards, or indeed for expressing the meaning of the words *I have sinned*:

> [I]f when they perceive that they are guilty of a fault which they had blamed in someone else the day before, they have a tendency to say, "That's not the same thing," this is because in fact "it is not the same thing." The one action is a given object of moral evaluation; the other is a pure transcendence which carries its justification in its very existence since its being is a choice. (BN 548–9)

From the external point of view they look identical. But 'the best will in the world will not allow him to realize this identity'. This is the source of many of the troubles of moral consciousness,

> in particular despair at not being able truly to condemn oneself, at not being able to realize oneself as guilty, at feeling perpetually a gap between the expressed meaning of the words: "I am guilty, I have sinned," etc., and the real apprehension of the situation. In short this is the origin of all the [anxiety] of a "bad conscience," that is, the consciousness of bad faith which has for its ideal a self-judgment— i.e., taking toward oneself the point of view of the Other. (BN 549)

For Sartre, the point of view of any other is bad faith. But this is Sartre's gravest misstep: for to refuse anything that comes 'from without' (BN 463) is to refuse the gaze of love; to refuse the collaborative, co-creative process of becoming that leads to human flourishing.

We will consider the last point in greater length in the final section of this chapter. But for now it is worth noting that this refusal has been the source of feminist criticism of Sartre's notion of the subject. Starting with Simone de Beauvoir, feminist authors have criticized Sartre's inviolable, autonomous consciousness, which Nancy Hartstock called a 'walled city'.[82] Beauvoir, by contrast, has a 'less dualistic and more relational view of the self' which tacitly rejects 'the notion of the "absolute subject" for a situated subject: a subject that is intrinsically intersubjective and embodied, thus always "interdependent" and permeable rather than walled'.[83]

In the *Ethics of Ambiguity*, Beauvoir articulates something closer to the Christian position, writing that 'A man who seeks being far from other men, seeks it against them at the same time that he loses himself.'[84] On her view, subjectivity is 'both constituting and constituted'; and consequently all forms of oppression affect more than their immediate 'victims' and require collective resistance.[85] In her late work *Old Age* Beauvoir writes that 'a society is a whole made up of individual parts. Its members are separate, but they are united by the need for reciprocal relationships.'[86]

> There are pursuits that are useful to mankind, and between men there are relationships in which they reach one another in full truthfulness. Once illusions have been swept away, these relationships, in which neither alienation nor myth form any part, and these pursuits remain.[87]

But Sartre adamantly rejects claims of useful pursuits and meaningful collectivity. Of the former, he famously concludes *Being and Nothingness* by saying that:

> Many men, in fact, know that the goal of their pursuit is being; and to the extent that they possess this knowledge, they refrain from appropriating things for their own sake and try to realize the symbolic appropriation of their being-in-itself. But to the extent that this attempt still shares in the spirit of seriousness and that these men can still believe that their mission of effecting the existence of the in-itself-for-itself is written in things, they are condemned to despair; for they discover at the same time that all human activities are equivalent (for they all tend

---

[82] Hartsock 1985: 241.   [83] Kruks 1992: 98.

[84] Beauvoir 2000: 66. See, e.g., Niebuhr 1937: 102: 'self-centred existence always disturbs the harmony and inter-relatedness of existence'.

[85] Kruks 1992: 104.

[86] Beauvoir 1977: 243. See Kirkpatrick 2014 on the applicability of her treatment of age to other experiences of 'being othered'.

[87] Beauvoir 1977: 547.

to sacrifice man in order that the self-cause may arise) and that all are on principle doomed to failure. Thus it amounts to the same thing whether one gets drunk alone or is a leader of nations.   (BN 646-7)

What matters, for him, is 'the degree of consciousness which the for-itself possesses of *its* ideal goal'. True freedom chooses 'not to recover itself but to flee itself, not to coincide with itself but to be always at a distance from itself' (BN 647).

But in so choosing it must also choose to be always at a distance from others. In the absence of God, appeals to collectivities—to 'Us-objects'—are unrealizable, for on Sartre's view we are only 'us' in the eyes of another, and without God no such 'witness' exists to bring collectivities into being.

> [I]t is in terms of the Others' look that we assume ourselves as "Us." But this implies that there can exist an abstract, unrealizable project of the for-itself toward an absolute totalization of itself and of *all* Others. This effort at recovering the human totality can not take place without positing the existence of a Third, who is on principle distinct from humanity and in whose eyes humanity is wholly object. This unrealizable Third . . . is one with the idea of God. But if God is characterized as radical absence, the effort to realize humanity as ours is forever renewed and forever results in failure.   (BN 444)[88]

On Sartre's hermeneutics of despair, optimism about such love or unity is utterly unwarranted.[89]

A HERMENEUTIC OF LOVE:
THE 'ORIGINAL OPTIMISM'

On one reading of Christianity, to be a true self is to be an object of love: to have as one's witness a God who *is* love; to love God above all

---

[88] He continues: 'Thus the humanistic "Us"—the Us-object—is proposed to each individual consciousness as an ideal impossible to attain although everyone keeps the illusion of being able to succeed in it by progressively enlarging the circle of communities to which he does belong.'

[89] As we saw in Chapter 6, Sartre did not rule out the possibility of an 'ethics of deliverance and salvation' entirely; he famously promised an ethics in the last line of BN: 'All these questions, which refer us to a pure and not an accessory (or impure) reflection, can find their reply only on the ethical plane. We shall devote to them a future work' (BN 647). But he did not publish one during his lifetime.

else; and to love all else through God.[90] The experience of being beheld by such clear-sightedness is not an experience of being beholden to an objectifying master—the God of this tradition is not the 'prying, judgmental tyrant' Keith Ward sees in Sartre.[91] Rather, this self is invited to a life of intersubjective co-creativity. It is an invitation to *know* that we are both constituted by and constitutive of the others in our lives, and to *acknowledge* our co-constitution in humility, love, and mercy. It is free, but its freedom is not 'strictly [to] be identified with nihilation' (BN 588): it is free also to affirm.

But a self in despair has a diseased view of these relations—doubting or denying their possibility. For Sartre, God's absence results in the impossibility of identity; there is no 'sinless love' (as Phèdre put it) to love us into being; our only witnesses are the fickle freedoms of others; and all human loves are irreparably tainted by the tyranny of *amour-propre*.[92] Although Sartre proposes auto-eklekticism as the answer to our not-being-chosen by God, he does not indulge in false optimism: we *choose ourselves*, all the while recognizing that self-choice amounts to useless passion.

It is here that the Jansenist note in Sartre's works is clearest: without God, the human can do nothing to save himself. Jansenism, as we have seen, took 'the extreme aspects of the Augustinian view of the self' without communicating 'the serenity of faith and the redemptive love that undergird Augustinian thought'.[93] As Mann writes, 'it is no part of Augustine's message that humans have been *shattered* by the fall'.[94] Bérulle wrote that 'péché originel' had 'ébran-lée, non pas ruinée' human nature—weakened, but not ruined. More-over, Bérulle taught that we should not despise the human nature which Christ Himself did not despise.[95]

As Reinhold Neibuhr writes, the 'measure of Christianity's success in gauging the full dimension of human life is given in its love perfectionism, on the one hand, and on its moral realism and pessimism, on the other'.[96] The original Augustinian optimism that is lacking in

---

[90] As William Wood writes (with respect to Pascal): 'Given that to be a true self is to be an object of love, it follows that a true self can only be called into being by a true, because rightly ordered, love' (Wood 2013: 219).

[91] Ward 2011: 98.

[92] See La Rochefoucauld's clearly Augustinian definitions of *amour-propre*: 'le(s) tyran(s) des autres', etc., in Thweatt 1980: 115.

[93] Thweatt 1980: 82.   [94] Mann 2001: 47.   [95] See Calvet 1938: 97.

[96] Niebuhr 1937: 75.

Sartre's Jansenist-inflected pessimism, therefore, is not only that there is a God who *is* love, but that there is a true self that can love and be loved. It is elusive; it must endure the ambiguities of existence and the ravages of time; but it is a self that was created by and for love. And it is a self that can, through imitating the love of Christ, become more truly itself—that can flourish and find rest.

Sartre's phenomenology of love clearly lacks the 'love-perfectionism' of the Christian tradition. But its moral realism and pessimism can fruitfully be used as a provocation to self-examination. William Wood writes of Pascal, that 'Just as a false self, a *moi*, paradoxically imitates God, so also a true self imitates Christ, who loves God above all things. By imitating Christ, the true self virtuously imitates God.'[97] The theological answer to Sartre, therefore, is that the rightly ordered self seeks to be *sicut Christus*: accepting her creaturely dependence, 'putting desire for God above all other desires', and 'judging human desires only in that light'.[98] As Cavell writes, it is in Christ's *acceptance* of this condition that we are to resemble him.[99] We must recognize that we cannot save ourselves from this situation, as Niebuhr writes, for that is the first step in being saved:

> It is possible for individuals to be saved from this sinful pretension, not by achieving an absolute perspective on their life, but by their recognition of their inability to do so. Individuals may be saved by repentance, which is the gateway to grace. The recognition of creatureliness and finiteness, in other words, may become the basis of man's reconciliation to God through his resignation to his finite condition.[100]

Recognition, Niebuhr writes, may become the basis of reconciliation. The Christian optimism that Sartre rejects is that 'when the self attains genuine self-knowledge it will not only love itself differently but will in fact become a different kind of self altogether'.[101]

Becoming that self requires accepting the gaze of love. We have already seen that the theme of having a witness preoccupied Sartre.[102] And in Kierkegaard's authorship, too, George Pattison notes that seeing and being seen are 'constant themes'.[103] What is at stake for Kierkegaard, on Pattison's reading, is 'not whether we are to see or to be seen. We will always see and be seen. The question is how we

---

[97] Wood 2013: 219.   [98] Coakley 2013: 11.   [99] Cavell 1976: 302.
[100] Niebuhr 1937: 99.   [101] Wood 2013: 219 (on Pascal).
[102] See Chapter 5; Gillespie 2016.   [103] Pattison 2013: 198.

choose to see and how we might let ourselves be seen.'[104] His point is worth quoting at length:

> If existing 'before Christ' in the mode of despair is thus 'offence', then truly to exist before Christ, existing before Christ with an understanding of what that meant and accepting what that meant, would be to exist with the knowledge of the forgiveness of sins... What we most truly 'are', then, is persons embraced by the forgiveness offered in Christ...[105]

It is only in the context of forgiveness (which Kierkegaard explicitly equates with love[106]) that we can love ourselves, and others, aright.

On Pascal's view, what is needed to see with the 'look of love', as Pattison calls it, is a transformation that is *imaginative*. Sartre's Garcin cannot 'set [his] life in order' by himself (NE 9). In Sartre's *Imaginary* he describes the imagination as a faculty which structures our reception of the world. 'It is only because I have the aim of being in a certain room that I see something as a door handle to be turned. Otherwise I might only see it as a metal protuberance from a piece of wood, or more simply as a chunk of matter.'[107] And it is precisely this faculty which, on Pascal's analysis, must be regenerated. Grace is required—which, on Pascal's view, is *aesthetic* and *affective*: it is 'received as a kind of pleasure: a delight in goodness and truth'.[108]

For Pascal, conversion brings an 'insight by which the soul considers things and herself in a manner wholly new'.[109] And to see with a 'look of love' that is free of *amour-propre*, 'we must imagine a body full of thinking members (for we are members of the whole), and see how each member ought to love itself'.[110] It is worth dwelling on this theme at greater length, for here we find the Christian conception of meaningful collectivity that Beauvoir found lacking in Sartre—a body that is both corporate and corporeal:[111]

> To be a member is to have no life, no being, and no movement except through the spirit of the body. And for the body, the separated member, no longer seeing the body to which it belongs, has only a wasted and moribund being. However, it believes itself to be whole, and, seeing no body on which it depends, it believes itself to be dependent only on itself and tries to make itself its own center and body. But not having in

---

[104] Pattison 2013: 199.   [105] Pattison 2013: 205, 206.
[106] See Pattison 2013: 209–11.   [107] Webber 2004: xxvi.
[108] Wood 2013: 212.   [109] Pascal 1653: paras 1–3.
[110] L368/B474.   [111] Anderson 2012: 143.

itself any principle of life, it only wanders about and becomes bewildered at the uncertainty of its being, feeling keenly that it is not the body and yet not seeing that it is a member of a body. Finally, it comes to know itself, it is as if it has returned home, and only loves itself for the body's sake.[112]

To use Augustine's terminology, participating in Being means reiterating the call of Being to other beings by the *regula amoris*.[113] It is not only to *know* wasted and moribund being when we see it in others and ourselves, but to *acknowledge* it: 'and do or reveal something on the basis of that knowledge'.[114]

This, on the Christian view, is what Sartre refuses in refusing grace: a 'new light' that enables the human to see that 'created things cannot be more lovely than their Creator; and her reason, aided by the light of grace, makes her understand that there is nothing more lovely than God, and that he can only be taken away from those who reject him, since to possess him is only to desire him, and to refuse him is to lose him'.[115]

In sum, Sartre's for-itself is free *to the extent that it refuses* anything that comes 'from without' (BN 463). Making this move enabled Sartre to escape a form of theological determinism: determination by unchosen grace. But Sartre's freedom does not escape the determinism of nothingness. Moreover, rejecting everything that comes from 'without' involves not only refusing grace, but the possibility of love.

[112] L372/B483.
[113] Mary Clark writes that Augustine is a radical 'philosopher of community': 'Man is neither an *en-soi* (an inhuman individual) nor a *pour-soi* (a human individual). Of course man-is-in-the-world and he is with-others, but man-is-for-God, yet for a God who creates and loves his world and all persons in it. This is why Augustinian otherworldliness can never be interpreted rightly as anti-world. In the Augustinian context man cannot fulfill his human vocation except by collaborating in the creative work of God. Man cannot really be for-God unless he is for-others. Other men ... mediate God's call to each man' (Clark 1970: 1, 2–3).
[114] Cavell 1976: 257.   [115] Pascal 1653: para. 11.

9

Sin is Dead, Long Live Sin!

The concept of sin may be used to damn others and ourselves. But it can also be used to form an individual and corporate imagination that resists determinism by cultivating humility, love, and mercy. So this final chapter raises two provocations: For even if—in the former sense—we wish to say 'Sin is Dead!'; might it nevertheless—in the latter sense—be worth adding, 'Long live sin!'?

In the *Pensées* Pascal wrote that it is 'equally dangerous for man to know God without knowing his own wretchedness as to know his wretchedness without knowing God'.[1] I have now made the case that Sartre retained a recognizable inheritance from the Christian doctrine of original sin in his concept of *le néant*; and that this concept has psychological, epistemological, and ethical insights in *Being and Nothingness* which leave it open to being read as a theology of refusal and a hermeneutics of despair. I have also argued that his phenomenological methods can usefully inform hamartiology, in particular that by evoking *recognition* of sin phenomenology can us lead to *acknowledgement* of it in new ways. By way of conclusion I offer two provocations to self-examination: on wretchedness without God and on God without wretchedness.

PROVOCATIONS

In a sermon on 'Salvation' Paul Tillich writes that 'the words which are most used in religion are also those whose genuine meaning is

---

[1] 'Il est . . . utile pour nous que Dieu soit caché en partie, et découvert en partie, puisqu'il est également dangereux à l'homme de connaître Dieu sans connaître sa misère, et de connaître sa misère sans connaître Dieu' (L446/B586).

almost completely lost and whose impact on the human mind is nearly negligible'.[2] Such words, he continues, must be either reborn or thrown away. For some readers of this work, the latter option will be preferable: the word 'sin' may seem ridiculous. At its worst, it has connotations of fundamentalist condemnation, psychological guilt, and spiritual suffering. In more banal instances of dismissal, it might be described, as Thomas Mann writes, as 'an amusing word, used to get a laugh'.[3]

But Sartre's account suggests that sin is considerably more than that—that it expresses something true about human experience which deserves greater scrutiny whether one professes faith or not. For Christian theologians, sin is a necessary concept because if—as the Christian faith proclaims—God sacrificed his Son to *save* us, then for that message to be coherent there must be something from which we need saving. But Sartre's insights in *Being and Nothingness* may usefully be read by anyone interested in anthropology (in the broad sense of what it means to be human): as Iris Murdoch wrote, Sartre performed 'the traditional task of the philosopher', namely 'reflecting systematically about the *human* condition'.[4]

I have argued that *Being and Nothingness* presents a portrait of fallenness without grace: an account of sin with no prospect of salvation. In drawing this book to a close, therefore, there are thus two senses in which I would like to complete this reading as a provocation to self-examination.[5] The first provocation is for those who do not believe in original sin, in the broad sense of ascribing to a form of Christian theism that includes the belief that we are 'fallen'.[6] The second is for those who do.[7] For the first readership, I argue, Sartre's account offers an invitation to look closely at sin before laughing at it. And for the second, I argue, Sartre's account reminds us that the gaze with which we regard sin should always be the 'look of love'.

---

[2] Tillich 1963: 94.   [3] Mann 1961 cited in Pieper 2001: back cover.
[4] Murdoch 1999: 137; emphasis added.   [5] McCord Adams 2013: 173.
[6] That is, in the broad that our 'sins' are not merely 'actual' (as discussed in Chapter 1), but that there is a social aspect to human fallenness, that we are all implicated in it, and that mere human effort will not eradicate it.
[7] This two-part division doesn't do justice to the variety of positions that can be held with respect to these topics, but constraints of space prevent a more comprehensive approach.

PROVOCATION I: SARTRE, SIN, AND
THE WARRANT OF OPTIMISM

Sartre's account of consciousness in general and love in particular demonstrates how absence and *lack*, despite being *nothing*, can have affective consequences. We saw in Chapter 4 that, as Morris writes, Sartre wanted to redress 'a widespread intellectual prejudice against the non-existent, the non-factual, the non-actual, and the absent, as well as the non-quantifiable and the non-measureable'; Morris summarizes this as the prejudice for the existent.[8] But Sartre's attention to the non-existent raises the problem of evil: How could a God *who is love* be consonant with the human experience of lovelessness?

We saw in the Introduction that Sartre objected to the distributive justice of grace and that the God he rejected was an arbitrary will—a Jansenist God, who might give and take away, and who *determines* the graced human, rendering her unfree. For many, Sartre's arbitrary God may seem more consonant with human experience—in which good does not appear to be distributed equally or justly—than the omni-benevolent God of Christian theism. This objection is not new, of course, and has led many to formulate arguments from evil, whether on account of the quantities or kinds of evil in the world. Sartre's ontology has the benefit, if one wishes to call it that, of being egalitarian. But its offering is an equality of lovelessness.

In such a world, I contend, optimism about human meaning-making is not rationally warranted. This is the first movement of the first provocation (mentioned above). After considering it in greater length, the second movement asks whether what I have called Sartre's pessimism may provoke the reader to consider whether some concept of sin might be a live option.

In her 2013 article 'God because of Evil', Marilyn McCord Adams constructs an *ad hominem* argument from evil for belief in God. Her target audience is non-theists, whether atheistic or agnostic, who are '*optimistic* and *purpose driven*, but who nevertheless insist that our worldviews and life projects should be *realistic*, most especially that they should reckon with empirical facts'.[9] Some of these non-theists take their realism to rule out religious belief on the grounds that it is irrational: either because it is (a) redundant in light of science having

---

[8] Morris 2008: 47.   [9] McCord Adams 2013: 160.

filled explanatory gaps; or (b) incoherent given evil. But McCord Adams argues that 'the latter are hoist on their own petard, because realism about evil is incompatible with such purpose-driven optimism unless it is undergirded by belief in God'.[10]

I have already said, in Chapter 1, that Sartre's atheism is not to be identified with the atheism discussed in contemporary (Christian) analytic philosophy of religion. Evil plays a role in Sartre's rejection of religion: as we saw in the Introduction and Chapter 7, he explicitly rejects the notion of grace. But as I have argued elsewhere, Sartre is concerned not with demonstrating God's existence through argument but with drawing an affective portrait of the consequences of God's *absence*.[11] In Nietzschean terms, we might say that where the analytic atheist is Apollonian in approaching the question of evil, setting out proofs to demonstrate the incompossibility of the classical divine attributes given evil, Sartre's atheism is Dionysian, presenting the reader with human suffering in a more immediate and affective way.[12]

Understood in this way, *Being and Nothingness* makes an interesting interlocutor with McCord Adams's argument. McCord Adams is emphatic that her *ad hominem* argument against a certain variety of atheism and agnosticism does not take the form of 'even your own false beliefs entail the existence of God'. Rather, it is intended to affect only a certain group of people: those non-theists who are 'optimistic and purpose-driven'.[13] She contends that 'given the way the world really is—it makes no sense to meet life this way apart from belief in God'.[14] It is worth quoting her at length:

> Atheological arguments from evil (such as that offered by Mackie 1955) are out to compel theists to "get real" about the evils in our world and their implications. My countercontention is that most parties that dispute have not been realistic enough (M. M. Adams 1999, 1–55). Robust realism requires more than the observation that our world is full of evils many and great (as well as trivial and miniscule); that pain and suffering may be instrumentally ordered to individual or species goods; that they are regularly consequent on natural causes and human choices and the (accidental or purposeful) intersection of the two; that in human

---

[10] McCord Adams 2013: 160.   [11] Kirkpatrick 2013.
[12] See Nietzsche 1993. As we saw in Chapter 1, Sartre wrote that 'thought conceals man', dismissing arguments as uninteresting unless they mask tears: 'The argument removes the obscenity from the tears; the tears, by revealing their origin in the passions, remove the aggressiveness from the argument' (WL 22).
[13] McCord Adams 2013: 161.   [14] McCord Adams 2013: 161.

life, "you have to take the bitter with the sweet." Robust realism demands confrontation with the horrendous, with the fact that our world is incessantly productive of evils of the prima-facie life-ruining kind.[15]

McCord Adams goes on to delimit her category of horrors,[16] arguing that human participation in horrors makes optimism (and the human attempt to make meaningful lives) irrational. Unless there is 'an agency powerful and resourceful, ready, willing, and able enough to make good on horrors, not only in the world as a whole but within the context of the individual horror-participants' lives',[17] she argues, such optimism is unwarranted.[18]

My reading of Sartre opens up a parallel argument. On Sartre's atheist account, optimism—about human meaning or relationality— is not rational. He, like Voltaire, would deride the view that this world is the best of all possible. But where the analytic argument from evil often discusses evils in terms of their external relations, what Sartre treats is the internal relations: the suffering that arises within and between human persons on account of their *néant*, which, in theological idiom, this book has called *sin*.

One of McCord Adams's points is that 'Many good and decent people have fruitful and enjoyable lives because they "abstract" from the possibility of horrors happening to them' because they 'adopt a policy of "avoiding unpleasantness"'.[19] They pay selective attention to the world in order to face it with the psychological outlook that they do. On the reading made here, Sartre's account lends credence to McCord Adams's view that optimism is not warranted if one takes a robust realist (and atheist) approach to evil. For a robust realist view of evil must take into account the ways human beings are alienated by and misuse freedom: or, in theological idiom, it must take into account our complicity in sin.

Read as such, Sartre presents a challenge. For the theist Kierkegaard's imperative of choice provides a way out: 'despair-or-choose-yourself!'

---

[15] McCord Adams 2013: 162.

[16] Where horrors are evils 'the participation in the doing or suffering of which constitutes *prima facie* reason to doubt whether the participant's life could (given their inclusion in it) be a great good to him/her on the whole' (McCord Adams 2013: 162).

[17] McCord Adams 2013: 166.

[18] He rejects Hegel's 'epistemological optimism' concerning the 'recognition' of the other and 'ontological optimism' regarding the ability of consciousness to know truth in BN 265–7. 'No logical or epistemological optimism can cover the scandal of the plurality of consciousnesses' (BN 268).

[19] McCord Adams 2013: 167.

implies that one should choose oneself from the hand of God—should choose a selfhood (that aspires to be) rightly ordered in relation to God, others and itself.[20] For the non-theist, Sartre's commendation of auto-eklekticism can be read as a secularized injunction to 'choose yourself'. But as we saw in Chapter 8, even Sartrean self-choice does not seem to absolve one of despair. When we die, we will live on only as the *paraître* perceived by other minds. On my pessimistic reading, even in *le choix originel* we must recognize that we are 'useless passions'.[21]

Moreover, even on the optimistic reading of Sartre, I take it, the rationality of human meaning-making is questionable: for Sartre does not touch on *horrors*—that is to say, situations in which individuals, for whatever reason, no longer have the capacities to self-choose and make meaning. But any optimistic reading of Sartre (as McCord Adams points out with respect to the atheisms of Camus, Russell, and Nagel) assumes 'that the individual's meaning-making faculties are intact'.[22] Sartre could thus be read in support of such pragmatic arguments for theistic faith: on his atheism, one cannot hold both a robust realist view of evil and a warranted optimism about things being made good.

I conclude the first provocation, therefore, by suggesting that as a phenomenologist of fallenness, Sartre may serve (to borrow a phrase from Mulhall) to 'hold open the possibility of taking religious points of view seriously'.[23] For if we find recognizable descendants of the concept of sin in some of the twentieth century's most prominent philosophers: *why*? If Sartre was simply wrong, then his pessimism need not trouble us. But if, as was argued in Chapter 8, his description of *lovelessness* is the lived experience of some members of humanity, it bears further consideration if one wishes to defend a warranted optimism about the meaning of human life.

PROVOCATION II: SET LOVE IN ORDER, THOU THAT LOVEST ME

The second provocation—on the question of wretchedness *with* God—builds on Cavell's distinction, introduced in Chapter 8, between

---

[20] See Chapter 3 and Wahl 1938: 83–4.   [21] See Chapter 7.
[22] McCord Adams 2013: 169.   [23] Mulhall 2005: Conclusion.

knowing and acknowledging.[24] I have argued that considering sin
abstractly is insufficient: knowing one's fallenness does not entail
acknowledging it. Acknowledgement requires that one knows, but
it goes beyond knowledge, prompting us, as Cavell writes, to 'do or
reveal something on the basis of that knowledge'.[25]

On the view defended in this book, to acknowledge sin is to 'set
love in order'. As discussed in Chapter 2, Augustine described sin as
'disorder':[26] as a shift of self's relatedness to itself and to its loves.
Love is what (as we saw in Chapter 8) 'creates'[27] the Two Cities; and
the existence of a love that is capable of ordering the self is precisely
what Sartre denies. In the *Confessions* Augustine wrote of the threefold concupiscence that 'the arrogance of pride, the pleasures of lust,
and the poison of vain curiosity are the impulses of a soul that is
dead'. But he does not leave it at that. For such a soul is not one 'so
dead that it lacks all impulse, but one that is dead because it has
forsaken the fountain of life and is swept along by the fleeting things
of this world, lending itself to their ways'.[28] There is no question, for
Augustine, of *whether* one should love: to love nothing is to be
'lifeless, dead, detestable, miserable'.[29] Rather, the question is *what*:
'Love, but be careful what you love.'

To Augustine's *what* I add a *how*: To set love in order we
must recognize—and *acknowledge*—our failures in love. And in this
Sartre's insights can support what Michael Theunissen calls 'the
negative method', according to which 'successful life is to be
explained by reference to failure'.[30] Sartre's pessimism can fruitfully
be used as a provocation to self-examination: where we recognize
ourselves in his account of anxiety, self-deception, and the desire to
dominate others, we can allow ourselves to be confronted with the
question: How have we failed in the ordering of our loves?

---

[24] The line quoted in the section heading is widely attributed to St Francis of Assisi,
'Cantica: Our Lord Christ of Order', trans. D. G. Rosetti, although the original poem,
'Amor di caritateâ', is the work of his follower, the mystic poet Jacopone da Todi
(1230?–1306).

[25] Cavell 1976: 257.   [26] Augustine 1953: I.ii.18.

[27] Augustine 2003: XIV.xxviii.593.   [28] Augustine 1961: XIII.21.

[29] *Enarr. In Ps.* 31.2.5; cited in Gilson 1961: 135. One of the 'capital themes'
that Augustinian theologians would give French Classicism was *l'amour de soi* (or
l'amour propre, in the idiom of the time).

[30] Theunissen, Michael, *Das Selbst auf dem Grund der Verzweiflung: Kierkegaards
negativistische Methode* (Frankfurt am Main: Anton Hain, 1991), 60–1, cited in (and
translated by) Hühn and Schwab 2013: 81.

It is hardly novel to claim that wisdom can come through the experience of failure. But for the Christian theist, Sartre's observations in *Being and Nothingness* can stimulate self-examination in several ways—psychologically, epistemologically, and ethically—where these categories are understood in relation to the order of our loves: of self, of knowledge, and of others. The boundaries of these ways are porous[31]—but they will be treated distinctly for the sake of making a few succinct gestures toward a constructive concept of sin: one which cultivates humility, love, and mercy.

Psychology

We saw in the Introduction that Sartre uses the word 'sin' with many meanings. In *Les Mouches*, a play rich in religious language, sin signifies bad faith. One conversation is particularly illustrative of this dimension: after entering Argos Orestes and the tutor meet two strangers: an old woman and a man—Zeus in disguise.

When Zeus asks the old woman why she wears black she responds that everyone does (F 53). Like *Bariona*'s Bethaura, Argos is a sick city, plagued by both external and internal pestilence: flies and guilt. When the old woman asks who Zeus is, he replies that she would 'do better to think of yourself and try to earn forgiveness by repenting of your sins' (F 54). It is worth quoting the exchange that follows at length:

OLD WOMAN: Oh, sir, I do repent, most heartily I repent. If you only knew how I repent, and my daughter too, and my son-in-law offers up a heifer every year, and my little grandson has been brought up in a spirit of repentance. He's a pretty lad, with flaxen hair, and he always behaves as good as gold. Though he's only seven, he never plays or laughs, for thinking of his original sin.

ZEUS: Good, you old bitch, that's as it should be—and be sure you die in a nice bitchy odor of repentance. It's your one hope of salvation. [*The* OLD WOMAN *runs away.*] Unless I am much mistaken, my masters, we have the real thing, the good old piety of yore, rooted in terror. (F 54)

---

[31] In delimiting the following stimuli to self-examination I am not claiming that these three categories (or the examples given of each) are comprehensive. They are intended to illustrate potential directions for future research.

Here is a god who, like Bariona's 'God of Vengeance and Anger' or Racine's merciless witness, is arbitrary and objectifying. His subjects are expected to attempt to *earn* forgiveness—even though merit is no guarantee that it will be granted. In his (supposedly) anonymous meeting with Orestes Zeus portrays the people of Argos as 'great sinners', reducing them to their past actions and holding them captive in a gaze of damnation.

Satirical though sin may be in *Les Mouches*, Sartre's account of bad faith in *Being and Nothingness*—as a temptation to overidentify with one's transcendence or facticity—can be used to illuminate the two poles of Pascal: 'pride and despair'.[32] Its message is that the battle between Pelagianism and *néantisme* is not just disputed in history books and faculties of theology, but within human persons: am I passive to the point of powerlessness, or active to the point of limitlessness? In Sartre's sin, the human person lives in a tensive state: only to try to escape its tension (qua *anxiety*) through the illusory reification of bad faith.

But neither extreme—*néantisme* or Pelagianism in the language of sin, identification with facticity or transcendence in the language of Sartre—can be consistently maintained. Human perfection (or unmitigated transcendence) is indefensible—for we are not only *internal* consciousnesses but also embodied, *situated* subjects, limited by our *external* situation. And if we are completely determined by circumstances (or sin)—that is to say, passive to the point of powerlessness—then how can we be held responsible for actions we could not have done (or existences we could not have lived) otherwise? On such a passive view of the human person we cannot possibly be *guilty*.

But rejecting *guilt* need not imply rejecting responsibility. As Niebuhr writes,

> The modern reaction to the religious sense of guilt has frequently tempted modern culture to deny the idea of moral responsibility completely. This was natural enough because modern culture is under the influence of the scientific method; and no scientific description of an act can ever disclose the area of freedom in which alternative choices are weighed. A scientific description of an act is both external and retrospective. For it every act is deterministically related to previous acts and conditions in an endless chain of natural causes and effects...[33]

---

[32] L192/B527. See Chapter 3.   [33] Niebuhr 1937: 90.

But if, as we saw in Chapter 5, the internal relations of human persons do not operate in the same manner as those of the external order, we may find ourselves responsible (internally) for a mess that is (externally) not of our making.

To return to the *Confessions*, Augustine himself admitted to poverty of speech when attempting to describe what it means that 'the love of God has been poured out in our hearts by the Holy Spirit, whom we have received',[34] asking:

> How shall I find words to explain how the weight of concupiscence drags us down in to the sheer depths and how the love of God raises us up through your Spirit, who moved over the waters? . . . The depths to which we sink, and from which we are raised, are not places in space.[35]

Sartre provides a language in which to discuss these depths: they are *internal*. Not places in space, but ways of being that are all but hidden from human eyes.

Between pride and despair there is a third way, a way characterized not only by the tension between freedom and limit but also by humility and hope. Humility because only God can—as Hugo's Monsieur Bienvenu is said to have done—'examine the road over which the fault has passed'.[36] And hope because, as Niebuhr writes, the optimism of the Christian faith is 'a type of optimism which places its ultimate confidence in the love of God and not the love of man, in the ultimate and transcendent unity of reality and not in tentative and superficial harmonies of existence which human ingenuity may contrive'.[37]

Epistemology

This brings us to the epistemological aspect of this provocation. For Sartre's warning against intellectual prejudices—for the external, for knowledge, and for the existent—may go some way in explaining why the doctrine of sin has been the subject of some embarrassment. For if its relations are internal, what can we *know* of it?

Chapter 8 showed that the prejudice for knowing excludes or devalues other forms of consciousness—particularly the lived experience of the world. For those in the grip of this prejudice, knowledge is

---

[34] Romans 5:5, cited in Augustine 1961: XIII.7. [35] Augustine 1961: XIII.7.
[36] See Chapter 3 and Hugo 1887: 24–5. [37] Niebuhr 1937: 131.

conceptual; it is connected to probability and empirical or conceptual validation. But on Sartre's view, proofs of this order do not convince. Drawing on Bergson, Sartre distinguishes between analysis as the method of the faculty of the intellect and intuition as the method of the faculty of intuition. He writes that:

> There is only intuitive knowledge. Deduction and discursive argument, incorrectly called examples of knowing, are only instruments which lead to intuition. When intuition is reached, methods utilized to attain it are effaced before it; in cases where it is not attained, reason and argument remain as indicating signs which point toward an intuition beyond reach; finally if it has been attained but is not a present mode of my consciousness, the precepts which I use remain as the results of operations formerly effected. (BN 195)

What Sartre calls 'the illusion of the primacy of knowledge' (BN 8, 10, 12) leads philosophers to consider existential relationships as epistemological ones. But if, for a person of faith, the phrase 'I have sinned' expresses not just a conceptual judgement of wrongdoing but a personal experience of broken relationship, then a conceptual approach to sin will not do it justice.

What is needed is a complimentary, *personal*, and phenomenological approach which aims to 'cultivate and develop your capacity faithfully to retrieve (for) yourself (as from the inside) a radically re-vis(ion)ed understanding of yourself and your place in the world and with others'.[38] This personal transformation takes into account the situatedness of our convictions and the importance of our conduct in relation to them: this is what is required if love is to be set in order. The person who *acknowledges* sin cannot be, like the philosophers of Marx's eleventh thesis on Feuerbach, content to 'interpret the world in various ways'; for acknowledgement entails the realization that they, too, are responsible for what it is—and for changing it.

As Westphal writes,

> By describing the goal of reflection as relearning to see the world, existential phenomenology reminds the theologian that, while 'seeing is believing', according to a familiar adage, believing is not necessarily seeing. I can sincerely believe, for example, that the lives of the homeless poor of New York and Calcutta and the shanty-town poor of Africa and Latin America are of equal value to the lives of highly educated, highly

---

[38] Glendinning 2007: 27.

affluent suburban Americans without seeing the former and myself in these terms. I can sincerely believe that my sins are forgiven by the grace of God and that justification is a gift and not a form of wages and still see myself as carrying a load of guilt that I must work off with pious practices.[39]

Ethics

This brings us to the ethical dimension of Sartre's challenge. One of the major twentieth-century shifts in the doctrinal locus of sin was its move from the doctrine of creation to the doctrine of redemption in liberation theology.[40] Earlier in the twentieth century, Niebuhr wrote that '[o]ne of the vices of a really profound religion is that its insights into the ultimate problems of the human spirit frequently betray it into indifference toward the immediate problems of justice and equity in human relations'.[41] On Niebuhr's view, we must insist against this tendency that 'the degree of imagination and insight with which disciplined minds are able to enter into the problems of their fellow men' can 'improve human happiness and social harmony'.[42]

One way in which this tendency can be resisted is by realizing that, as Westphal writes, 'having my doxastic house in order is not the ultimate goal of theological discourse. It is rather *to bring my seeings (and thereby feelings and actions, since these arise more from my seeings than from my believings) into conformity with my best judgments about what is true*'.[43]

One cannot set one's love in order per se, by oneself. For as *situated* beings, corporate and corporeal, our loves are ordered and disordered by a web of relationships, some of which pre-exist us and some of which will outlast us. Some of the relationships we inhabit are internal, and some of them are external, concerning the material circumstances in which we and others live. We saw in Chapter 5 that externally related things are what they are independently of other things. But internal relations are brought into being by a witness. Sartre's ethical challenge, therefore, is twofold: First, what kind of witness will you be? His philosophical account theorizes what we find in literary form in Hugo and elsewhere: the sentiment that 'True or false, that which is

---

[39] Westphal 2009: 271–2.   [40] See Kelsey 1993.   [41] Niebuhr 1937: 103.
[42] Niebuhr 1937: 103.   [43] Westphal 2009: 271–2.

said of men often occupies as important a place in their lives, and above all in their destinies, as that which they do.'[44]

When we look on others, therefore, we must take care with our gaze, remembering when the defining gazes in our lives have not been looks of love. This is what it means to be merciful: to show compassion to those whom it is within our power to harm. We must resist the constant temptation to take others hostage in objectification, reducing them to the external relations of sex, gender, age, race, nationality, education, beauty, ugliness, poverty, or wealth. Rather, in faith, we must cultivate a vision of the other that sees them as a member of Christ's body—of *our* body—in order to bring, as Westphal writes, our believings into line with our seeings.

The second challenge concerns one's own internal relations, namely: 'What kind of witness will you accept?' In *Le Diable et le bon dieu* we find a dramatic—and poignant—expression of one man's answer to this question:

> GOETZ: Hilda, I need to be put on trial. Every day, every hour, I condemn myself, but I can never convince myself because I know myself too well to trust myself. I cannot see my soul any longer, because it is under my nose; I need someone to lend me his eyes.
>
> HILDA: Take mine.
>
> GOETZ: You don't see me either; you love me. Heinrich hates me, therefore he can convince me; when my own thoughts come from his mouth, I will be able to believe. (LL 177–8)

Sartre's Goetz succumbs to *néantisme*, refusing the gaze of love because it 'doesn't see'. Between being and nothingness, each individual has to choose whose eyes see most clearly when their own can no longer be trusted: Is it those of love and mercy, or hate and condemnation?

THE LAST WORD

One of the reasons religion has had so many 'cultured despisers' is because its speech can be troubling to those who do not understand it from within. This is particularly so now, in the context of what Rowan

---

[44] Hugo 1887: 17.

Williams calls a 'damaging cultural amnesia about what religious commitment looks like in practice'.[45]

I have argued that the theological categories sin and love cannot be known merely conceptually, but must be acknowledged personally. Sartre's phenomenology suggests that sin is not dead: the temptation to objectify others and ourselves—reducing human beings to aspects of their bodies, to a single one of their actions, or to their utility for our purposes—is no less fictive now than it was when *Being and Nothingness* was published in 1943.

Williams points out that 'the forming of a corporate imagination is something that continues to be the more or less daily business of religious believers'. And especially in the case of *sin*, I contend, 'this is a process immeasurably more sophisticated than the repetitive dogmatism so widely assumed to be the sole concern of those who employ religious language'.[46] For this particular religious word has the potential to shape a corporate imagination which *acknowledges* the situatedness and relatedness of each self, cultivating humility, love, and mercy. That is its optimism: our failures don't have the last word.

[45] Williams 2008: xi.   [46] Williams 2008: xi.

References

Abercrombie, Nigel (1936) *The Origins of Jansenism*, Oxford: Clarendon Press.

Anders, Günther Stern (1950) 'Emotion and Reality', *Philosophy and Phenomenological Research* 10(4) (June): 553–62.

Anderson, Gary (2010) *Sin: A History*, London: Yale University Press.

Anderson, Pamela Sue (2012) *Revisioning Gender in Philosophy of Religion: Reason, Love, and Epistemic Locatedness*, Farnham: Ashgate.

Anderson, Thomas C. (2010) 'Atheistic and Christian Existentialism: A Comparison of Sartre and Marcel', in Adrian Mirvish and Adrian van den Hoven (eds), *New Perspectives in Sartre*, Newcastle: Cambridge Scholars Publishing.

Aristotle (1979) *Metaphysics*, trans. Hugh Tredennick, Loeb Classical Library, Cambridge, MA: Harvard University Press.

Augustine (1947) *Enchiridion: On Faith, Hope, and Love* [*Enchiridion de fide, spe, et caritate*], trans. Bernard M. Peebles, Fathers of the Early Church 4, New York: Cima Publishing Co.

Augustine (1948) *Soliloquies*, trans. T. F. Gilligan, in Fathers of the Early Church 5, Washington, D.C.: Catholic University of America Press.

Augustine (1953) 'To Siplician' [*Ad simplicianum*], trans. J. H. S. Burleigh, in *Augustine: Earlier Writings*, Philadelphia: Westminster.

Augustine (1957) *Against Julian* [*Contra Julianum*], trans. Matthew A. Schumacher, in Fathers of the Early Church 35, Washington, D.C.: Catholic University of America Press.

Augustine (1959) *Of True Religion* [*De vera religione*], trans. J. H. S. Burleigh, Chicago: Regnery.

Augustine (1961) *Confessions*, trans. R. S. Pine-Coffin, London: Penguin.

Augustine (1982) *The Literal Meaning of Genesis* [*Genesis ad literam*], Ancient Christian Writers 41, trans. John Hammond Taylor SJ, New York: Paulist Press.

Augustine (1998) *On Marriage and Concupiscence* [*De nuptiis et concupiscentia*], trans. Roland J. Teske, *Answer to the Pelagians II*, vol. I/24 of *The Works of Saint Augustine*, New York: New City Press.

Augustine (1999) *Against Julian, an Unfinished Work* [*Contra Julianum opus imperfectum*], trans. Roland J. Teske, in *Answer to the Pelagians III*, vol. I/25 of *The Works of Saint Augustine: A Translation for the 21st Century*, ed. John E. Rotelle, New York: New City Press.

Augustine (2003) *City of God*, trans. Henry Bettenson, London: Penguin.

Augustine (2010) *The Free Choice of the Will* [*De liberio arbitrio*], trans. Robert P. Russell, in *The Teacher; The Free Choice of the Will; Grace and Free Will*, The Fathers of the Church 59, Washington, D.C.: Catholic University of America Press.

Aumann, Jordan, OP (1985) *Christian Spirituality in the Catholic Tradition*, London: Sheed & Ward.

Ayer, A. J. (1945) 'Novelist-Philosophers, V: Jean-Paul Sartre', *Horizon*, 12: 12–26.

Babcock, William S. (1988) 'Augustine on Sin and Moral Agency', *The Journal of Religious Ethics* 16: 28–55.

Bachmann, Jakob (1964) *La Notion du temps dans la pensée de Pierre de Bérulle*, Winterthur: Éditions P. G. Keller.

Badiou, Alain, with Nicolas Truong (2012 [2009]) *In Praise of Love*, trans. Peter Bush, London: Serpent's Tail.

Barnes, Hazel (1958) 'Introduction' to *Being and Nothingness*, London: Methuen & Co.

Barth, Karl (1956–75) *Church Dogmatics*, trans. T. F. Torrance and G. W. Bromiley, Edinburgh: T. & T. Clark. [*CD*].

Baruzi, Jean (1924) *Saint Jean de la Croix et le problème de l'éxperience mystique*. Paris: Alcan.

Beauvoir, Simone de (1960) *La Force de l'age*, Paris: Gallimard.

Beauvoir, Simone de (1962) *The Prime of Life*, trans. Peter Green, London: Penguin.

Beauvoir, Simone de (1977) *Old Age*, trans. Patrick O'Brian, Harmondsworth: Penguin.

Beauvoir, Simone de (1984) *Adieux: A Farewell to Sartre*, trans. Patrick O'Brian, New York: Pantheon.

Beauvoir, Simone de (1990) *Lettres à Sartre*, vols. 1–2, ed. Sylvie le Bon de Beauvoir, Paris: Gallimard.

Beauvoir, Simone de (1991) *Letters to Sartre*, trans. Quentin Hoare, London: Vintage.

Beauvoir, Simone de (2000) *The Ethics of Ambiguity*, trans. Bernard Frechtman, New York: Citadel.

Beauvoir, Simone de (2006) *Diary of a Philosophy Student Volume I, 1926–27*, ed. Barbara Klaw et al., Chicago: University of Illinois Press.

Bellemare, Rosaire (1959) *Le Sens de la créature dans la doctrine de Bérulle*, Paris: Desclée de Brouwer.

Bénichou, Paul (1948) *Morales du Grand Siècle*, Paris: Gallimard.

Bernasconi, Robert (2006) *How to Read Sartre*, London: Granta.

Bérulle, Pierre de (1856) [1597] *Bref discours de l'abnégation intérieur*, Paris: Migne. [Citations to this work refer to the column number in the Migne ed., *Œuvres complètes*.]

Bérulle, Pierre de (1859) *Discours de l'Etat des Grandeurs de Jésus*, Paris: Gauine.

Bérulle, Pierre de (1944) *Opuscules divers de piété*, ed. Gaston Rotureau, Paris: Aubier.

Bérulle, Pierre de (1987 [1624]) *Un Néant capable de Dieu*, Paris: Arfuyen.

Blair, Gordon (1970) 'Sartre in British and American Literary Criticism', *ADAM International Review* 343–5: 100–4.

Bonhoeffer, Dietrich (1998) *Creation and Fall*, Minneapolis: Augsburg Fortress.

Boorsch, Jean (1948) 'Sartre's View of Cartesian Liberty', *Yale French Studies* 1, *Existentialism*: 90–6.

Boulé, Jean-Pierre and Benedict O'Donohoe (eds) (2011) *Jean-Paul Sartre: Mind and Body, Word and Deed*, Newcastle: Cambridge Scholars Publishing.

Briggs, Robin (2001) *Communities of Belief*, Oxford: Clarendon Press.

Busch, Thomas W. (1989) *The Power of Consciousness and the Force of Circumstances in Sartre's Philosophy*, Bloomington: Indiana University Press.

Butler, Judith (1990) *Gender Trouble: Feminism and the Subversion of Identity*, New York: Routledge.

Cabestan, Philippe, and Tomes, Arnaud (2001) *Le Vocabulaire de Sartre*, Paris: Ellipses.

Calvet, Jean (1938) *La Littérature religieuse de François de Sales à Fénelon*, vol. 5 of *Histoire de la littérature française*, Paris: J. de Gigord.

Calvin, Jean (1980) *Institutes of the Christian Religion*, ed. J. T. McNeill, trans. and indexed by F. L. Battles, Philadelphia, PA: Library of Christian Classics.

Cannon, Betty (2013) 'Psychoanalysis and Existential Psychoanalysis', in Steven Churchill and Jack Reynolds (eds), *Jean-Paul Sartre: Key Concepts*, Durham: Acumen.

Catalano, Joseph (1985) *A Commentary on Jean-Paul Sartre's Being and Nothingness*, Chicago: University of Chicago Press.

Catalano, Joseph (1990) 'Successfully Lying to Oneself: A Sartrean Perspective', *Philosophy and Phenomenological Research* 50(4): 673–93.

Catalano, Joseph (1998) 'The Body and the Book: Reading *Being and Nothingness*', in J. Stewart (ed.), *The Debate between Sartre and Merleau-Ponty*, Evanston, IL: Northwestern University Press.

Catalano, Joseph (2009) 'The Body and the Book: Reading *Being and Nothingness*', in Katherine J. Morris (ed.), *Sartre on the Body*, London: Palgrave MacMillan.

Catalano, Joseph (2010) *Reading Sartre*, Cambridge: Cambridge University Press.

Cavell, Stanley (1976) *Must We Mean What We Say?*, Cambridge: Cambridge University Press.

Caws, Peter (1979) *Sartre*, London: Routledge.

Chabot, Alexis (2016) 'Cruel Atheism', *Sartre Studies International* 22(1): 58–68.

Churchill, Steven (2013) 'Contingency and Ego, Intentionality and Nausea', in Steven Churchill and Jack Reynolds (eds), *Jean-Paul Sartre: Key Concepts*, Durham: Acumen.

Clark, Kelly James (1998) 'Foreword', in Merold Westphal, *Suspicion and Faith: The Religious Uses of Modern Atheism*, New York: Fordham University Press.

Clark, Mary (1970) *Augustinian Personalism*, Villanova, PA: Villanova University Press.

Coakley, Sarah (2013) *God, Sexuality, and the Self: An Essay on the Trinity*, Cambridge: Cambridge University Press.

Cochois, Paul (1963) *Bérulle et l'École française*, Paris: Éditions du Seuil.

Cognet, Louis (1949) *La Spiritualité française au XVIIe siècle*, Paris: La Colombe.

Cohen-Solal, Annie (1987) *Sartre: A Life*, London: Heinemann.

Connor, Peter Tracey (2000) *Georges Bataille and the Mysticism of Sin*, London: Johns Hopkins University Press.

Contat, Michel, and Rybalka, Michel (1974) *The Writings of Jean-Paul Sartre*, 2 vols, Evanston, IL: Northwestern University Press.

Cooper, Terry D. (2003) *Sin, Pride, and Self-Acceptance: The Problem of Identity in Theology and Psychology*, Downers Grove, IL: IVP.

Coorebyter, Vincent de (2005) 'Bariona, ou la nativité d'un athée', *Revue internationale de philosophie* 2005/1(231): 15–49.

Coorebyter, Vincent de (2008) 'Le manuscrit "Liberté–Égalité"', *Études sartriennes* 12: 155–63.

Coorebyter, Vincent de (2010) '"Liberté–Égalité": Une genèse non marxiste de l'idéologie bourgeoise', *Études sartriennes* 14: 27–54.

Copleston, Frederick (1974) *A History of Philosophy*, vol. 9 : *Modern Philosophy from the French Revolution to Sartre, Camus, and Levi-Strauss*, New York: Doubleday.

Cormann, Grégory (2015) 'Alain au prisme de l'ontologie phénoménologique: Relectures croisées d'Alain et de Sartre', in N. Depraz (ed), *Alain philosophe rouennais*, Rouen: Presses de l'Université de Rouen.

Cox, Gary (2009) *Sartre and Fiction*, London: Continuum.

Dagens, Jean (1953) 'Le XVIIe siècle, siècle de Saint Augustin', *Cahiers de l'Association internationale des études françaises*, 3(3–5): 33–8.

Daniel-Rops, Henri (ed.) (1941) *Mystiques de France: Textes choisis et commentés*, Paris: Éditions Corréa.

Delacroix, Henri (1938 [1908]) *Les Grand Mystiques chrétiennes*, Paris: Alcan.

Dennett, Daniel C. (1991) *Consciousness Explained*, New York: Little, Brown.

Descartes, René (1969) *The Philosophical Works of Descartes*, 2 vols, ed. and trans. Elizabeth Haldane and G. R. T. Ross, Cambridge: Cambridge University Press.

Descartes, René (1981) *Méditations métaphysiques*, avec présentation et introduction par Jean-Paul Marty, Paris: Hachette.

Descartes, René (1988) *Selected Philosophical Writings*, trans. John Cottingham, Robert Stoothoff, and Dugald Murdoch, with an introduction by John Cottingham, Cambridge: Cambridge University Press.

Donneau, Olivier (2010) 'Christianisme, bourgeoisie, modernité: Sartre accumulateur critique de matériaux historiques', *Études sartriennes* 14: 55–70.

Doyle, William (2000) *Jansenism: Catholic Resistance to Authority from the Reformation to the French Revolution*, New York: St. Martin's Press.

Dunning, Stephen N. (1985) 'Kierkegaard's Systematic Analysis of Anxiety', in Robert Perkins (ed.), *International Kierkegaard Commentary: The Concept of Anxiety*, Macon: Mercer University Press.

Dupré, Louis, and Don. E. Saliers (eds) with John Meyendorff (1989) *Christian Spirituality: Post-Reformation and Modern*, London: SCM Press.

Economist (2003) 'Hands across a century: Review of *Sartre: The Philosopher of the Twentieth Century* by Bernard-Henri Lévy' (August 28).

Elmarsafy, Ziad (2003) *Freedom, Slavery, and Absolutism: Corneille, Pascal, Racine*, Lewisburg, PA: Bucknell University Press.

Emerson, Ralph Waldo (1983) 'Uses of Great Men', in *Essays and Lectures*, selected by Joel Porte, New York: The Library of America.

Esslin, Martin (1970) 'Sartre's Nativity Play', *ADAM International Review* 343–5.

Fénelon, François de Salignac de La Mothe (1827) *Correspondance de Fénelon*, 11 vols, Paris: Ferra et Leclerc.

Fénelon, François de Salignac de La Mothe (1880) *De l'existence de Dieu, Lettres sur religion, etc.*, avec introduction par le Cardinal de Bausset, Paris: Garnier Frères.

Ferreyrolles, Gérard (2000) *Les Reines du monde: Imagination et coutume chez Pascal*, Paris: Honoré Champion.

Fingarette, Herbert (1969) *Self-Deception*, London: Routledge.

Firestone, Shulamith (1970) *The Dialectic of Sex: The Case for Feminist Revolution*, New York: William Morrow.

Flynn, Thomas (1986) *Sartre and Marxist Existentialism: The Test Case of Collective Responsibility*, Chicago: University of Chicago Press.

Flynn, Thomas (2013) 'Jean-Paul Sartre', *The Stanford Encyclopedia of Philosophy* (Fall 2013 Edition), Edward N. Zalta (ed.), <http://plato.stanford.edu/archives/fall2013/entries/sartre/>.

Flynn, Thomas (2014) *Sartre: A Philosophical Biography*, Cambridge: Cambridge University Press.

Foreaux, Francis (2010) *Dictionnaire de culture générale*, Paris: Pearson Education France.

Friedman, Michael (2010) 'Descartes and Galileo', in Janet Broughton and John Carriero (eds), *A Companion to Descartes*, Oxford: Wiley.

Fullbrook, Edward, and Kate Fullbrook (2008) *Sex and Philosophy: Jean-Paul Sartre and Simone de Beauvoir*, London: Continuum.

Fulton, Ann (1999) *Apostles of Sartre: Existentialism in America, 1945–1963*, Evanston, IL: Northwestern University Press.

Gardner, Sebastian (2009) *Sartre's Being and Nothingness: A Reader's Guide*, London: Continuum.

Gazier, Augustin (1915) *Jeanne de Chantal et Angélique Arnauld: Étude historique et critique*, Paris: Honoré Champion.

Gellman, Jerome (2009) 'Jean-Paul Sartre: The Mystical Atheist', *European Journal for Philosophy of Religion* 1(2): 127–37.

Geroulanos, Stefanos (2010) *An Atheism That Is Not Humanist Emerges in French Thought*, Stanford: Stanford University Press.

Gillespie, John H. (2013) 'Sartre and God: A Spiritual Odyssey, Part 1', *Sartre Studies International* 19(1): 71–90.

Gillespie, John H. (2014) 'Sartre and God: A Spiritual Odyssey, Part 2', *Sartre Studies International* 20(1): 45–56.

Gillespie, John H. (2016) 'Sartre and the Death of God', *Sartre Studies International*, 22:1: 41–57.

Gilson, Etienne (1913) *La Doctrine cartésienne de la liberté et la théologie*, thesis, Paris.

Gilson, Etienne (1961) *The Christian Philosophy of Saint Augustine*, London: Victor Gollancz Ltd.

Girard, René (1994) *Quand ces choses commenceront . . . Entretiens avec Michel Treguer*, Paris: Arléa.

Glendinning, Simon (2007) *In the Name of Phenomenology*, London: Routledge.

Goldmann, Lucien (1964) *The Hidden God: A Study of the Tragic Vision in the Pensées of Pascal and the Tragedies of Racine*, trans. Philip Thody, London: Routledge.

Goldthorpe, Rhiannon (1984) *Sartre: Literature and Theory*, Cambridge: Cambridge University Press.

Grimaldi, Nicolas (1987) 'Sartre et la liberté cartesienne', *Revue de Métaphysique et de Morale* 92(1), Philosophie et réception I: Descartes en phénoménologie (Janvier–Mars): 67–88.

Guicharnaud, Jacques (1967) *Modern French Theatre: From Giraudoux to Genet*, London: Yale University Press.

Guigot, André (2000) *Sartre et l'existentialisme*, Toulouse: Éditions MILAN.

Hackel, Manuela (2011) 'Jean-Paul Sartre: Kierkegaard's Influence on His Theory of Nothingness', in Jon Stewart (ed.), *Kierkegaard's International Reception*, vol. 9: *Kierkegaard and Existentialism*, Farnham: Ashgate.

Hanby, Michael (2003) *Augustine and Modernity*, London: Routledge.

Harnack, Adolf von (2005) *The History of Dogma*, vol 5., trans. Neil Buchanan, Grand Rapids: Christian Classics Ethereal Library.

Harries, Karsten (1995) 'Authenticity, Poetry, God', in William J. Richardson and Babette Babich (eds), *From Phenomenology to Thought, Errancy, and Desire*, Dordrecht: Springer.

Harries, Karsten (2004) 'Sartre and the Spirit of Revenge', *Sartre Studies International* 10(1): 25–38.

Hartmann, Klaus (1966) *Sartre's Ontology: A Study of Being and Nothingness in the Light of Hegel's Logic*, Evanston, IL: Northwestern University Press.

Hartsock, Nancy (1985) *Money, Sex, and Power: Toward a Feminist Historical Materialism*, Boston, MA: Northeastern University Press.

Haynes-Curtis, Carole (1988) 'The "Faith" of Bad Faith', *Philosophy* 63(244): 269–75.

Hegel, G. W. F. (1977) *Phenomenology of Spirit*, trans. A. V. Miller, Oxford: Clarendon Press.

Helm, Bennett (2013) 'Love', *The Stanford Encyclopedia of Philosophy* (Fall 2013 Edition), Edward N. Zalta (ed.), <http://plato.stanford.edu/archives/fall2013/entries/love/>.

Helms, Chad (2006) 'Introduction' to Fénelon, François de Salignac de La Mothe, *Fénelon: Selected Writings*, ed. and trans. Chad Helms, New York: Paulist Press.

Hong, Howard, and Hong, Edna (1998) 'Introduction' to Søren Kierkegaard, *Works of Love*, trans. H. Hong and E. Hong, Princeton: Princeton University Press.

Hopkins, Jasper (1994) 'Theological Language and the Nature of Man in Jean-Paul Sartre's Philosophy', in *Philosophical Criticism: Essays and Reviews*, Minneapolis: Arthur J. Banning Press.

Howells, Christina (1981) 'Sartre and Negative Theology', *Modern Language Review* 76(3) (July): 549–55.

Howells, Christina (1988) *Sartre: The Necessity of Freedom*, Cambridge: Cambridge University Press.

Howells, Edward (2009) 'Relationality and Difference in the Mysticism of Pierre de Bérulle', *Harvard Theological Review* 102(2): 225–43.

Hugo, Victor (1887) *Les Misérables*, New York: Crowell & Co.

Hühn, Lore, and Philip Schwab (2013) 'Kierkegaard and German Idealism', in John Lippit and George Pattison (eds), *The Oxford Handbook of Kierkegaard*, Oxford: Oxford University Press.

Idt, Geneviève (1971) *La Nausée*, Paris: Hatier.

Ihde, Don (1971) *Hermeneutic Phenomenology: The Philosophy of Paul Ricoeur*, Evanston, IL: Northwestern University Press.

Imbert, Henri-François (1970) *Stendahl et la tentation janséniste*, Paris: Librarie Droz.

Izumi-Shearer, Shigeko (1976) 'Le Corps ambigu chez Jean-Paul Sartre', *Études de langue et de littérature françaises* 28: 96–115.

Jambor, Mishka (1990) 'Sartre on Anguish', *Philosophy Today* 34(2): 111–16.

Jansen, Cornelius (1640) *Augustinus, seu doctrina S. Augustini de humanae sanitate, aegritudine, medicina adversus pelagianos et massilienses, De statu naturae lapsae*, Leuven: J. Zeger.

Jeanson, François (2005 [1966]) *Sartre devant Dieu*, Paris: Éditions Cécile Defaut.

Jedrazweski, Marek (1989) 'On the Paths of Cartesian Freedom: Sartre and Levinas', *Analecta Husserliana* 27: 671–83.

Jenson, Matt (2007) *The Gravity of Sin: Augustine, Luther, and Barth on homo incurvatus in se*, Edinburgh: T. & T. Clark.

Judaken, Jonathan (2006) *Jean-Paul Sartre and the Jewish Question*, Lincoln, NE: University of Nebraska Press.

Jüngel, Eberhard (2001) *Justification*, trans. Jeffrey F. Cayzer, Edinburgh: T. & T. Clark.

Kelsey, David (1993) 'Whatever Happened to the Doctrine of Sin', *Theology Today* 50(2): 169–78.

Kierkegaard, Søren (1929) *Le Journal du séducteur*, trans. Jean-Jacques Gateau, Paris: Stock.

Kierkegaard, Søren (1932) *Le Traité du désespoir (ou La Maladie jusqu'à la mort)*, trans. Jean-Jacques Gateau, Paris: Gallimard.

Kierkegaard, Søren (1935) *Le Concept de l'angoisse*, trans. Knud Ferlov and Jean-Jacques Gateau, Paris: Gallimard.

Kierkegaard, Søren (1980) *The Concept of Anxiety*, trans. Reidar Thomte, Princeton: Princeton University Press.

Kierkegaard, Søren (1983) *The Sickness unto Death*, trans. H. Hong and E. Hong, Princeton: Princeton University Press.

Kierkegaard, Søren (1987) *Either/Or*, vol. 2, trans. H. Hong and E. Hong, Princeton: Princeton University Press.

Kierkegaard, Søren (1998) *Works of Love*, trans. H. Hong and E. Hong, Princeton: Princeton University Press.

King, Thomas (1974) *Sartre and the Sacred*, Chicago: University of Chicago Press.

Kirkpatrick, Kate (2013) 'Jean-Paul Sartre: Mystical Atheist or Mystical Antipathist?', *European Journal for Philosophy of Religion* 5(2): 159–68.

Kirkpatrick, Kate (2014) 'Past her Prime? Simone de Beauvoir on Motherhood and Old Age', *Sophia* 53(2): 275–87.

Kirkpatrick, Kate (2015) 'Sartre: An Augustinian Atheist', *Sartre Studies International* 21(1): 1–20.

Kirkpatrick, Kate (2017) *Sartre and Theology*, London: Bloomsbury/ T. & T. Clark.

Kleist, Aaron J. (2008) *Striving with Grace: Views of Free Will in Anglo-Saxon England*, Toronto: University of Toronto Press.

Kojève, Alexandre (1980) *Introduction to the Reading of Hegel: Lectures on the Phenomenology of Spirit*, trans. James H. Nichols Jr, New York: Cornell.

Kołakowski, Leszek (1995) *God Owes Us Nothing: A Brief Remark on Pascal's Religion and on the Spirit of Jansenism*, Chicago: University of Chicago Press.

Kouvélakis, Stanthis (2008) 'Penser le dieu absent, du Tintoret de Sartre au Pascal de Goldmann', *Marxismes au XXIe siècle*, presentation at King's College London.

Krailsheimer, A. J. (1980) *Pascal*, Oxford: Oxford University Press.

Krishek, Sharon (2009) *Kierkegaard on Faith and Love*, Cambridge: Cambridge University Press.

Kruks, Sonia (1992) 'Gender and Subjectivity: Simone de Beauvoir and Contemporary Feminism', *Signs* 18(1): 89–110.

Lafarge, Jacques (2000) 'L'Edition des Oeuvres complètes de Kierkegaard en français: contexte—historique—objectifs—conception—réalisation', in Niels Jørgen Cappelørn, Hermann Deuser, and Jon Stewart (eds), *Kierkegaard Studies Yearbook* (2000), New York: de Gruyter.

Lançon, Philippe (2014) 'Sartre, l'enfer de je', *Libération*, 3 August, http://www.liberation.fr/livres/2014/08/03/sartre-l-enfer-du-je_1075016.

Landkildehus, Søren (2009) 'Blaise Pascal: Kierkegaard and Pascal as Kindred Spirits in the Fight against Christendom', in Jon Bartley Stewart (ed.), *Kierkegaard and the Renaissance and Modern Traditions*, vol. 1: *Philosophy*, Aldershot: Ashgate.

Langford, Wendy (1999) *Revolutions of the Heart: Gender, Power and the Delusions of Love*, London: Routledge.

Lavelle, Louis (1948) *Bérulle et Malebranche*, Paris: Association Fénelon.

Leak, Andrew (2006) *Jean-Paul Sartre*, London: Reaktion.

Leduc-Lafayette, Denise (1996a) *Fénelon et l'amour de Dieu*, Paris: Presses Universitaires de France.

Leduc-Lafayette, Denise (1996b) 'Vouloir ne vouloir pas', in *Fénelon: Philosophie et spiritualité*, ed. Denise Leduc-Lafayette, Geneva: Librairie Droz.

Levinas, Emmanuel (1981) *Otherwise than Being*, trans. Alphonso Lingis, The Hague: Martinus Nijhoff.

Levinas, Emmanuel (1988) 'Useless Suffering', in *The Provocation of Levinas*, ed. R. Bernasconi and D. Wood, London: Routledge.

Lévy, Bernard-Henri (2003) *Sartre: The Philosopher of the Twentieth Century*, trans. A. Brown, Cambridge: Polity.

Lewis, Philip E. (1994) 'Jansenist Tragedy', in Denis Hollier and R. Howard Bloch (eds), *A New History of French Literature*, Cambridge, MA: Harvard University Press.

Louandre, Charles (1847) 'L'Histoire du Jansénisme', *Revue des Deux Mondes* 19: 713–27.

Louette, Jean-François (2002–3) 'Jean-Paul Sartre en classe', *Revue d'histoire littéraire de la France* 102: 417–41.

Lubac, Henri de (1969) *Augustinianism and Modern Theology*, trans. Lancelot Sheppard, London: Geoffrey Chapman.

Lukács, George (1974 [1920]) *The Theory of the Novel*, Cambridge, MA: MIT Press.

Macquarrie, John (1973) *Existentialism*, London: Pelican.

Magnard, Pierre (1996) 'La Querelle des augustinismes', in Denise Leduc-Lafayette (ed.), *Fénelon: Philosophie et spiritualité*, Geneva: Librairie Droz.

Mann, Thomas (1961) *The Holy Sinner*, trans. H. T. Lowe-Porter, London: Penguin.

Mann, William E. (2001) 'Augustine on Evil and Original Sin', in Eleonore Stump and Norman Kretzman (eds), *The Cambridge Companion to Augustine*, Cambridge: Cambridge University Press.

Manser, Anthony (1983) 'Unfair to Waiters?', *Philosophy* 58 (223): 102–6.

Marcel, Gabriel (2002) *The Philosophy of Existentialism*, New York: Citadel Press.

McBride, William L. (1995) 'Sartre's Debts to Kierkegaard: A Partial Reckoning', in Merold Westphal and Martin J. Matuštík (eds), *Kierkegaard in Post/Modernity*, Bloomington, IN: Indiana University Press.

McCord Adams, Marilyn (2000) *Horrendous Evils and the Goodness of God*, Ithaca, NY: Cornell University Press.

McCord Adams, Marilyn (2013) 'God because of Evil: A Pragmatic Argument from Evil for Belief in God', in Justin P. McBrayer and Daniel Howard-Snyder (eds), *The Blackwell Companion to the Problem of Evil*, Malden, MA: Wiley Blackwell.

Melzer, Sara E. (1986) *Discourses of the Fall: A Study of Pascal's Pensées*, Berkeley: University of California Press.

Menn, Stephen (2002) *Descartes and Augustine*, Cambridge: Cambridge University Press.

Mesnard, Jean (1992) 'Jansenism et littérature', in *La Culture de XVIIe siècle: Enquêtes et synthèses*, Paris: PUF.

Meszaros, Istvan (2012) *The Work of Sartre*, New York: NYU Press.

Michalson, Gordon E. (1990) *Fallen Freedom: Kant on Radical Evil and Moral Regeneration*, Cambridge: Cambridge University Press.

Mohanty, Christine (1974) 'Bariona, the Germination of Sartrean Theatre', *The French Review* 47(6): 1094–109.

Moran, Dermot (2000) *Introduction to Phenomenology*, London: Routledge.

Moran, Dermot (2009) 'Husserl, Sartre and Merleau-Ponty on Embodiment, Touch and the "Double Sensation"', in Katherine J. Morris (ed.), *Sartre on the Body*, London: Palgrave MacMillan.

Moran, Dermot (2011) 'Sartre's Treatment of the Body in *Being and Nothingness*: The "Double-Sensation"', in Jean-Pierre Boulé and Benedict O'Donohoe (eds), *Jean-Paul Sartre: Mind and Body, Word and Deed*, Newcastle: Cambridge Scholars Publishing.

Moran, Dermot (2013) '"Let's Look at It Objectively": Why Phenomenology Cannot Be Naturalized', *Royal Institute of Philosophy Supplements* 72: 89–115.

Moriarty, Michael (2006) *Fallen Nature, Fallen Selves: Early Modern French Thought II*, Oxford: Oxford University Press.

Morris, Katherine J. (1997) 'Ambiguity and Bad Faith', *American Catholic Philosophical Quarterly* 70(4): 467–84.

Morris, Katherine J. (2008) *Sartre*, Oxford: Blackwell.

Morris, Katherine J. (ed.) (2009) 'Introduction', in *Sartre on the Body*, London: Palgrave MacMillan.

Mui, Constance (2009) 'Sartre and Marcel on Embodiment: Re-evaluating Traditional and Gynocentric Feminisms', in Katherine J. Morris (ed.), *Sartre on the Body*, London: Palgrave MacMillan.

Mulhall, Stephen (2005) *Philosophical Myths of the Fall*, Princeton: Princeton University Press.

Murdoch, Iris (1999) *Sartre: Romantic Rationalist*, London: Vintage.

Neu, Jerome (1988) 'Divided Minds: Sartre's "Bad Faith" Critique of Freud', *The Review of Metaphysics* 42(1): 79–101.

Newman, John Henry (1907) *The Idea of a University*, London: Longmans, Green, and Co.

Niebuhr, Reinhold (1937) *An Interpretation of Christian Ethics*, London: SCM Press.

Nietzsche, Friedrich (1984) *Human, All Too Human*, trans. Marion Farber, Lincoln, NE: University of Nebraska Press.

Nietzsche, Friedrich (1993) *The Birth of Tragedy*, trans. Shaun Whiteside, London: Penguin.

Noudelmann, François, and Gilles Philippe (eds) (2013) *Dictionnaire Sartre*, Paris: Champion Classiques.

O'Connell, David (1994) 'Bourgeois Sin', in Denis Hollier and R. Howard Bloch (eds), *A New History of French Literature*, Cambridge, MA: Harvard University Press.

O'Neil, M. A. (1999) 'Pascalian Reflections in *Les Misérables*', *Philological Quarterly* 78(3): 335–48.

Olivera, Philippe (2002) 'Commémorer Pascal en 1923 (I)', *Les Cahiers du Centre de Recherches Historiques*, 28–9: 'Quelques "XVIIème siècle": Fabrications, usages et réemplois'.

Onaf, Christian (2013) 'Sartre's Understanding of the Self', in Steven Churchill and Jack Reynolds (eds), *Jean-Paul Sartre: Key Concepts*, Durham: Acumen.

Parish, Richard (1989) *Pascal's Lettres Provinciales: A Study in Polemic*, Oxford: Clarendon Press.

Pascal, Blaise (1653) 'On the Conversion of the Sinner', in *Minor Works*, trans. O. W. Wright, Cambridge, MA: Harvard Classics (1909–14), http://www.bartleby.com/48/3/5.html.

Pascal, Blaise (1909) *Pensées et Opuscules*, ed. Léon Brunschvicg, Paris: Hachette.

Pascal, Blaise (1964–92) *Blaise Pascal, Oeuvres complètes*, Texte établi, présenté et annoté par Jean Mesnard, édition du Tricentenaire, Paris: Desclée de Brouwer, Bibliothèque européenne. [OCM]

Pascal, Blaise (1995a) *Pensées and Other Writings*, trans. Honor Levi, Oxford: Oxford University Press.

Pascal, Blaise (1995b) *Pensées*, trans. A. Krailsheimer, London: Penguin.

Patrick, Denzil G. M. (1947) *Pascal and Kierkegaard: A Study in the Strategy of Evangelism*, London: Lutterworth Press.

Pattison, George (1996) *Agnosis: Theology in the Void*, Basingstoke: Palgrave Macmillan.

Pattison, George (2013) *Kierkegaard and the Quest for Unambiguous Life: Between Romanticism and Modernism*, Oxford: Oxford University Press.

Pearson, Roger (2006) 'Explanatory Notes' in Voltaire's *Candide and Other Stories*, Oxford: Oxford University Press.

Perrin, Marius (1980) *Avec Sartre au stalag 12D*, Paris: Jean-Pierre Delarge.

Peters, Renate (1997) 'Sartre, White America, and the Black Problem', *Canadian Review of American Studies* 27(1): 21–41.

Phillips, D. Z. (1981) 'Bad Faith and Sartre's Waiter', *Philosophy* 56(215): 23–31.

Philonenko, Alexis (1981) 'Liberté et mauvaise foi chez Sartre', *Revue de Métaphysique et de Morale* 86(2): 145–63.

Pieper, Josef (2001) *The Concept of Sin*, South Bend, IN: St. Augustine's Press.

Plantinga, Alvin, and Nicholas Wolterstorff (eds) (1983) *Faith and Rationality: Reason and Belief in God*, Notre Dame: University of Notre Dame Press.

Poole, Roger (1998) 'The Unknown Kierkegaard: Twentieth-Century Receptions', in Alastair Hannay and Gordon D. Marino (eds), *The Cambridge Companion to Kierkegaard*, Cambridge: Cambridge University Press.

Quinones, Ricardo J. (2007) *Dualisms: The Agons of the Modern World*, Toronto: University of Toronto Press.

Racine, Jean (1963) *Phaedra and Other Plays*, trans. John Cairncross, London: Penguin.

Read, Herbert (2012) *The Sense of Glory: Essays in Criticism*, Cambridge: Cambridge University Press.

Rex, Walter (1977) *Pascal's Provincial Letters: An Introduction*, London: Hodder and Stoughton.

Richmond, Sarah (2004) 'Introduction' to Jean-Paul Sartre, *The Transcendence of the Ego*, trans. Andrew Brown, London: Routledge, 2011.

Richmond, Sarah (2013) 'Nothingness and Negation', in Steven Churchill and Jack Reynolds (eds), *Jean-Paul Sartre: Key Concepts*, Durham: Acumen.

Ricoeur, Paul (1967) *The Symbolism of Evil*, trans. Emerson Buchanan, New York: Harper & Row.

Ricoeur, Paul (1970) *Freud and Philosophy*, trans. D. Savage, New Haven: Yale University Press.

Ricoeur, Paul (1974) *The Conflict of Interpretations: Essays in Hermeneutics*, ed. Don Ihde, trans. Willis Domingo et al., Evanston, IL: Northwestern University Press.

Ricoeur, Paul (1992) *Oneself as Another*, trans. Kathleen Blamey, Chicago: University of Chicago Press.

Royle, Peter (2005) *L'Homme et le néant chez Jean-Paul Sartre*, Saint-Nicolas, Québec: Presses de l'Université Laval.

Šajda, Peter (2009) 'Fénelon: Clearing the Way for *The Sickness unto Death*', in Jon Bartley Stewart (ed.), *Kierkegaard and the Renaissance and Modern Traditions*, vol. 2: *Theology*, Aldershot: Ashgate.

Salvan, Jacques (1967) *The Scandalous Ghost: Sartre's Existentialism as Related to Vitalism, Humanism, Mysticism, Marxism*, Detroit: Wayne State University Press.

Santoni, Ronald E. (1995) *Bad Faith, Good Faith, and Authenticity in Sartre's Early Philosophy*, Philadelphia: Temple University Press.

Sartre, Jean-Paul, and Pierre Verstraeten (2010) 'Je ne suis plus réaliste', *Études sartriennes*, 14: 3–26.

Schrift, Alan D. (2008) 'The Effects of the *Agrégation de Philosophie* on Twentieth-Century French Philosophy', *Journal of the History of Philosophy* 46(3) (July): 449–73.

Schroeder, William R. (1984) *Sartre and His Predecessors: The Self and the Other*, London: Routledge.

Scruton, Roger (1986) *Sexual Desire: A Moral Philosophy of the Erotic*, New York: Free Press.

Scruton, Roger (2014) 'Roger Scruton's Quotes on Nonsense', *The Guardian*, 15 August.

Sellier, Philippe (1970) *Pascal et Saint Augustin*, Paris: Armand Colin.

Sellier, Philippe (2000) *Port-Royal et la littérature*, 2 vols, Paris: Champion.

Sève, Bernard (1996) 'Le Possible dans *L'Etre et le néant*', *Raison présente*, 'Sartre', no. 117: 87–106.

Shelley, Christopher Acton (2008) *Transpeople: Repudiation, Trauma, Healing*, Toronto: University of Toronto Press.

Sicard, Michel (1990) 'Carnet Midy: Notice', in Jean- Paul Sartre, *Écrits de jeunesse*, ed. M. Contat and M. Rybalka, Paris: Gallimard.

Simont, Juliette (1992) 'Sartrean Ethics', in Christina Howells (ed.), *The Cambridge Companion to Sartre*, Cambridge: Cambridge University Press.

Simont, Juliette (1999) 'Sartre's Critique of Humanism', in James Giles (ed.), *French Existentialism: Consciousness, Ethics, and Relations with Others*, Amsterdam: Rodopi.

Smart, Carol (2007) *Personal Life*, Cambridge: Polity Press.

Smith, David Woodruff (2013) 'Phenomenology', in *The Stanford Encyclopedia of Philosophy* (Winter 2013 edition), ed. Edward N. Zalta, http://plato.stanford.edu/archives/win2013/entries/phenomenology/.

Smith, James K. A. (2001) 'Confessions of an Existentialist: Reading Augustine after Heidegger, Part I', *New Blackfriars* 82(964), 335–47.

Solomon, Robert (1988) *About Love: Reinventing Romance for Our Times*, New York: Simon & Schuster.

Solomon, Robert C. (2006) *Dark Feelings, Grim Thoughts: Experience and Reflection in Camus and Sartre*, Oxford: Oxford University Press.

Stephens, Bradley (2011) *Victor Hugo, Jean-Paul Sartre, and the Liability of Liberty*, Oxford: Legenda.

Stevenson, Leslie (1983) 'Sartre on Bad Faith', *Philosophy* 58(224): 253–8.

Stewart, Jon (2009) 'France: Kierkegaard as a Forerunner of Existentialism and Poststructuralism', in Jon Stewart (ed.), *Kierkegaard's International Reception*, vol. 1: *Northern and Western Europe*, Farnham: Ashgate.

Stump, Eleonore (2010) *Wandering in Darkness: Narrative and the Problem of Suffering*, Oxford: Oxford University Press.

Surya, Michel (2002) *Georges Bataille: An Intellectual Biography*, trans. Krzysztof Fijalkowski and Michael Richardson, London: Verso.

Taveau, Claude (1933) *Le Cardinal de Bérulle: Maître de vie spirituelle*, Paris: Desclée de Brouwer.

Teboul, Margaret (2005) 'La Réception de Kierkegaard en France, 1930–1960', *Revue des sciences philosophiques et théologiques* 89(2): 315–36.

Theunissen, Michael (2005) *Kierkegaard's Concept of Despair*, trans. Barbara Harshav and Helmut Illbruck, Princeton: Princeton University Press.

Thiher, Allen (2013) *Understanding Marcel Proust*, Columbia, SC: University of South Carolina Press.

Thompson, William M. (1989) 'Introduction' to Bérulle, Pierre de, *Bérulle and the French School: Selected Writings*, ed. William M. Thompson, trans. Lowell M. Glendon, SS, New York: Paulist Press.

Thweatt, Vivien (1980) *La Rochefoucauld and the Seventeenth-Century Concept of the Self*, Geneva: Librarie Droz.

Tillich, Paul (1953) *Systematic Theology*, vol. 1, London: Nisbet & Co.

Tillich, Paul (1957) *Systematic Theology*, vol. 2, London: Nisbet & Co.

Tillich, Paul (1963) *The Eternal Now*, London: SCM.

Tolstoy, Leo (2010) 'The Death of Ivan Ilyich', in *The Death of Ivan Ilyich and Other Stories*, trans. Larissa Volokhonsky and Richard Pevear, London: Vintage.

Tomes, Arnaud (2013) 'Choix', in *Dictionnaire Sartre*, ed. François Noudelmann and Gilles Philippe, Paris: Honoré Champion.

Valéry, Paul (1960) 'Tel Quel', in *Oeuvres complètes*, vol. 2, Paris: Pléiade.

Van Den Abbeele, Georges (1994) 'Moralists and the Legacy of Cartesianism', in Denis Hollier and R. Howard Bloch (eds), *A New History of French Literature*, Cambridge, MA: Harvard University Press.

Van Kley, Dale (2006) 'The Rejuvenation and Rejection of Jansenism in History and Historiography: Recent Literature on Eighteenth-Century Jansenism in French', *French Historical Studies* 29(4): 649–84.

Van Stralen, Hans (2005) *Choices and Conflict: Essays on Literature and Existentialism*, Oxford: Peter Lang.

Voltaire (1819 [1728]) *L'Anti-Pascal*, in *Oeuvres complètes de Voltaire*, vol. 29, Paris: Antoine-Augustin Renouard.

Voltaire (2006) *Candide*, trans. Roger Pearson, Oxford: Oxford University Press.

Von Harnack, Adolf (2013) *History of Dogma*, 5 vols, London: Forgotten Books.

Wahl, Jean (1932–3) 'Heidegger et Kierkegaard: Recherche des elements originaux de la philosophie de Heidegger', *Recherches Philosophiques*, publiées par A. Koyré, H.-C. Puech, A. Spaier, Paris: Boivin.

Wahl, Jean (1938) *Études Kierkegaardiennes*, Paris: Aubier.

Wahl, Jean (2012) 'The Roots of Existentialism: An Introduction by Jean Wahl', in Jean-Paul Sartre, *The Philosophy of Existentialism: Selected Essays*, New York: Open Road Media. [Kindle edition: All citations refer to the Kindle location.]

Walsh, Sylvia (2009) *Kierkegaard: Thinking Christianly in an Existential Mode*, Oxford: Oxford University Press.

Wang, Stephen (2009) *Aquinas and Sartre: On Freedom, Personal Identity, and the Possibility of Happiness*, Washington, D.C.: Catholic University of America Press.

Ward, Keith (2011) *Is Religion Irrational?*, Oxford: Lion.

Warnock, Mary (1965) *The Philosophy of Sartre*, London: Hutchinson.

Webber, Jonathan (2004) 'Philosophical Introduction' to Jean-Paul Sartre, *The Imaginary*, trans. Jonathan Webber, London: Routledge.

Webber, Jonathan (2009) *The Existentialism of Jean-Paul Sartre*, London: Routledge.

Weightman, John (1970) 'Sartre Catalogued', *ADAM International Review* 343–5: 29–32.

Westphal, Merold (1998) *Suspicion and Faith: The Religious Uses of Modern Atheism*, New York: Fordham University Press.

Westphal, Merold (2009) 'Hermeneutics and Holiness', in Oliver Crisp and Michael Rea (eds), *Analytic Theology: New Essays in the Philosophy of Theology*, Oxford: Oxford University Press.

Westphal, Merold (2010) 'Phenomenology and Existentialism', in Charles Taliaferro, Paul Draper, and Philip L. Quinn (eds), *A Companion to Philosophy of Religion*, Oxford: Wiley-Blackwell.

Williams, Rowan (2000) 'Insubstantial Evil', in Robert Dodaro and George Lawless (eds), *Augustine and His Critics: Essays in Honour of Gerald Bonner*, London: Routledge.

Williams, Rowan (2008) *Dostoevsky: Language, Faith, and Fiction*, London: Continuum.

Wood, William (2013) *Blaise Pascal on Duplicity, Sin and the Fall: The Secret Instinct*, Oxford: Oxford University Press.

Zum Brunn, Emilie (1988) *St. Augustine: Being and Nothingness*, New York: Paragon House.

Index